THOMAS H

Literary Lives
General Editor: Richard Dutton, Professor of English
Lancaster University

This series offers stimulating accounts of the literary careers of
the most admired and influential English-language authors.
Volumes follow the outline of writers' working lives, not in
the spirit of traditional biography, but aiming to trace
the professional, publishing and social contexts which
shaped their writing.

A list of the published titles in this series follows overleaf.

Published titles

Morris Beja
JAMES JOYCE

John Mepham
VIRGINIA WOOLF

Cedric C. Brown
JOHN MILTON

Michael O'Neill
PERCY BYSSHE SHELLEY

Peter Davison
GEORGE ORWELL

Leonée Ormond
ALFRED TENNYSON

Richard Dutton
WILLIAM SHAKESPEARE

George Parfitt
JOHN DONNE

Jan Fergus
JANE AUSTEN

Gerald Roberts
GERARD MANLEY HOPKINS

James Gibson
THOMAS HARDY

Felicity Rosslyn
ALEXANDER POPE

Kenneth Graham
HENRY JAMES

Tony Sharpe
T. S. ELIOT

Paul Hammond
JOHN DRYDEN

Grahame Smith
CHARLES DICKENS

W. David Kay
BEN JONSON

Gary Waller
EDMUND SPENSER

Mary Lago
E. M. FORSTER

Cedric Watts
JOSEPH CONRAD

Alasdair D. F. Macrae
W. B. YEATS

John Williams
WILLIAM WORDSWORTH

Joseph McMinn
JONATHAN SWIFT

Tom Winnifrith and Edward Chitham
CHARLOTTE AND EMILY
BRONTE

Kerry McSweeney
GEORGE ELIOT (MARIAN
EVANS)

John Worthen
D. H. LAWRENCE

Thomas Hardy

A Literary Life

James Gibson

First published 1996 by
MACMILLAN PRESS LTD
Houndmills, Basingstoke, Hampshire RG21 6XS
and London
Companies and representatives
throughout the world

ISBN 0–333–43830–2 hardcover
ISBN 0–333–43831–0 paperback

A catalogue record for this book is available from the British Library.

10   9   8   7   6   5   4   3
05   04   03   02   01   00

Printed and bound in Great Britain by
Antony Rowe Ltd
Chippenham, Wiltshire

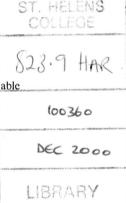

Published in the United States of America 1996 by
ST. MARTIN'S PRESS, INC.,
Scholarly and Reference Division
175 Fifth Avenue, New York, N.Y. 10010

ISBN 0–312–15945–5

To My Hardy Society Friends

Contents

Preface

It is a measure of the difference between Edmund Gosse and Thomas Hardy that Gosse could describe Hardy's life as 'uneventful'. Hardy was so interested in every aspect of the human situation that he would have seen no human – or animal – life as 'uneventful', and time has not confirmed Gosse's assumption. At a rough calculation the three major biographies of Hardy published in the past twenty years total some 2000 pages, not really an indication of a shortage of events about which to write.

Two problems have confronted me: how to keep my selection of events to the number of pages available – and Hardy lived considerably longer than almost all other writers in this series – and how to avoid being too dependent on what all serious scholars now regard as the definitive biography – Michael Millgate's *Thomas Hardy: A Biography*. My debt to Michael, I immediately acknowledge is enormous, not just for his biography but for his edition of Hardy's letters and his many other contributions to Hardy scholarship. I have not completely solved either problem but it is my hope that I may have written a biography that will prove of value to the student because of its concentration on the literary side of Hardy's life. And I have not tried to hide my affection for Hardy and almost all his works even though enthusiasm is out of fashion in modern criticism. Nearly seventy years after his death Hardy is being increasingly seen as one of the very greatest of English writers because of his achievement in *both* the novel and poetry. I have tried to defend him against the attacks of those who through ignorance or prejudice dismiss him as a gloomy pessimist and recluse and an inhospitable miser. For my book on Hardy in Macmillan's 'Interviews and Recollections' series I have collected nearly two hundred accounts of people who met him, and they almost all talk of him with affection as a man of kindness and generosity with a sense of humour and a great interest in others.

Many other debts must be acknowledged both to the writers of the books mentioned in the Bibliography and to so many friends and scholars whose books I have read or with whom I have talked about Hardy at Hardy Society functions. These include Claudius Beatty, Jean Brooks, Joanna Cullen Brown, Peter Coxon, Simon Curtis, John

Doheny, Ronald Draper, Suguru Fukasawa, Simon Gatrell, Ian Gregor, Graham Handley, Timothy Hands, Melissa Hardie, Desmond Hawkins, Samuel Hynes, Michael Irwin, Bill and Vera Jesty, Trevor Johnson, David and Nancy Jones, Denys Kay-Robinson, Bill King, Elizabeth Lawrence, Andrew and Marilyn Leah, Phillip Mallett, Rosemarie Morgan, Harold Orel, Norman Page, Charles Pettit, Frank Pinion, Harry Polley, Jack Schwarz, Robert Schweik, Ruth Skilling, Len Smith, Rosemary Sumner, Furse Swann, Dennis Taylor, Richard Taylor and Tessa Taylor, and, sadly, several who are now 'friends beyond'. Hardy was not only a friendly man, he was a cause of friendship in others.

There remain three people who require very special mention. My wife, Helen, has saved me weeks of work by somehow deciphering my sheets of near-illegible manuscript and producing from her computer a text which I could hand to the publisher without shame. For that I am immensely grateful and left wondering what we textual students of Hardy's works would have done if Florence Hardy had possessed a computer. Finally, a special vote of thanks goes from me to Richard Dutton, the General Editor of the Literary Lives Series, and to Charmian Hearne, my editor at Macmillan, for their patience, efficiency and support.

JAMES GIBSON
Cerne Abbas

A Note on Texts

References to Hardy's novels are to the New Wessex paperback edition, abbreviated *N.W.E.* References to the poems are to *The Complete Poems of Thomas Hardy* (edited by James Gibson), abbreviated *C.P.* *The Collected Letters* are referred to as *C.L.* (full details in the Bibliography).

Introduction

Thomas Hardy was born at Higher Bockhampton in the parish of Stinsford, about two miles from Dorchester, on 2 June 1840. The place of his birth was a small country cottage at the end of a lonely lane surrounded by trees and heathland. It had been built in 1801 by his great-grandfather as a house for his son Thomas (the first), who had recently married Mary Head. The Hardys were mastermasons and had a small building business which placed them in the social scale above the 'workfolk' but meant that they were still comparatively humble people. The writer's father Thomas (the second), was born in 1811 and lived in the Bockhampton cottage in the parish of Stinsford all his life, marrying Jemima Hand in 1839 only six months before Thomas (the third), the writer, was born. Nothing in the circumstances of the baby's birth in this small, secluded cottage could have indicated that nearly eighty-eight years later he would be recognised at his death as the 'Grand Old Man' of English literature and that one hundred and fifty years later he can be seen as one of the greatest of literary geniuses.

This was not a flower that was born to blush unseen far from the madding crowd. Yet looking back now, it can be recognised that much about these circumstances was propitious, that there were certain influences on him which, given the nature of the child and his background, would strongly dispose him to success in life as a writer. His life can best be studied if it is thought of as being composed of three phases, each of approximately thirty years. The first phase began with his birth in 1840 and lasted until the writing of his first published novel, *Desperate Remedies*, in 1871. This was a period of growth and development in which the young Hardy consciously and assiduously prepared himself to be a writer, and tried his hand by writing a little poetry and an unpublished first novel. The second phase lasted from 1870 until 1897 and during those years fourteen of his novels, some fifty of his short stories and almost all his other prose writings were published and he achieved fame as a novelist. It was a period which can now be seen as further preparation for his ultimate aim of being a poet. The third and final phase began in 1898 with the publication of his first book of poems *Wessex Poems* and ended on 11 January 1928 with his death in Dorchester, close to the place of his birth. During those final thirty years he wrote nearly one thousand poems and *The Dynasts* and convinced the world that he was a great poet as well as a great novelist, a distinction rare indeed.

Phase the First: Preparing to Be a Writer (1840–70)

What we inherit from our parents plays a vital part in shaping us and Hardy was particularly fortunate here. His forefathers were masons and did small building jobs. They would have had some interest in creativity and Hardy inherited their creative spirit and interest in structures, materials and carving, and their determination to do a job well. From his father's side too there came a wide-ranging love of music. Both father and grandfather had played viols and violins and had a love of music, religious and secular, which played an important part in their lives. In *The Life and Work of Thomas Hardy* by Thomas Hardy (edited by Michael Millgate, published by Macmillan, and hereafter referred to as *Life*, see pages 175–6) Hardy describes his grandfather's devotion both to church music and to country dances:

> On removing with his wife in 1801 to this home provided by his father John, Thomas Hardy the First (of these Stinsford Hardys) found the church music there in a deplorable condition, it being conducted from the gallery by a solitary old man with an oboe. He immediately set himself, with the easy-going vicar's hearty concurrence, to improve it, and got together some instrumentalists, himself taking the bass-viol as before, which he played in the gallery of Stinsford Church at two services every Sunday from 1801 or 1802 till his death in 1837, being joined later by his two sons who, with other reinforcement, continued playing till about 1842, the period of performance by the three Hardys thus covering inclusively a little under forty years. (p. 13)

Many years later Hardy was to write a poem 'To My Father's Violin', in which he remembers those distant days:

3

In the gallery west the nave,
But a few yards from his grave,
Did you, tucked beneath his chin, to his bowing
     Guide the homely harmony
          Of the quire
     Who for long years strenuously –
          Son and sire –
Caught the strains that at his fingering low or higher
From your four thin threads and eff-holes came outflowing.
                    (*Complete Poems*, hereafter *C.P.*, 381)

Hardy inherited this love of music to full measure. While of 'quite tender years' he was, he tells us, 'extraordinarily sensitive to music' so much so that there were 'among the endless jigs, hornpipes, reels, waltzes and country-dances that his father played of an evening . . . three or four that always moved the child to tears, though he strenuously tried to hide them' (*Life*, p. 19). This sensitivity is also to be found in his love of literature and in his own writing. But he was not just a passive listener. His father taught him to tune a fiddle and when only a boy he used to accompany his father to weddings and parties. At one New Year's Eve party when he was about 13 or 14 he was so carried away that he played a favourite country-dance, 'The New-Rigged Ship', for an unbroken three-quarters of an hour and had to be stopped then by his hostess who was frightened that he would 'burst a bloodvessel' (*Life*, p. 28). This participation in music on weekdays and holidays was on Sundays reinforced by regular attendance at Stinsford church. By the early 1840s the instrumentalists in the old church-choirs had mostly been replaced by barrel-organs and Hardy had to rely on the memories of his older relatives for the material he was later to use in *Under the Greenwood Tree*. But his family were regular in their attendance at church and Hardy talks of himself as having a 'dramatic sense of the church services'. The music of the hymns and the liturgy was an ever-living presence to him and he mentions church music in his writing with the authority of close acquaintanceship over a long period.

He inherited, then, a love of music from his father and this was developed by his own musical interests as a boy both in the secular and religious aspects of his life. Music was to come into his writing both as something that is often mentioned directly and allusively and, more subtly, in the lyricism of his verse. He was particularly resentful of critics who described him as having an ear deaf to music, and repeatedly defended himself by referring to his 'sensitivity to a melody' (*Life*, p. 21). Some of his poems are based upon the rhythms and structures of well-known Victorian hymns, and few today would deny the song-like quality of many such poems as 'When I Set out for Lyonnesse' or 'Great Things' or 'The Voice'.

Among the fine collection of Hardy items in the Dorset County Museum one of the most interesting is the music-book which belonged to his father and grandfather. Today music comes to us so easily from compact discs and the radio that it is easy to forget the difficulties our forefathers in the last century had to face in recording their music. Printed music in the early nineteenth century was expensive and difficult to come by, and just as ballads and songs were often passed on orally so those who played music had to copy it down themselves from the music-books of their friends. The Hardy music-book is a remarkable tribute to the knowledge and industry of the two men but it also illustrates the wide range of their interest, and the manner in which serious religious songs can be put next to sexually suggestive folk-songs without any sense of incongruity. This tradition of juxtaposing the sacred and the profane, the serious and the comic, is one that goes back to English medieval drama where knockabout humour can be followed quite naturally by religious scenes of the utmost piety. There was felt to be no need of a unity of mood, and Shakespeare, in the same tradition, had no hesitation in introducing comedy into the most tragic moments of his plays because he knew that life is a mixture of the comic and the tragic and that the one articulates the other. Hardy talks of the comedy underlying the sorriest things, and his youthful days and nights, with the juxtaposition of church and secular music, were to influence him profoundly as a writer. In one of his most humorous short stories, 'Absent-Mindedness in a Parish Choir', the humour results from a situation in which the church instrumentalists all fall asleep under the influence of a furtive drink of hot brandy and beer, wake up suddenly in the dark of a winter afternoon in the church gallery, think they are at a party they had attended the previous evening, and start playing a bawdy folk tune.

The three Thomas Hardys, grandfather, father, son, were closely linked by music, but there was one way in which the writer could not be like his father. The latter seems to have been a happy-go-lucky man who would rather play his violin then get on with his daily work, who liked his drink and the ladies, and married his wife when she was already three months pregnant. In his poem 'Night in the

Old Home' (*C.P.*, 222) Hardy, describing himself as 'A thinker of
crooked thoughts upon Life in the sere', hears his 'perished people'
answer that he should:

> 'Take of Life what it grants without question. . . .
> Enjoy, suffer, wait: spread the table here freely like us,
> And satisfied, placid, unfretting, watch Time away beamingly!'

His father's fatalistic approach to life could be envied by Hardy
and understood by him. He portrays this fatalism in characters
in his novels and it is typical of his ambivalent approach that he
repeatedly questions what has been gained by education and social
and material advancement, most notably in his poem 'Afternoon
Service at Mellstock' (*C.P.*, 356).

> On afternoons of drowsy calm
>   We stood in the panelled pew,
> Singing one-voiced a Tate-and-Brady psalm
>   To the tune of 'Cambridge New'.
>
> We watched the elms, we watched the rooks,
>   The clouds upon the breeze,
> Between the whiles of glancing at our books,
>   And swaying like the trees.
>
> So mindless were those outpourings! –
>   Though I am not aware
> That I have gained by subtle thought on things
>   Since we stood psalming there.

But by temperament and upbringing he was fated not to be 'satisfied, placid, unfretting'. When he was no more than about five years
of age he lay on his back in the sun and thought how useless he
was and wished that he did not have to grow up (*Life*, p. 20). He
was already sensitive to the 'ongoing' nature of time and the sadness of the tears of things, and this at an age when most children are longing to grow up and be adults. Much of this part of
his character must have come from his mother – Jemima. She was
one of a family of several children whose father died when Jemima
was a young girl, leaving his family in impoverished circumstances.
The hardships of her childhood were such that she was reluctant in

later life to talk about them. Hardy describes her as being of 'unusual ability and judgement' (*Life*, p. 12) and, to escape from her troubles, she became an omnivorous reader. She married Hardy's father in 1839 when she was 25 after having been in service as a maid and cook, and bore her husband four children. That at a time of such high infant mortality all her children survived is a tribute to her good health and toughness. Her influence on Thomas was immense. It became the driving force in his life, and before he was 10 she had him reading Dryden's *Works of Virgil* and Johnson's *Rasselas*.

Tom's was a difficult birth – one account of it tells how the doctor decided that he was dead and it took a watchful midwife to decide that there was life in him – and it was as if the mother had decided that her eldest son for whom she had suffered so much should be more of a success in his life than his easy-going father. There are similarities here with the life of D. H. Lawrence, and, like Lawrence, Hardy's obvious interest in, regard for, and understanding of, women results to some extent from his close association with his mother. Hardy was very near to her as a son and inherited much of her character – her dourness, her interest in people, her love of a good story, her dry sense of humour, and her expectation that life would have as many buffets as rewards. Hardy's note of 30 October 1870 is revealing: 'Mother's notion and also mine: That a figure stands in our van with an arm uplifted, to knock us back from any pleasant prospect we indulge in as probable.' No matter what success and happiness may follow, suffering in childhood is never forgotten and Hardy shared his mother's early sufferings with her as she recollected them.

When Hardy was born there was living in the Bockhampton cottage not just his mother and father but his paternal grandmother, Mary, who talked a great deal to him of the past. The poem 'One We Knew' (*C.P.*, 227) illustrates this:

> She told of that far-back day when they learnt astounded
> > Of the death of the King of France:
> Of the Terror; and then of Bonaparte's unbounded
> > Ambition and arrogance. . . .

> With cap-framed face and long gaze into the embers –
> > We seated around her knees –
> She would dwell on such dead themes, not as one who remembers,
> > But rather as one who sees.

> She seemed one left behind of a band gone distant
>   So far that no tongue could hail:
> Past things retold were to her as things existent,
>   Things present but as a tale.

Hardy's love of anecdote, and his fascination with the past, were
nurtured in his growing-up years by the constant talking together
of mother and grandmother. His earliest surviving poem, which he
claims was written when he was about 18, not only provides a physical picture of the cottage's surroundings in those early years, but
introduces us to Mary Hardy and has her talking about the past.

DOMICILIUM

> It faces west, and round the back and sides
> High beeches, bending, hang a veil of boughs,
> And sweep against the roof. Wild honeysucks
> Climb on the walls, and seem to sprout a wish
> (If we may fancy wish of trees and plants)
> To overtop the apple-trees hard by.
>
> Red roses, lilacs, variegated box
> Are there in plenty, and such hardy flowers
> As flourish best untrained. Adjoining these
> Are herbs and esculents; and farther still
> A field; then cottages with trees, and last
> The distant hills and sky.
>
> Behind, the scene is wilder. Heath and furze
> Are everything that seems to grow and thrive
> Upon the uneven ground. A stunted thorn
> Stands here and there, indeed; and from a pit
> An oak uprises, springing from a seed
> Dropped by some bird a hundred years ago.
>
>   In days bygone –
> Long gone – my father's mother, who is now
> Blest with the blest, would take me out to walk.
> At such a time I once inquired of her
> How looked the spot when first she settled here.
> The answer I remember. 'Fifty years

Have passed since then, my child, and change has marked
The face of all things. Yonder garden-plots
And orchards were uncultivated slopes
O'ergrown with bramble bushes, furze and thorn:
That road a narrow path shut in by ferns,
Which, almost trees, obscured the passer-by.

'Our house stood quite alone, and those tall firs
And beeches were not planted. Snakes and efts
Swarmed in the summer days, and nightly bats
Would fly about our bedrooms. Heathcroppers
Lived in the hills, and were our only friends;
So wild it was when first we settled here.'

(C.P., 1)

It is worth quoting because we witness here not only the close relationship with his grandmother but the living presence of his childhood environment. The cottage surroundings are economically but
observantly described with emphasis on the difference between the
view to the west of trees, flowers and cottages, and the wild heathland which lay behind it, a difference which is to some extent symbolic of that conflict in Hardy's own life between the primitive and
rustic and the sophisticated and urban. A sly touch of humour is
found in the passing reference to 'such hardy flowers\ As flourish
best untrained' and the use of a word like 'esculents' tells us something about Hardy's knowledge of plants.

But the country by itself is never enough for Hardy and he almost
always introduces figures in order to provide significance. Here it
is 'my father's mother' who used to take him out for walks, and
in answer to a question which reveals Hardy already interested
in the past she talks about the changes she has seen in fifty years
of living in the cottage. To her they are considerable. The wildness,
remoteness and loneliness of the cottage in these early days are what
she remembers, and we can understand the effect on Hardy of such
reminiscing. In his own life he was to see changes on a scale as yet
undreamt of and he was to be the chronicler of those changes as
they were to affect the Wessex he knew so well. Later, in *Tess of the
d'Urbervilles* he was to write 'Between the mother, with her fast-
perishing lumber of superstitions, folk-lore, dialect, and orally
transmitted ballads, and the daughter, with her trained National
teachings and Standard knowledge under an infinitely Revised Code,

there was a gap of two hundred years as ordinarily understood' (New Wessex Edition, hereafter *N.W.E.*, p. 43). That gap he had personally observed in talking to his older relatives and to understand his writings we should appreciate that his early years at Bockhampton were largely spent with people who would have been in many ways as much at home in the seventeenth and eighteenth centuries as in the Victorian period of accelerating change in which he was growing up.

'Domicilium' is not a great poem but it is a remarkable achievement for a young man still in his teens, and it tells us a great deal about him. He had read widely among the Romantic poets and knew Wordsworth's style well enough to do a passable pastiche. The blank verse is competent, the vocabulary wide-ranging, the control of rhythmic effects impressive. There is already an interest in such poetic techniques as alliteration and assonance, and a strong sense of structure. How has it come about that this Hardy flower, born in what at first glance might seem such unpropitious circumstances is already showing such talent?

Some of the influences on him have already been described, and the most powerful was his mother's determination that her son should do well in life. It was not enough just to surround him with books; he had to be educated. As he was growing up at a time when there was no State education this entailed paying for him, and Jemima somehow or other found the money to do so. At first he had been a frail child but at 8 he was thought strong enough to be sent to the village school in Lower Bockhampton. This was a National (Church of England) school which had only just been opened. It had been paid for by Julia Augusta Martin who with her husband had bought the adjoining large estate of Kingston Maurward in 1844. Mrs Martin's interest in the school made it, according to Hardy, 'far superior to an ordinary village school', and he tells us in *The Life* (p. 23) that, not having children of her own, 'she had grown passionately fond of Tommy almost from his infancy – said to have been an attractive little fellow at this time – whom she had been accustomed to take into her lap and kiss until he was quite a big child. He quite reciprocated her fondness.' His later fascination with attractive aristocratic ladies may have originated here. Certainly, later he was to recall 'the thrilling "frou frou" of her four grey silk flounces when she used to bend over him' (*Life*, p. 104).

Mrs Hardy seems to have been jealous of the attention the Lady of the Manor gave to her precocious son and in 1849 she took him away from the Bockhampton school; after a visit to relatives in Hertfordshire, he was sent in 1850 to the Dorchester British School, an elementary school established by the Nonconformist British and Foreign Bible Society. This involved a walk of two to three miles each way every day, but he was now stronger and thus began a habit and love of walking which was to be life-long. His astonishingly detailed knowledge of the whole of Dorset – its history, topography and natural life – was largely acquired by extensive walking which gave him the opportunity to observe in detail, to become 'a man who used to notice such things'. Public transport in the early years of Hardy's life was by the stage-coach for long journeys and the tranters' carts for short distances. The railway did not reach Dorchester until the late 1840s. Hardy's novels often begin with characters walking along a road and a character like Tess is repeatedly seen journeying along thoroughfares which may often have symbolic undertones. On his own journey from the Bockhampton cottage to the centre of Dorchester, a journey he made almost every day from 1848 until 1862, he would have observed the changing of the seasons, the activities of the workfolk in the fields, the habits of birds and butterflies, and have stored in his mind memories which were later to be used in his writing. At the end of the lane leading to the cottage he passed the barton built by his father shortly before he was born and mentioned in his poem 'The Oxen', and as he entered Dorchester, bustling with life and so different from the quietness of Higher Bockhampton, he crossed Grey's bridge, later to be portrayed in both *Under the Greenwood Tree* and in *The Mayor of Casterbridge*. Stopping for a moment he would have noticed the green weed stretched out by the flow of the river Frome. In *Under the Greenwood Tree* Parson Maybold, looking from that same bridge, saw 'how the water came rapidly from beneath the arches, glided down a little steep, then spread itself over a pool in which dace, trout, and minnows sported at ease among the long green locks of weed that lay heaving and sinking with their roots towards the current' (*N.W.E.*, p. 187). They still do so to this day. Then in High East Street is The King's Arms hotel where Henchard sits in state as Mayor, unaware that Nemesis is about to strike him.

Dorchester was the county town and there was much for a keen-sighted child to observe – the judges coming to the Assizes, the soldiers in the barracks, the hiring fairs, the markets. Public executions still occurred outside the massive red-brick gaol and Hardy witnessed two of these. The first was on 9 August 1856 when Martha

Browne was executed for murdering her husband. In *The Life* Hardy says no more than that he stood close to the gallows, but in 1919 in a talk with a visitor called Elliott Felkin he recalled:

> The hanging itself did not move me at all. But I sat on after the others went away, not thinking, but looking at the figure . . . turning slowly round on the rope. And then it began to rain, and then I saw – they had put a cloth over the face – how as the cloth got wet, *her features came through it*. That was extraordinary. A boy had climbed up into a tree nearby, and when she dropped he came down in a faint like an apple dropping from a tree. It was curious the two dropping together. (*Encounter*, April 1962)

Freudian interpretations by some biographers of this and a reference in one of his letters to the way in which the woman's 'light black silk gown set off her shape' have led to accusations that Hardy secretly enjoyed the spectacle which gave him a morbidly erotic thrill and revealed something sick in his imagination. But these were really no more than the very natural observations of a highly sensitive and perceptive young man. Dickens and many thousands of others watched public executions in those days without the same accusations being made about them. In fact, Dickens referred to the 'fascination of the repulsive', something most of us have experienced. The second hanging took place about two years later and was observed by Hardy from a hill behind the cottage. He used a big brass family telescope and 'At the moment of his placing the glass to his eye the white figure dropped downwards, and the faint note of the town clock struck eight. The whole thing had been so sudden that the glass nearly fell from Hardy's hands. He seemed alone on the heath with the hanged man and he crept homeward wishing he had not been so curious' (*Life*, p. 33). The short story 'The Withered Arm' ends with an execution at the gaol for which Hardy draws on his first-hand knowledge of such occasions, and it was to this gaol that Boldwood walked after he had shot Sergeant Troy in *Far from the Madding Crowd*.

Isaac Last, the schoolmaster at the British School, was a stern disciplinarian who would 'frequently chase a boy round the room lashing him with his cane until he was white in the face'. Hardy describes him as an able teacher and he soon recognised Hardy's promise as a student. He taught Hardy Latin as an extra and when in 1853 Last opened a more advanced school called an Academy,

Hardy went with him. The syllabus included elementary drawing, advanced arithmetic, geometry and algebra, and he won prizes in 1854 for diligence and good behaviour, and in 1855 for his progress in Latin. His 'bookishness', as he describes it, and his love of study were a vital part of his preparation to be a writer. He was beginning to acquire that vast erudition which distinguishes his work, but that would not have been enough without the human touch. He knew that 'He has read well who has learnt that there is more to read outside books than in them' (*Life*, p. 110) and he was at this time actively playing his fiddle at parties and village festivities where he could both entertain and watch the behaviour of the local folk. He was to be no reclusive bookworm.

His study, his music and his intensive observation of the life around him did not interfere, however, with his falling in love and he was only 14 when he fell in love for the first time with a pretty girl, glimpsed on horseback in Dorchester. For several days he wandered about looking for her, miserably and unsuccessfully, and, in his own self-mocking words 'was more than a week getting over this desperate attachment' (*Life*, p. 29). This was the first of several adolescent attachments which seem to have been of the kind where 'he never told his love' and, as so often at that age, admired at a distance. One of the girls is the subject of his poem 'To Lizbie Browne' (*C.P.*, 94). Significantly, this is partly a lament for an action not taken, an opportunity missed:

VII

Dear Lizbie Browne,
I should have thought,
'Girls ripen fast,'
And coaxed and caught
You ere you passed,
Dear Lizbie Browne!

VIII

But, Lizbie Browne,
I let you slip;
Shaped not a sign;
Touched never your lip
With lip of mine,
Lost Lizbie Browne!

It is a motif which sounds again and again in his novels and poems.

His full-time scholastic education ended in July 1856. Although it had lasted eight years and provided him with an education far better than 'someone of his class' could have expected, it had not provided him with the classical qualifications needed to go on to university. A sense of inferiority resulted which was to receive literary expression in *Jude the Obscure* where Jude is advised by the Master of Biblioll College to remain 'in your own sphere', that of a 'working-man'. His mother's influence was felt at this stage of his life because it was she, anxious as always that her son should do well in life, who found the money for him to be articled to an architect, Mr John Hicks of Dorchester. Architects at that time did not have quite the professional status they have today, but they were higher up the social scale than builders. Hicks recognised Hardy as a promising pupil and agreed to accept him for a lower premium than usual. The £40 which Mrs Hardy paid would have been at least £1000 in today's money and it must have required some sacrifice on her part to find even that amount. Moreover, there was the loss of income that would result from not sending Hardy out to earn his living and contribute to the family budget. By such altruism Jemima Hardy did much to bind her son's loyalty and love to her.

The choice of architecture for Hardy and his articling to John Hicks can now be seen, paradoxically, as another important step in his preparation to be a writer even though he himself would not have seen it as so at that time. Mr Hicks was himself a well-educated man and his office was a relaxed and happy one where Hardy found himself among fellow pupils whose discussions challenged and stimulated him in much the way that might have happened at a good university. Both Hicks and one of his pupils, Henry Barstow, were enthusiastic about the Classics. Barstow was a keen Baptist and he and Hardy sharpened their minds by lengthy discussions about such matters as infant baptism. These discussions entailed a detailed study of the Greek New Testament and this, together with his regular attendance at church, meant that he was acquiring a profound and comprehensive knowledge of the Bible on which he would draw for many purposes when he became a writer. In *Thomas Hardy: Distracted Preacher?* Timothy Hands describes how the words Hardy 'uses are greatly affected by his religious past' and he finds more than 600 biblical allusions in the fourteen published novels, while F. B. Pinion, in his invaluable *A Hardy Companion*, tells us that 'No other book, not even the works of Shakespeare, informed the

thought and character of Hardy as much as the Bible.' At this stage
of his life Hardy even considered becoming a candidate for the ministry and he was later to describe himself as 'churchy'. However,
some indication of the future is to be found in his observation that
with the departure of Barstow to New Zealand at the end of his
training he returned with some pleasure to 'pagan writers' such as
Homer and Virgil. Next door to Hicks's architectural office in South
Street, Dorchester, lived William Barnes, the characterful Dorset
poet, philologist, engraver, teacher, and, later, minister of the Church.
Hardy's admiration for Barnes's poetry must have begun about this
time, and it is likely that his deep interest in language, etymo-
logical and semantic, dates from then. Here again was a piece of good
fortune for the incipient writer, for Barnes had much to teach him
about the history and use of the English language, and about poetic
techniques. Most of Barnes's poetry is written in the Dorset dialect
and, although it may appear simple, it is based upon profound
knowledge and the use of a wide range of vocabulary, alliteration,
assonance, rhyme and rhythm. In his Toucan Press Monograph
William Barnes: Friend of Thomas Hardy, Aneirin Talfan Davies describes Barnes's interest in Welsh poetry and in particular the
cynghanedd, a literary device using similar sounds in an elaborate
and symmetrical way. Barnes died in 1886 and Hardy wrote a poem
called 'The Last Signal' (*C.P.*, 412) in memory of him. As Hardy
walked across the fields towards Came Church where Barnes was
to be buried, he saw the sun flash on the coffin as if Barnes were
sending him a signal. The poem makes special use of *cynghanedd* as
a tribute to his old friend, and Hardy used the device repeatedly in
his poetry. It is a fascinating aspect of English literature that Gerard
Manley Hopkins, another poet active like Thomas Hardy in the 1860s
and 1870s, and like him unpublished and unrecognised at that time,
admired Barnes's poetry and learnt from it.

Hicks was primarily an ecclesiastical architect and a good deal of
his concern was with the restoration of old Gothic churches. Many
of these had been so neglected during the preceding two or three
hundred years that when the religious revival took place in the
1840s and 1850s some degree of restoration had to take place. Hardy
was assigned by Hicks to this restoration work and he spent many
hours in churches and churchyards 'sketching, with another pupil,
and we had many pleasant times at the work. Probably this explains
why churchyards and churches never seem gloomy to me' (*C.L.*, 6,
p. 122). He later regretted that he had been involved in what he felt

was at times unnecessary destruction of fine old Gothic work. As a pupil Hardy would have done little more than copying but he would then have moved on to making surveys and taking measurements, and he proved himself to be, as might be expected, a meticulous and conscientious draughtsman. His *Architectural Notebook* was published in 1966 and in an informative introduction the editor, Claudius Beatty, writes of the influence his first profession, architecture, undoubtedly had on his development as a writer. He was actively involved in architecture for twenty years and what he learnt from this first profession never left him. Although he repeatedly denied that there were any autobiographical references in his novels, in at least one of them, *A Laodicean*, architecture plays a large part both literally and symbolically, and leading characters in *Desperate Remedies, A Pair of Blue Eyes* and *A Laodicean* are architects. Architecture comes into several of his poems, and one of them 'The Abbey Mason' (*C.P.*, 332), is about the 'Inventor of the "Perpendicular" style of Gothic Architecture' and is inscribed '(With Memories of John Hicks, Architect)'. Architecture is present in the novels in the countless descriptions of buildings of many kinds – cottages, barns, churches, castles, country houses. Hardy writes about them with a knowledge which gives interest and authority to the story, and impresses the reader. When he describes Knapwater House in *Desperate Remedies* or Weatherbury church in *Far from the Madding Crowd* he is describing, with some imaginative licence, buildings which he knows, and it seems as if often his imagination needs to begin with a *real* building before he can create his *imaginative* one. He is also fascinated by the parts of buildings, and windows and doors have a large part to play. Thus, in *Far from the Madding Crowd*, at the shearing supper the distance between the farmer and her employees is indicated by her sitting just inside the window while the workfolk sit at the same long table, but outside.

There was yet another way in which his architectural studies were to be carried over into his writing. Defending himself against the cruel and often ignorant attacks on his early books of verse, he wrote in *The Life* (p. 323):

In the reception of this and later volumes of Hardy's poems there was, he said, as regards form, the inevitable ascription to ignorance of what was really choice after full knowledge. That the author loved the art of concealing art was undiscerned. For instance, as to rhythm. Years earlier he had decided that too regular a beat was bad art. He had fortified himself in his opinion by thinking of the analogy of architecture, between which art and that of poetry he had discovered, to use his own words, that there existed a close and curious parallel, each art, unlike some others, having to carry a rational content inside its artistic form. He knew that in architecture cunning irregularity is of enormous worth, and it is obvious that he carried on into his verse, perhaps unconsciously, the Gothic art-principle in which he had been trained – the principle of spontaneity, found in mouldings, tracery, and such-like – resulting in the 'unforeseen' (as it has been called) character of his metres and stanzas – that of stress rather than of syllable, poetic texture rather than poetic veneer; the latter kind of thing, under the name of 'constructed ornament', being what he, in common with every Gothic student, had been taught to avoid as the plague. He shaped his poetry accordingly, introducing metrical pauses, and reversed beats; and found for his trouble that some particular line of a poem exemplifying this principle was greeted by one of those terrible persons, the funny man of the critical press, with a jocular remark that such a line 'did not make for immortality', the writer being probably a journalist who had never heard of pauses or beats of any kind. The same critic might have gone to one of our cathedrals (to follow up the analogy of architecture), and on discovering that the carved leafage of some capital or spandrel in the best period of Gothic art strayed freakishly out of its bounds over the moulding, where by rule it had no business to be, or that the enrichments of a string-course were not accurately spaced; or that there was a sudden blank in a wall where a window was to be expected from formal measurement, have declared with equally merry conviction, 'This does not make for immortality'.

This passage is worth quoting in full because it reveals not only Hardy's natural sensitivity to hostile reviewing but also the close relationship he saw between what appear at first to be two quite different art-forms. His poems are full of examples of what he calls 'cunning irregularity' where, for example, a repeated structure is subtly changed towards the end. Thus in 'The Colour' (*C.P.*, 657) the first four stanzas all begin with a line ' "What shall I bring you?" ' but the fifth and final stanza is slightly changed to ' "What shall I bring you/ Then?" ' where the run-over provides a satisfying variant on the normal pattern.

And there was yet another way in which we might possibly deduce from the novels and poems that he had had architectural training. He is passionately interested in structure. His greatest novels are all constructed with the care an architect would give to a building. *The Mayor of Casterbridge* is a fine example of this, and the internal division of his novels under such headings as 'Books' and 'Phases' is also worthy of study. But it is in the poems that this keen awareness of the shape of things is most fully exploited. Some poets have written almost entirely in couplets, others in quatrains, others in blank verse. Hardy uses a multitude of different line-lengths and stanza forms, and to look at the 947 poems in his *Complete Poems* is to be aware of the remarkable variety of poetic structures he employs. So aware is he of the pattern the words make on the page that he once instructed his printers to move the opening and closing lines of the two stanzas in his poem 'A Broken Appointment' (*C.P.*, 99) 'two em', that is the space taken by two 'm's, to the right.

In all his work there is a strong sense of place and time. The sense of place comes partly from his work as an architect. A strong sense of time, and particularly of time passing, seems to have been with him from his earliest childhood. His first novel, *Desperate Remedies*, is divided up not by chapters but by periods of time, and in all his work he takes care to make his readers aware of where the action is taking place, and when. In the poems he is frequently writing in the present about time past and this results in interesting temporal structures. Thus the first two stanzas of 'The Oxen' (*C.P.*, 403) describe the past, the second two the present. In 'Beyond the Last Lamp' (*C.P.*, 257) the first three stanzas seem to be describing the present, but in the fourth and fifth stanzas we suddenly learn that all this was, in fact, thirty years ago. In 'Beeny Cliff' (*C.P.*, 291) the pattern is similar, with a powerful temporal break after the third stanza. This has the same effect as the volta, the break after the first eight lines, in a Petrarchan sonnet, and one of the delights of Hardy's verse is the powerful structural sense.

These years, from 1856 to 1862, from the ages of 16 to 22, were immensely important to Hardy's mental and cultural growth. His life was now so full that much of his reading 'was done between five and eight in the morning before he left home for the office' (*Life*, p. 32). His programme of self-education was such that he read widely, and particularly among the classical authors. It continued even on his walks to and from the office in Dorchester as he used

to soliloquise in Latin on his various projects. His mother's determination that he should succeed in life was now his, and he seems
to have been driven by ambition to raise himself from his humble
background. In a passage of particular importance in *The Life* (p. 36)
he describes how he was able to see the activities of town and country in a peculiarly close juxtaposition. In Dorchester there were now
railways and telegraphs and daily London papers, while in Bockhampton there was a world of shepherds and ploughmen who
thought of these modern developments as wonders.

> To these externals may be added the peculiarities of his inner life,
> which might almost have been called academic – a triple existence
> unusual for a young man – what he used to call, in looking back,
> a life twisted of three strands – the professional life, the scholar's
> life, and the rustic life, combined in the twenty-four hours of one
> day, as it was with him through these years. He would be reading
> the *Iliad*, the *Aeneid*, or the Greek Testament from six to eight in
> the morning, would work at Gothic architecture all day, and then
> in the evening rush off with his fiddle under his arm – sometimes
> in the company of his father as first violin and uncle as 'celloist
> – to play country-dances, reels, and hornpipes at an agricultur-
> ist's wedding, christening, or Christmas party in a remote dwell-
> ing among the fallow fields, not returning sometimes till nearly
> dawn . . .' (*Life*, p. 36)

In his auto-didacticism Hardy would have had the full support
of his mother whose strength of character was such that they were a
close-knit family. There were now four children. Mary had followed
Tom in 1841 and then, after a gap of ten years, Henry was born in
1851 and Katharine (always known as Kate) in 1856. As might be
expected, Hardy was very close to Mary and there was a strong
bond of affection between them. Both were earnest and introspect-
ive and they had more of their mother in them than did the two
later children who had the easy-going nature of their father. Mary
began training as a schoolteacher at Salisbury Training College in
April 1860 and Hardy drew upon his knowledge of her experience
to provide material for *Jude the Obscure*.

There is one other friend who must be mentioned because of
the effect he was to have on Hardy's life. Fordington St George is a
Dorchester parish on the Bockhampton side of the town. To it came
as vicar in 1829 the Reverend Henry Moule, a young man of strongly

Evangelical ideas who during his fifty-one years as vicar acquired
national recognition because of the outspokenness of his views on
the 1854 cholera outbreak in Dorchester and the courage he showed
at that time. He was a vigorous man of wide interests, and of his
seven sons two became Bishops, one a President of a Cambridge
College, and another a distinguished archaeologist and then Curator
of the Dorset County Museum. Horace Moule, his fourth son, had
become a friend of Hardy's by 1857 when he presented Hardy with
a copy of Jabez Hogg's *Elements of Experimental and Natural Philosophy*. He was a gifted and generous author, of whom one of his
brothers said about him as a teacher of the Classics, 'Wonderful
was his subtle faculty for imparting, along with all due care for
grammatical precision, a living interest in the subject-matter, and
for shedding an indefinable glamour of the ideal over all we read'
(H. J. Moule, *Memories of a Vicarage*, p. 35). His academic distinction
was such that he won the Hulsean Prize at Cambridge in 1858 and
had a book on the Roman Republic published in 1860. In addition,
he was a poet, loved music, and wrote essays and reviews which
appeared in national periodicals. Although eight years older than
Hardy he seems to have recognised in him qualities which were
worthy of nourishing, and Hardy must have regarded Horace with
a mixture of admiration, worship, envy and love. He was an intellectual, a scholar, a teacher, a man whose world included not only
London but Oxford and Cambridge. And yet he was not above making a friend out of Hardy, stimulating his mind and awakening him
to new areas of intellectual and cultural experience. It may have
been he who first made Hardy aware of the geological discoveries
which were to challenge the literal truth of some passages of the
Old Testament and they would certainly have discussed together
Darwin's *The Origin of Species* which, published in 1859, did so much
to destroy Hardy's religious beliefs. A dispute between Horace and
his father in which he was rebuked for buying theologically unsound
books provided Hardy with the substance of the scene in which in
Tess of the d'Urbervilles Angel Clare is rebuked in a similar way by
his father.

Such tension between father and son must have been disturb-
ing to Horace Moule who greatly respected his father even if he
could not subscribe completely to his rigidly held views. It almost
certainly contributed to his alcoholism, which may also have been
the result of the taking of opium when overworked while reviewing
books. As so often happens with alcoholism, there were times of

abstinence – he even lectured on temperance in 1861 – and then a
return to despair and drunkenness. Rumours exist about his sexual
behaviour but here we can only accept Millgate's just and objective
opinion: 'What cannot be so precisely pinned down is the part played
in his personal tragedy by that ambiguous sexuality which seems
to have constituted the obverse, so to speak, of his gifts as a teacher
and his devotion to the boys and young men who were his pupils'
(Michael Millgate, *Thomas Hardy: A Biography*, hereafter 'Millgate',
p. 70) Hardy would certainly have known this other side of Moule's
character and the drunken outbursts of Jude in *Jude the Obscure* may
owe something to his observation of Moule's lapses. Their friendship, however, survived such moments and contributed a great deal
to the widening of Hardy's interests and his earnest desire to succeed in the world. Yet, at the same time, the friendship must have
strengthened the ambivalence of his approach to study and the intellectual life. Might Moule, he may have asked, have been happier if
he hadn't been so well-educated and intellectual?

In 1860 Hardy completed his architectural training but he continued to work as a paid assistant for Hicks, earning 15 shillings
a week. Now he could afford to take lodgings in Dorchester and
although the Bockhampton cottage remained his home – he had
lived there almost continuously for twenty years – his visits to it
were mostly at weekends. London had been brought much closer
by the railway and a new element of mobility manifested itself in
the lives of Dorset's inhabitants. A visit with his mother to Hatfield
when he was 9 had already given him some experience of travelling and by the early 1860s he was hungry for more. In *The Life*
(p. 38) he describes how he was attracted to one of Hicks's pupils
by his visits to London and

> his return thence whistling quadrilles and other popular music,
> with accounts of his dancing experiences at the Argyle Rooms
> and Cremorne – both then in full swing. Hardy would relate that
> one quadrille in particular his precursor Fippard could whistle
> faultlessly, and while giving it would caper about the office to
> an imaginary dance-figure, embracing an imaginary Cremorne or
> Argyle *danseuse*. The fascinating quadrille remained with Hardy
> all his life, but he never could identify it.

The lure of London to the young Hardy was great. *There*, he could
continue his education and widen it still further, *there*, were to be

found experiences unknown in Dorchester, *there*, he could continue
his preparation for what was perhaps just beginning to take shape
in his mind, the career of a writer. He had already written some
poetry, including 'Domicilium', and he had had one or two small
prose-pieces published in local papers. He would need to continue
to earn his living by architecture but London would provide opportunities that could be found nowhere else, so on 17 April 1862, at
the age of 21 he set out for London.

LONDON, 1862–67

Hardy, who described himself at the time as being 'quite a pink-
faced youth even now', cannot have had any certainty of his ability
to earn his living in what must have seemed to him a vast, noisy
and bustling town, and he took a return railway ticket presumably
as some kind of insurance against failure. Calling on an acquaintance he could not have felt encouraged by 'Wait till you have walked
the streets a few weeks . . . and your elbows begin to shine, and the
hems of your trousers get frayed, as if nibbled by rats! Only practical men are wanted here' (*Life*, p. 40). But good luck was with
him and he soon found lodgings while one of his two letters of introduction led to his being sent to meet Arthur Blomfield, son of a
bishop, a Cambridge graduate and a well-known church designer
and restorer. He needed someone to help him with this work, and
Hardy had exactly the qualifications needed. Blomfield was then a
comparatively young man of 33 and, like Hicks, he ran a happy
and relaxed office, which was situated at 8 Adelphi Terrace from
where, Hardy informed a correspondent later in life, he could see
'the Embankment and Charing-Cross Bridge built'. Blomfield was
a good architect and a cultured man. He loved singing glees and
catches with his staff during office hours, something that must have
delighted the musical Hardy.

But there were unpleasanter aspects to the work. As the son of
a bishop, Blomfield was given the job of supervising the removal of
bodies where a new railway line at St Pancras required a cutting
through a churchyard. Victorian propriety demanded that this
morbid job should be 'done decently and in order', and Blomfield
was thought to be the right man for the job. Checking up that the
work had been done properly Blomfield was horrified to find that
there was no evidence that the bodies had been reinterred and that

there were rumours that sacks of bones had been sold to the bone-mills. He appointed a clerk-of-works who was never to leave the site during working hours, and deputed Hardy to keep a watch on the clerk-of-works.

'The plan,' Hardy writes, 'worked excellently,' and throughout the late autumn and early winter (of probably the year 1865 or thereabouts) Hardy attended at the churchyard – each evening between five and six, as well as sometimes at other hours. There after nightfall, within a high hoarding that could not be over-looked, and by the light of flare-lamps, the exhumation went on continuously of the coffins that had been uncovered during the day, new coffins being provided for those that came apart in lifting, and for loose skeletons; and those that held together being carried to the new ground on a board merely; Hardy supervising these mournful processions when present – with what thoughts may be imagined, and Blomfield sometimes meeting him there. In one coffin that fell apart was a skeleton and two skulls. He used to tell that when, after some fifteen years of separation, he met Arthur Blomfield again and their friendship was fully renewed, among the latter's first words were 'Do you remember how we found the man with two heads at St Pancras?' (*Life*, p. 47)

It has been remarked that churchyards and graves play a sub-stantial part in Hardy's novels and poems. That is so but it should be remembered that his work as an architect specialising in church restoration meant that he spent many hours drawing in church-yards – one of his poems is entitled 'Copying Architecture in an Old Minster' (*C.P.*, 369) – and that his ghoulish experiences in Old St Pancras Churchyard must have made a lifelong impression on him. Hardy's dry sense of humour would have helped him here, and we meet that humour in a poem which would have had its origins in those macabre nights in St Pancras Churchyard.

IN THE CEMETERY

'You see those mothers squabbling there?'
Remarks the man of the cemetery.
'One says in tears, "'Tis mine lies here!"
Another, "Nay, mine, you Pharisee!"
Another, "How dare you move my flowers
And put your own on this grave of ours!"

But all their children were laid therein
At different times, like sprats in a tin.

'And then the main drain had to cross,
And we moved the lot some nights ago,
And packed them away in the general foss
With hundreds more. But their folks don't know,
And as well cry over a new-laid drain
As anything else, to ease your pain!'

(C.P., 342)

Hardy's comic satire is deployed here against the inability of so many of us to face reality – and particularly the reality of death. His early life in a rural environment where hardship was endemic had taught him the uselessness and dangers of self-delusion and sentimentality. One has to live in the real world, not one of euphemisms.

As an assistant architect, he was not at this time entrusted with designing, and as much of his work was monotonous and mechanical copying, he threw himself into his out-of-work activities with relief and enthusiasm, and, as in Dorchester, he wasted not a moment. Soon after arriving in London he called on Mrs Martin, who had left Kingston Maurward House and was living in London. He expected to find her unaltered but she had, of course, aged and he was no longer the 'rosy-cheeked, innocent little boy' she had known all those years before at the Bockhampton school. The meeting was not a success and Hardy never repeated his call, but it taught him something about the difference between dream and reality. He made frequent visits to the International Exhibition at South Kensington where there were many items of interest to the architect and a fine collection of English paintings. He had his head read by a phrenologist and was told that it 'would lead him to no good' (*Life*, p. 43). He got to know some of the leading coffee-houses and restaurants, being particularly fond of Bertolini's. He saw Charles Kean and his wife performing Shakespeare, and at Drury Lane followed the Phelps series of Shakespeare plays with the text in his hand. He heard Dickens do one of his famous readings. One would have liked to know what Hardy made of Dickens but, alas, he is very sparing and discreet in his comments on other writers and he does not tell us. Just occasionally there is an echo of Dickens's style in Hardy's novels and Hardy is fond of the dramatic incident in dialogue, as Dickens was, but they are very different kinds of novelist.

Music still featured largely in Hardy's life and in addition to singing in the office glee-club he bought himself an old fiddle and practised pieces from the foreign operas which were then in vogue at Covent Garden and Her Majesty's Theatre, operas by such composers as Rossini, Donizetti, Verdi, Meyerbeer and Bellini. He went to the opera two or three times a week and heard singers as famous as Tietjens, Nilsson and Patti. In an article in *The Thomas Hardy Journal* (January 1990) Colin Boone has shown that Hardy's love of music was not confined to religious, folk and popular music of that time, but that he also possessed a considerable knowledge of classical music, so much so that he could later entitle a poem 'Lines to a Movement in Mozart's E-Flat Symphony' and make the comment that Tchaikovsky's music exactly expressed the modern tone of unrest. In lighter mood he went to balls at Willis's Rooms, which had previously been known as Almack's and to the Cremorne Gardens in Chelsea and the Argyle Rooms in Great Windmill Street.

Robert Gittings in his *Young Thomas Hardy* (p. 58) describes the girls there as prostitutes and he quotes the words of a French visitor to the Argyle Rooms who saw it as 'a kind of lust-casino'. In his poem 'Reminiscences of a Dancing Man' (*C.P.*, 165) Hardy looks back forty years and paints a lively picture of the dancing and gaiety at these places, seemingly innocent until in the last lines he wonders whether those dancing damsels of old are now dancing as spectres within 'The smoky halls of the Prince of Sin'.

Every experience in that London period, even those at the cemetery and the ballroom, was later to be grist to Hardy's writer's mill but the more serious side of him was still concerned with his own self-education. He was already keeping a personal notebook in which entries such as the following appear: 'End of Dec. 1865 – To insects the twelvemonth has been an epoch, to leaves a life, to tweeting birds a generation, to man a year.' (*Life*, p. 56) and 'More conducive to success in life than the desire for much knowledge is the being satisfied with ignorance on irrelevant subjects' (*Life*, p. 50), a maxim which he does not seem to have observed himself at this period of his life. He felt that he should know more French so he took French classes at King's College. An educated man needed to have a knowledge of art history so he went to the National Gallery whenever he could and devoted 'twenty minutes after lunch to an inspection of the masters hung there, confining his attention to a single master on each visit, and forbidding his eyes to stray to any other . . . he used to recommend the plan to young people, telling

them that they would insensibly acquire a greater insight into
schools and styles by this means than from any guide books to
the painters' works and manners' (*Life*, p. 53). What is impressive
here is the planning and discipline it reveals and this is a very
noticeable part of Hardy's character. Although he says that it is all
done for 'sheer liking', the precision of the planning hints at sub-
conscious, if not conscious, wishes for self-improvement. We know
that about this time, probably influenced by his study of architectural periods, he had thought of becoming an art critic and writing
for the press.

Not that there is any reason to doubt Hardy's great love of art
and his understanding of it, and all these twenty-minute periods
spent in the National Gallery were invaluable to him when he began to write and must have contributed to his astonishing visual
awareness. He was no mean artist himself and a number of his
sketches in watercolours of places in Dorset still survive. London
offered him the opportunity to study art in a way he could never
have done in Dorchester and he took full advantage of it, as indeed
he did of almost everything that would help him in that as yet
uncertain career towards which he was slowly feeling his way. There
still exists (reproduced in Richard Taylor's edition of *The Personal
Notebooks of Thomas Hardy*) a notebook headed 'Schools of Painting'
which he began in 1863 and which contains brief factual material
about the work of major painters. In the novels he frequently draws
upon his knowledge of art by using paintings as images and analogies that enrich description. Sometimes, especially in the earlier
novels, these allusions are too esoteric and smack of name-dropping,
but at their best they add an extra dimension to his writing. Sometimes the description in the novel seems to have begun with a painting which his retentive memory had stored away for later use. Thus
in *Far from the Madding Crowd* it has been pointed out that the
description of Gabriel Oak, the shepherd, standing with his lamp
by his shepherd's hut, is a visual echo of Holman Hunt's 'The Light
of the World' in which Christ stands beside a hut with a lantern,
while Arabella standing behind the bar of the inn at Christminster in *Jude* bears a strong resemblance to the barmaid in Manet's
painting 'A Bar at the Folies-Bergère'. But his knowledge of art is
used not only in this fairly direct way, it is also used to suggest
ways of seeing. In *The Woodlanders* Marty is seen by the hairdresser
through the window of her cottage as part of an 'impression-picture'
and we know that Hardy had visited an exhibition of paintings by

the French Impressionists shortly before he wrote that novel. In 1889 he attended the Old Masters Exhibition at the Royal Academy, and made a note: 'Turner's water-colours; each is a landscape *plus a man's soul*. . . . What he paints chiefly is *light as modified by objects*. He first recognises the impossibility of really reproducing on canvas all that is in a landscape; then gives for that which cannot be reproduced a something else which shall have upon the spectator an approximative effect to that of the real' (*Life*, pp. 225–6). This highly perceptive comment on Turner's work also tells us something about Hardy's last novels which are novels *plus a man's soul* and aim at providing something other than completely realistic description.

Music, architecture, art – they are all becoming important components of Hardy's mind. What about literature? Here again London is important because it was while he was there between 1862 and 1867 that the idea of being a writer began gradually to become significant. As we have seen, he had written some prose and verse while in Dorchester but he had not taken this at all seriously. In London he showed that he could write a good essay by being presented in 1863 with the Royal Institute of British Architects' Silver Medal for an essay he had written 'On the Application of Coloured Bricks and Terra Cotta to Modern Architecture'. In 1865 *Chambers's Journal* published anonymously what he called rather disparagingly – but then he was always modest about his own work – 'a humorous trifle' called 'How I Built Myself a House'. This was his first professional appearance as a writer and it earned him the sum of £3.15.0. Robert Gittings quite rightly says of this almost forgotten article that it is of 'great charm and is worth noticing' and indeed it is. About the same time he decided that he would take up poetry seriously. It is possible that this action was given final motivation by the short talks on poets and poetry which he gave to Blomfield's pupils and assistants 'on afternoons when there was not much to be done, or at all events when not much was done!' (*Life*, p. 49) Although Hardy has always been better-known as a novelist it should not be overlooked that his first wish was to be a poet, that he took up novel-writing only because he could not earn a living as a poet, that he returned to writing poetry as soon as he had an assured income from his novels, that in later life he more than once pointed out that he had spent more years in writing poetry than in writing novels, and that he frequently said that it was as a poet that he wished to be remembered. Nothing would have pleased him more than to know how widely read his poetry is today, so many years after his death.

To understand this we need to appreciate that he was born not long after the great Romantic Period of English verse had ended, and before the great period of the English novel had arrived, and that his formative years saw him reading a great deal of Wordsworth and Coleridge, Shelley and Keats. Since the days of the great Classical writers poetry had been regarded as the supreme form of expression. To Shelley poets were 'the unacknowledged legislators of the world'. For Keats poetry 'should strike the reader as a wording of his own highest thoughts', while for Wordsworth poetry was 'the breath and finer spirit of all knowledge'.

Hardy inherited much of the Romantics' vision of poetry and to him the poet was a seer, because he saw into and expressed the heart of things. 'In verse was concentrated the essence of all imaginative and emotional literature', he wrote in *The Life* (p. 51), and in his 'Apology' to his 1922 book of verse, *Late Lyrics and Earlier* he talked about poetry and religion touching each other. When in 1865 he set out to be a poet there must have been in his mind the fact that even though his growing criticism of the Church and many of its works made it increasingly unlikely that he would ever now be a benevolent influence on mankind as an ordained minister, nevertheless through poetry he could do something similar. His preparation for his writing of poetry had all the thoroughness of a training for the ministry. He set about acquiring volumes of poetry and with an infinite capacity for taking pains kept a notebook, headed 'Studies, Specimens etc', which contained lists of words and epithets old and new, which he might use in poems. He even bought copies of Nuttall's *Standard Pronouncing Dictionary* and Walker's *Rhyming Dictionary*.

He might have said that at this time his was a life twisted into four strands – the professional life of an architect, the life of study, because he continued to read widely in literature, philosophy and theology, the life of leisure and participation in the multifarious activities of London, and the life of poetry. At this time he tells us that his mind was 'deeply immersed in the study and function of English poetry' (*Life*, p. 52). It took a man of Hardy's exceptional energy and ability to find enough time in the twenty-four hours of each day to write at all.

The poetry-writing began in 1865 and by 1866 he was sufficiently confident to send some poems to magazines, and when they were

rejected – as they appear all to have been – he accepted the judgement of editors and never sent them out twice. Later he regarded
this as a fortunate thing because when he began to publish poetry
in the 1890s many of these poems had been preserved (he seems to
have had a capacious bottom-drawer) and he was able 'by the mere
change of a few words or the rewriting of a line or two, to make
them quite worthy of publication' (*Life*, p. 49). These poems of the
1860s are varied in quality. At least one, 'Neutral Tones' (*C.P.*, 9)
is regarded as among his best and another 'The Ruined Maid'
(*C.P.*, 128) is among his most popular. Overall there is a preoccu-
pation already with irony and such themes as the large part played
in life by sheer chance (referred to as 'crass casualty' in 'Hap' (*C.P.*, 4),
the sufferings of lovers, the tears of things, and the passing of time.
Love is the major subject, as it was to be when he became a professional writer. Many of these early poems are obviously exercises in
writing certain conventional forms. For example, his sonnets, as
Professor Dennis Taylor has shown in his *Hardy's Metres and Victorian Prosody* (p. 78), 'tend to show a development from conventional imitation [of such writers of sonnets as Petrarch, Spenser
and Shakespeare] through modified convention to original forms'.
It is often difficult to know to what extent Hardy is using autobiographical material but Professor Millgate has confidently related
the four 'She to Him' sonnets as growing out of Hardy's emotional involvement with an Eliza Nicholls to whom he was 'more or
less formally engaged from about 1863 until 1867' (Millgate, p. 84).
Others, which might be described as 'the enigma variations', are
likely to remain an insoluble problem to the biographer. It should
not always be assumed as evidence that when Hardy uses the word
'I' in a poem he is the 'I': he thinks in dramatic terms and in his
poetry he is continually creating characters who speak to us in the
first person and may be completely Hardy, partly Hardy or not
Hardy at all.

Part of his greatness results from an extreme sensitivity to many
aspects of life, but that sensitivity made him a shy, diffident, even
secretive, person and meant that he hid behind many veils. As we
have seen his first piece of writing in *Chambers's Journal* was published anonymously, as were his first two novels. He wrote his own
life-story, and passed it off as having been written by his second
wife, partly in the hopeless hope of preventing too much enquiring
into his private life. To confuse the issue he added to the difficulties
of future biographers by burning a great deal of the evidence in a

series of bonfires on the Max Gate lawn. A writer's private life was his own affair, and, it was up to the writer to decide how much of it was revealed. He could never forget, in many ways did not want to, his own humble background, but the snobberies of the time made him delicately aware of it and, interestingly, in *The Life* he tries to hide just how humble it was. The fact that in the 1851 census Hardy's father was described as a bricklayer was not mentioned, Hardy preferring to describe him as being in the building and masonry business. By some genealogical gymnastics he connected his branch of the Hardy family with the better-class Hardys and made his father's business sound far more substantial than it was. Ironically, today, when to have had a father who was a miner or a manual worker is regarded as a status symbol to be proud of, he might well have been emphasising the lowly conditions of his birth and childhood.

In any judgement of Hardy we must remember the ambivalences of that background, one which we can now see to have been rich in influences on the developing writer even if it was comparatively poor in material resources and the so-called refinements of life. When the young Hardy uses a Latin title for his poem 'Domicilium' or a little too obviously shows off his knowledge in his earliest novels, or enjoys mentioning in *The Life* the upper-class ladies with whom he dined, it really won't do for critics in these days of inverted and different snobberies to be severe in their judgements. His defence must be – and it is a good one – that he grew up a very sensitive young man at a time when the class system was rigid and could be merciless on those who aimed to rise in the world. His awareness of the class differences which he saw around him and which he encountered in his own life is one of the most pervasive influences on his novel-writing.

There were undoubtedly experiences which Hardy had to endure in those formative years, which do much to explain what Millgate very nicely calls 'the extraordinary discrepancy between the public boldness of his literary presence and the defensive reticence of his private self' (Millgate, p. 45). As the idea of a literary career became ever stronger in Hardy's mind in the mid-1860s, that 'defensive reticence' is a vital element of it. Every writer has to draw upon personal experiences, often of a delicate and painful kind, and Hardy is an intensely personal writer. He is faced with the problem that he has to reveal and yet wishes to conceal, and this explains the often enigmatic way in which he writes, the deliberate ambiguities and contradictions, the way in which *The Life* was almost entirely his own work even if it was passed off as having been written by Florence. The four 'She to Him' poems might have been written by a woman to a lover who had proved faithless and found someone else. In fact, they are written by a man who has the imaginative ability to express such a woman's feelings. Hardy would certainly not have wanted us to know to what extent these poems refer to a living woman, although it is natural that with both protagonists long dead we should want to do so. As the poems are obviously an exercise in writing a pastiche of the Elizabethan sonnet, he may have thought that most of his readers would assume that it was no more than a literary exercise, particularly as from the outset we know that a man provides the words, not a woman. If, as seems likely, they were sent by Hardy to a journal editor with the intention that they should be published anonymously, Hardy might then have assumed that the public would assume that they were written by a woman, and this would have resulted in yet more ambiguity and confusion and concealment. Simple as Hardy's writings might seem they are really anything but simple.

DORSET, 1867–70

Hardy gives as a reason for his return to Dorset in July 1867, after five immensely busy years in the capital, that his health had deteriorated either because of the stench from the mud in the River Thames which still acted as a main drain for the community, or because 'he had been accustomed to shut himself up in his rooms at Westbourne Park Villas every evening from six to twelve reading incessantly, instead of getting out for air after the day's confinement' (*Life*, p. 54). It seems probable, too, that the attractions of London and of architecture as a profession had begun to pall, so he took his leave of Blomfield, who strongly advised him not to stay too long in the country, and set off for his mother's cottage at Bockhampton. Again he was fortunate. His old employer, John Hicks, was looking for a good assistant accustomed to church-restoration and Hardy was offered the post. The return to his old way of life and the five years of rapid maturing in London meant that he began to look very closely into what he was doing and what his future was likely to be. He was now 27 and back in the rural retreat where he had begun. Where, if anywhere, did it all lead?

Perhaps he felt within him the powerful influences which it has been the purpose of the first part of this book to record, influences which found him in his late twenties in control of literary forces as yet untapped and waiting to be used. The university had not been for him – he had had neither the right qualifications nor, probably, the money: the Church was not for him because his reading in London had convinced him that he could not accept with honour the Thirty-Nine Articles of the Anglican Church: architecture had interested him but he was still no more than an architect's assistant and it was unlikely that there would be more than a limited future there. But literature called and here was a potential career of mental and material rewards – but not in poetry. Only a rare few like Wordsworth and Tennyson had earned a living from writing poetry. However, there was the novel, that remarkable and comparatively new arrival on the literary scene which had already produced giants like Dickens and Thackeray and George Eliot, and which had a rapidly growing market of readers and could provide rich rewards for the successful. It was, in Hardy's eyes, an inferior genre of literature and not to be compared with poetry but if it had to be the novel, the novel it should be. 'Thus,' as he said in *The Life* (p. 58), 'under the stress of necessity he had set about a kind of literature in which he had hitherto taken but little interest – prose fiction', and he settled down to write his first novel in that late summer of 1867.

Almost inevitably it was to be largely autobiographical, based very much upon his experiences in Dorset which he considered he knew fairly well in 'its less explored recesses', and in London. The story would be about 'the life of an isolated student cast upon the billows of London with no protection but his brains' (*Life*, p. 58) and it was to be about love, which Hardy once said was almost the only subject worth writing about. Significantly he tells us that he aimed at writing 'a striking socialistic novel'. This was a remarkably early use of the word 'socialistic' and tells us a great deal about the way in which Hardy's thoughts were developing at that time. He would have come to London with a sympathetic appreciation of the hardships suffered by the agricultural workers of Dorset, and in London he would have known of the activities of the Reform League whose offices were immediately below Blomfield's at 8 Adelphi Terrace. Swinburne described the League as 'a body of extreme reformers' with 'advanced democratic or republican opinions' (*Life*, p. 42). Hardy's reading in the 1860s of a translation of the French socialist Charles Fourier's *Passion of the Human Soul*, might also have contributed to the radical views expressed in this first unpublished novel.

The inverted Cinderella theme emerges in Hardy's title, 'The Poor Man and the Lady . . . by the Poor Man' and readers will meet it again in his later novels. (It is interesting to trace its development through D. H. Lawrence and on to John Braine's *Room at the Top*.) Later he was to write a poem called 'A Poor Man and a Lady' (*C.P.*, 766) which has a footnote to the effect that 'The foregoing was intended to preserve an episode in the story of "The Poor Man and the Lady", written in 1868, and, like these lines, in the first person; but never printed, and ultimately destroyed.' The young man in the poem is 'a striver with deeds to do,/And little enough to do them with' while the young woman is 'a comely woman of noble birth,/With a courtly match to make . . .'. He places a ring on her finger and although the marriage can have no legal validity it is, she says, 'sanct in the sight of God'. But a man of 'illustrious line and old' comes along and she marries him, and sees no validity in her past vow, and they part for ever. The manuscript of the novel was destroyed by Hardy but evidence exists that its hero was a young man from a poor background, with the name Will Strong (very Hardy!), and the heroine the daughter of the local squire. He studies to become an architect and goes to London where he addresses meetings of workers. They become secretly married but her father arranges for her to marry the son of a landowner and the heroine is saved from a fate almost as bad as death only by conveniently dying on the eve of her wedding.

We know from what Hardy tells us that the story was written – unusually for him – in the first person and crude though the story may have been it obviously contained a good deal of Hardy. The hero is poor, of humble parents, deeply conscious of class distinction and an architect who goes to London where the most important scenes occur. Hardy's own feelings in the past for Mrs Martin are developed into the love of the poor man for the lady, and that in itself contains the germ of yet another theme which is found again and again in the later novels – the search for the unattainable, the pursuit of the well-beloved who, when found, never quite matches up to the ideal. The first title of the work was

> *The Poor Man and the Lady*
> A Story with no plot;
>
> Containing some original verses.

Hardy was determined to get some poetry in somehow! It is not known what the poems were to be but we can guess that they would have included some of the 1860s poems which have survived, and, as Trevor Johnson showed in *The Thomas Hardy Journal* (January 1985), Hardy's first published novel, *Desperate Remedies*, does contain prose versions of some of his poems, and these may have been the ones it was intended to include in *The Poor Man and the Lady*.

He worked away at his novel through the last months of 1867 and made a fair copy in the first six months of 1868. On 25 July the manuscript was posted to the then very distinguished publisher, Macmillan, and Hardy 'now being free of it lent some more help to Mr Hicks in his drawings for church-restoration, reading the Seventh Book of the *Aeneid* between whiles' (*Life*, p. 59).

It is a tribute to Macmillan's efficiency at that time that he had a reply, dated 10 August, written in Alexander Macmillan's own hand. In a letter accompanying his manuscript, Hardy had tried to soften what was inescapably an attack on the behaviour of the upper classes by claiming that the satire was subtle and indirect and that upper-class readers would continue reading the book because the attack was 'half-concealed beneath ambiguous expressions, or at any rate written as if they were not the chief aims of the book (even though they may be)' (*Collected Letters* 1, hereafter *C.L.*, p. 7). This is perhaps a little over-ingenious and the 'at any rate' reveals the weakness of Hardy's defensive position. Alexander Macmillan, close to being one of the upper classes himself, was not taken in, and his reply tells us so much about this lost novel that it is worth quoting at length. He began by saying that he had read the novel,

with care, and with much interest and admiration, but feeling at the same time that it has what seem to me fatal drawbacks to its success, and what, I think, judging the writer from the book itself, you would feel even more strongly – its truthfulness and justice. . . .

The utter heartlessness of *all* the conversation you give in drawing-rooms and ball-rooms about the working-classes, has *some* ground of truth, I fear, and might justly be scourged as you aim at doing, but your chastisement would fall harmless from its very excess. Will's speech to the working men is full of wisdom – (though, by the way, would he have told his own story in public, being, as you describe him, a man of substantially good taste?)

– and you there yourself give grounds for condemning very much that is in other parts of the book. Indeed, nothing could justify such a wholesale blackening of a class but large and intimate knowledge of it. Thackeray makes them not greatly better in many respects, but he gave many redeeming traits and characters; besides, he did it all in a light, and chaffy way that gave no offence – and I fear did little good – and he soothed them by describing the lower class, which he knew nothing of and did not care to know, as equally bad when he touched them at all. He meant fun, you *'mean mischief.'* (*The House of Macmillan* by Charles Morgan [London, 1943], pp. 88–9)

Hardy could have drawn some encouragement from Alexander Macmillan's admiration and his remark that 'If this is your first book I think you ought to go on.' However, waiting to hear further – the book had not been finally rejected – worried him, as it would any new young writer, and on 10 September he wrote a rather poignant letter to Macmillan expressing his anxiety. He didn't care what happened to the book so long as something did; he had in mind another tale 'which would consist entirely of rural scenes and humble life' (obviously *Under the Greenwood Tree* was beginning to evolve) and he ended by asking rather pathetically for suggestions of the kind of story he could do best or, in fact of 'any literary work I should do well to go on upon' (*C.L.*, I, p. 8). The manuscript was then returned to him, revised so as to make it 'less offensive to the upper classes' and resubmitted, and finally declined by Macmillan in November. In February 1869 it was sent to Chapman and Hall, who at first agreed to publish it if Hardy would pay part of the cost. Although Hardy agreed to this arrangement, the idea of publication was finally dropped after Hardy had met Chapman and Hall's reader who was the distinguished writer, George Meredith. He described the novel as 'a sweeping dramatic satire of the squirearchy and nobility, London society, the vulgarity of the middle class, modern Christianity, church restoration and political and domestic morals in general'. He warned Hardy, whom he described as 'a young man with a "passion for reforming the world"' (*Life*, p. 63), that he would be viciously attacked by the press if he published the novel and that this would be a handicap to his career as a writer. He should either rewrite the novel in a milder form or try to write a novel with no ulterior motives and with a more complicated plot. The Victorians liked their plots!

Hardy was later to agree that the satire went too far but at the time he did not give up and the manuscript went to a further publisher, Tinsley, in the spring of 1869. Tinsley offered to publish it, but needed a guarantee of a sum of money, which Hardy regarded as excessive.

The Poor Man and the Lady was not entirely abandoned. Life had taught Hardy the virtues of hard work and thrift. Nothing should be wasted. His 'pictures of Christmas Eve in the tranter's house', mentioned as being 'really good quality' in Macmillan's report, were adapted for use in *Under the Greenwood Tree*, and the Rotten Row scene, also praised by Macmillan, provided the basis for much of Chapter 14 of *A Pair of Blue Eyes*. In 1878 he used part of it for a novella entitled 'An Indiscretion in the Life of an Heiress', which was published in the *New Quarterly Magazine*. Hardy's love of playing with names is seen in the new name of Will Strong who becomes Egbert Mayne, where Mayne (i.e. main) has the hidden meaning *strength*. It must have given Hardy some satisfaction that he could 'cannibalise' his first major attempt to be a writer but the influence on him of this failure made him realise that he was, like Jude and Sue, fifty years ahead of his time and that the polite world of the novel could not yet accept his kind of criticism of its palpable weaknesses. It was a hard lesson for him and one that he did not forget. If he wished to reform the world, and earn a living, it would have to be done more subtly and gently.

Love is present as a theme in all of Hardy's novels and is a major force in almost all of them. Women often play a dominating part, and a close awareness and knowledge are revealed. As a result, his own relationships with women have frequently been examined by biographers anxious to find something which might help us to understand him better and also provide the substance of a book or article. But at this distance of time, and bearing in mind Hardy's extreme reticence about his private life and the steps he took to burn, or have burnt, so much of the evidence it is extremely unlikely that any new information will turn up that will tell us more than we know already about the years before his marriage in 1874.

What we do know seems to show that he was a very natural male. As already mentioned, at puberty he fell in love with a number of young ladies, admired them from a distance, and, as so often happens at this age, lacked the courage and experience to do anything about it. We now know of his love affair with Eliza Nicholls, the daughter of a coast-guard at one time living in Kimmeridge Bay on the Dorset coast. Whether or not this led to sexual intercourse we shall never know, but the opportunities in London at that time for lovers in the situation of Hardy and Miss Nicholls could not have been many. What is certain is that Hardy did have a great interest in women, did fall in love on a number of occasions, and that in his novels he writes so sensitively about women that this in itself seems to provide evidence of a number of close relationships with them. Just how close we shall never know. Robert Gittings argues that because Hardy visited the Argyle Rooms in Great Windmill Street and the Cremorne Gardens in Chelsea where dancing was one of the entertainments, and because there were 80 000 prostitutes in London at that time, it seems almost certain that Hardy would have been tempted to indulge. However, the evidence of the 80 000 prostitutes – so often quoted – is based upon what seems to have been a very unrepresentative sample multiplied to give an answer which no statistician would be willing to accept as sound mathematics, and who would 'scape whipping if just to attend a dance-hall known to attract 'women of easy virtue' were to be taken as proof positive of fornication?

One of the women with whom his relationship was very close was Tryphena Sparks, the subject of a book by Terry Coleman and Lois Deacon, published in 1966 and called *Providence and Mr. Hardy*. The title refers to Edmond Gosse's question in his 1896 review of *Jude the Obscure*,

> What has Providence done to Mr Hardy that he should rise up in the arable land of Wessex and shake his hand at his Creator? (*Cosmopolis*, January 1896)

Lois Deacon was convinced that Hardy's whole life and most of his writing were affected by his hopeless passion for his young cousin, Tryphena Sparks. Hardy's mother's older sister, Maria, married James Sparks and Tryphena was the youngest of her children. She was born in 1851 and was some ten years younger than Hardy. Their passionate love affair is supposed to have begun about 1867 when she was only 16 and to have led to a secret engagement frowned on by Hardy's mother possibly because Tryphena was not really the daughter of Maria but the illegitimate daughter of Maria's oldest daughter, Rebecca, registered as Maria's child to avoid disgrace to Rebecca. This may be, but on top of this we are asked to believe that Rebecca was really Jemima's illegitimate child also registered by Maria to save Jemima disgrace. If this were so, and it seems highly improbable, even if one has to admire the ingenuity of the argument, Rebecca was Hardy's sister and Tryphena his niece and any sexual relationship would have been incestuous. It also led, it is said, to a baby with the name Randy, who obligingly disappears to Australia. There is even supposed to be a photograph of the said Randy, but unfortunately evidence shows that the photograph must have been taken years later than these events.

When the book was published it received the kind of massive exposure that any so-called revelation of a writer's sex-life always receives from the media. However, Robert Gittings and others soon found much to question in the story. Michael Millgate, in his customary fair and objective way, comments, 'For none of this speculation is there any evidence capable of withstanding scholarly or even common-sensical scrutiny' (Millgate, p. 105). He suggests that Hardy was attracted by Tryphena's good looks and happy personality, that she may have been 'courted mildly by her grown-up cousin' and that as the two were often alone together 'it would not be extraordinary if they made love. But there was certainly no child, probably no formal engagement, and perhaps not even a dramatic parting but simply a gradual erosion of intimacy, and eventual relapse into the friendly and cousinly terms of the past' (Millgate, p. 106). And that is common-sensical.

During these amorous adventures and literary probings in poetry and the novel, Hardy continued his architectural work. He also found time to press on with his self-education and we learn from *The Life* that at about this time he 'read a good many books' including 'various plays of Shakespeare, Walpole's *Letters to Sir Horace Mann* in six volumes, Thackeray, Macaulay, Walt Whitman, Virgil's *Aeneid* (of which he never wearied), and other books . . .' (*Life*, p. 61). He was now more than ever exercised in his mind about the future. Should he be cautious and practical and devote himself to architecture and economic security, or do what he really wanted to do, what his natural instinct told him to do, be a writer? So difficult was the choice that he seems rather to have waited to see what would turn up than to have reached a definite decision. John Hicks died in the winter of 1868 and his practice was taken over by a Weymouth architect, Mr G. R. Crickmay who in April 1869 asked Hardy to assist him with some of Hicks's unfinished restoration work. Crickmay's office was in the seaside town of Weymouth and

Hardy took lodgings there. Since returning from London his health had been restored and he took full advantage of the pleasures of this seaside resort made fashionable by George III. Every morning at seven he had a swim and every evening he went rowing. He loved lying on his back on the 'surface of the waves, rising and falling with the tide in the warmth of the morning sun' (*Life*, p. 65). He seems to have been happy, too, in his architectural work and with Hicks's death he was able to take a larger and more responsible part in the rebuilding of Turnworth church which was the main project at the time. In *The Life* he talks of his lightness of heart and of hearing Johann Strauss's 'Morgenblätter' waltz played by the town band. The poem 'At a Seaside Town in 1869' (*C.P.*, 447) has a footnote 'From an old note' and it seems to date from this time. It describes how the inner memories of 'my Love' are obscured by

> The boats, the sands, the esplanade.
> The laughing crowd;
> Light-hearted, loud
> Greeting from some not ill-endowed;
>
> The evening sunlit cliffs, the talk,
> Hailings and halts
> The keen sea-salts,
> The band, the Morgenblätt Waltz.

Weymouth was to become the Budmouth of the novels and the location of a number of poems, including 'On the Esplanade' (*C.P.*, 682). 'Her Father' (173), 'At Waking' (174) and 'Singing Lovers' (686) have 'Weymouth' subscriptions. Although not published until more than thirty years later they may well have been drafted at that time. Hardy joined a quadrille class where 'a good deal of flirtation went on, the so-called "class" being, in fact a gay gathering for dances and love-making by adepts of both sexes' (*Life*, p. 66). In his poem, 'Great Things' (*C.P.*, 414) the first 'great thing', cider, is drunk in a hostelry while travelling to Budmouth town and the other two great things are 'the dance' and 'love'. Memories of the past in Weymouth must have come vividly before him while writing it.

While living and working in Weymouth Hardy continued with

his poetic exercises and began work on a story to be called *Desperate Remedies*. It was to be his first published novel. He was now 29 and, although he did not know it, the initial period of preparation to be a writer was ending. On 2 June 1865, he had written in his notebook 'My 25th birthday. Not very cheerful. Feel as if I had lived a long time and done very little'. In fact, he had done a great deal in those opening years of his life and a big change was on the way.

Phase the Second: The Novelist (1870–97)

The first mention in *The Life* of *Desperate Remedies* is of the character Edward Springrove who was said by Hardy to be based on a new assistant who had joined Mr Crickmay's office staff in August or September 1869 (p. 65). In the novel Springrove is a young architect from a humble background who loves books, writes poetry, and has a comprehensive knowledge of Shakespeare. He may well be speaking for Hardy when he says that to succeed as an architect depends upon 'an earnestness in making acquaintances, and a love for using them'. The similarity to Hardy himself is so close that the 'new assistant' may be just another attempt to throw the biographical sleuths off the trail. Again we meet Hardy's resentment of what is, unfortunately, the very natural desire of many people to know more about the writer and his life. Again and again he denied – even when it was obvious that he was not being strictly accurate – that his novels contained autobiographical material. They all do. His objections to a biographical chapter in F. A. Hedgcock's *Thomas Hardy: penseur et artiste* (Paris, 1911) was so great that he managed to stop the publication of an English translation, and he commented in the margin of his own copy 'All this is too personal, and in bad taste.' Writing to a correspondent on 30 October 1919 on behalf of her husband, Florence Hardy again indignantly denies that *Jude* is autobiographical, adding the very questionable 'there is not a scrap of personal detail in it, it having the least to do with his own life of all his books'. Then she goes on with the remarkable statement, again very questionable, that 'Speaking generally, there is more autobiography in a hundred lines of Mr Hardy's poetry than in all the novels' (*Life*, p. 425). This letter would almost certainly have been written out in draft by Hardy for his wife to copy, and it is strange that he could have believed that such statements would be taken at their face-value. Why was he so obsessively anxious to

41

conceal the autobiographical aspects of the one literary form and yet willing to acknowledge the large part it played in the other? There seems to be no easy answer, but it may tell us something about Hardy's differing attitudes to the two genres.

In writing *Desperate Remedies* Hardy was responding to George Meredith's suggestion that he should 'attempt a novel with a purely artistic purpose, giving it a more complicated "plot" than was attempted with *The Poor Man and the Lady*' (*Life*, p. 64). There is a certain comic cynicism about Hardy's approach, and a good deal of humour in the book results from his undercutting of the tradition of the mystery story in which he is being forced to write.

One influence on him was Wilkie Collins who had been very successful with his 'whodunnit?' stories in the 1850s and 1860s. The plot is, indeed, complicated and ingenious in an almost Dickensian way. It contains melodrama, mystery, surprise, and could be described as the first of the many 'Who wins her?' stories that Hardy was to write, stories in which the heroine is loved by more than one man and the reader's hopes and fears are aroused by whether Mr Right will triumph over Mr Wrong. It is a very old recipe but a very sound one, and it depends upon the reader's interest in and sympathy with the heroine. Here Hardy does not fail. Cytherea's character is central to the novel and we really do care that this innocent and helpless maiden should not marry the sinister Manston. The two protagonists in *Desperate Remedies* are a young architect, Edward Springrove, the hero, and Aeneas Manston, another architect, the villain. Both wish to marry the beautiful Cytherea who works for the wealthy lady of the manor, Miss Aldclyffe, who for some at-first undivulged reason does everything to force Manston's suit, and he, for some at-first undivulged reason appears to have an impediment . . . but one must not spoil the story.

Budmouth (i.e. Weymouth) figures largely in the story as does Knapwater House, which is based upon Kingston Maurward House so well-known to Hardy since his infancy. Although so crude and laughable in plot – perhaps deliberately so – it is a very readable story and shows us Hardy, in the words of Virginia Woolf, 'feeling his way to a method'. And even if at times he feels it necessary to show off his knowledge, thus revealing the very understandable inferiority complex resulting from his humble background, there is much of the later mature Hardy to be found even in this piece of apprentice work.

In the very first pages the reader is conscious that there is an acute mind at work which revels in the penetrating observation of life. To love at first sight, writes Hardy, is to do a thing 'the blissfulness of which was only eclipsed by its hazardousness'; and 'With all, the beautiful things of the earth become more dear as they elude pursuit.' His descriptions are often striking, his images drawn from the countryside. Cytherea, the heroine, is 'like a single bright red poppy in a field of brown stubble', and white sunlight shines 'in shaft-like lines from a rift in a slaty cloud'. The man with the watching eye, as Hardy once described himself, is now beginning to use the vast storehouse of impressions which his early years in Dorset have given him. As Cytherea turns her face landward on the boat taking her from Lulwind Cove to Budmouth 'The wide concave which lay at the back of the hill in this direction was blazing with the western light, adding an orange tint to the vivid purple of the heather, now at the very climax of bloom, and free from the slightest touch of the invidious brown that so soon creeps into its shades' (*N.W.E.*, p. 60). He is already making use of places he knows which are given fictitious names that scarcely conceal their origins but allow him to treat them imaginatively and, if necessary, alter them to meet his fictional needs. Quotations and allusions abound – particularly from the Bible, the Classics and Shakespeare – sometimes obtrusively but they usually enrich meaning. His characterisation can be incisive and pleasing as when he describes Springrove's father:

He was a poet with a rough skin: one whose sturdiness was more the result of external circumstances than of intrinsic nature. Too kindly constituted to be very provident, he was yet not imprudent. He had a quiet humorousness of disposition, not out of keeping with a frequent melancholy, the general expression of his countenance being one of abstraction. Like Walt Whitman he felt as his years increased –

I foresee too much; it means more than I thought.

On the present occasion he wore gaiters and a leathern apron, and worked with his shirt-sleeves rolled up beyond his elbows, disclosing solid and fleshy rather than muscular arms. They were stained by the cider, and two or three brown apple-pips from the pomace he was handling were to be seen sticking on them here and there. (*N.W.E.*, p. 154)

There are memories here of Hardy's father making cider at Bockhampton.

Perhaps most impressive of all in this first novel is the portrayal of his rustic chorus, and here he has combined his close observation of the Dorset workfolk and their manner of speech.

'... She's in love wi' the man, that's what she is.'

'Then she's a bigger stunpoll than I took her for,' said Mr Springrove. 'Why, she's old enough to be his mother.'

'The row'll be between her and that young Curly-wig, you'll see. She won't run the risk of that pretty face beën near.'

'Clerk Crickett, I d'fancy you d'know everything about everybody,' said Gad.

'Well so's,' said the clerk modestly. 'I do know a little. It comes to me.'

'And I d'know where from.'

'Ah.'

'That wife o' thine. She's an entertainen woman, not to speak disrespectful.'

'She is: and a winnen one. Look at the husbands she've had – God bless her!'

'I wonder you could stand third in that list, Clerk Crickett,' said Mr Springrove.

'Well, 't has been a power o' marvel to myself often-times. Yes, matrimony do begin wi' "Dearly beloved," and ends wi' "Amazement," as the prayer-book says. But what could I do, naibour Springrove? 'Twas ordained to be. Well do I call to mind what your poor lady said to me when I had just married. "Ah, Mr Crickett," says she "your wife will soon settle you as she did her other two: here's a glass o' rum, for I shan't see your poor face this time next year." I swallered the rum, called again next year, and said "Mrs Springrove, you gave me a glass o' rum last year because I was going to die – here I be alive still, you see." "Well said, clerk! Here's two glasses for you now, then," says she. "Thank you, mem," I said, and swallered the rum. Well, dang my old sides, next year I thought I'd call again and get three. And call I did. But she wouldn't give me a drop o' the commonest. "No, clerk," says she, "you be too tough for a woman's pity." ... Ah, poor soul, 'twas true enough! Here be I, that was expected to die, alive and hard as a nail, you see, and there's she moulderen in her grave.' (Osgood, McIlvaine Edition, 1896, pp. 148–9)

Many readers may find it sad that in later editions Hardy removed some of the dialect found in this 1896 edition. Early in March 1870 the almost complete manuscript of *Desperate Remedies* was sent to Macmillan and a month later returned by them, as Hardy thought, because of their disapproval of its more sensational incidents. After all, to begin a novel with a seduction, even if it is only hinted at, and an illegitimate child who doesn't die or get sent to Australia but survives was not really Macmillan's line, and not even the fact that the illegitimate child came to no good could make it more acceptable. Hardy must have felt he couldn't win. However, he then sent the manuscript to the much less distinguished publisher, William Tinsley, and he agreed to publish if Hardy would put up an advance of £75 (say about £2000 in present-day money) to cover any loss that might occur. The novel was completed and a fair copy made in the autumn and sent to Tinsley in December. It says a good deal about his sensitivity that Hardy wanted it to be published anonymously and it appeared without his name on the title-page in an edition of 500 copies on 25 March 1871.

Hardy's feelings must have been a mixture of pride, pleasure, fear and foreboding. He had put most of his life's savings into the venture and had written a book which was 'a sort of thing he had never contemplated writing, till, finding himself in a corner, it seemed necessary to attract public attention at all hazards' (*Life*, p. 87). He awaited the reviews with anxiety and the early ones in *The Athenaeum* and *Morning Post* were pleasing, but *The Spectator* review of 22 April was damning. The novel was so bad, the reviewer claimed, that it was no wonder the writer had decided to remain anonymous. 'Here are no fine characters, no original ones to extend one's knowledge of human nature, no display of passion except of the brute kind. . . . The story is disagreeable, and not striking in any way.' Finally, the readers of the magazine were warned 'against this book'. Hardy describes how he read the review while sitting on a stile on the edge of Kingston Maurward ewe-leaze and wished himself dead, and he would have felt much the same when in June he 'received a fresh buffet from circumstances in seeing at Exeter Station *Desperate Remedies* in Messrs Smith & Son's surplus catalogue for 2s. 6d. the three volumes, and thought *The Spectator* had snuffed out the book, as it probably had done' (*Life*, p. 87). At that time the novel market was very much in the control of the large circulating libraries and it suited them to have novels published in three volumes (known as 'three-deckers'). The normal price for the three volumes was £1.11.6d, a great deal of money at that time, but the circulating libraries were given large discounts. The remainder price of 2s. 6d. was very low and it is ironic that first-editions of *Desperate Remedies* are eagerly sought after today by collectors who will pay thousands of pounds for them.

Horace Moule kindly wrote and begged Hardy not to take the review too much to heart but such advice is easier to give than to take. It has become customary to talk about Hardy's extraordinary sensitivity to adverse criticism and it is true that in *The Life* and the *Letters* there are frequent comments on the unfairness and stupidity of many reviewers and critics. But he had to put up with a great deal that was unfair and bigoted, even gratuitously unpleasant, as was the offending *Spectator* review which wondered how the writer had dared to suppose 'that an unmarried lady owning an estate could have an illegitimate child'. And what writer is not sensitive to the bad review? One of the sternest critics of Hardy on this point once admitted to me that he never read reviews of his own books if he could help it – he found them too painful. One bad review is remembered when ten good ones have been forgotten. Those of us who live in glasshouses ought to be careful about throwing stones. There is much truth in Hardy's epigrammatic comment: 'But criticism is so easy and art so hard.'

If the outlook was poor on the book front it seemed much improved in his personal life, for while *Desperate Remedies* was being written, published and reviewed, probably the most important single event in his life occurred. He met Emma Lavinia Gifford and fell in love with her. She was later to become his wife. It was a strange chance that brought them together. In February 1870 Hardy, almost at the end of his restoration work for Crickmay, gave up his lodgings in Weymouth and returned once again to the Bockhampton cottage. But there was one more job that Hicks had agreed to do before his death and Crickmay asked Hardy to help him with it. The church at St Juliot, near Boscastle in Cornwall, was in a very dilapidated condition, so bad that the existing tower, north aisle and north transept were unsafe. The new rector, the Rev. Caddell Holder, required it to be restored as soon as possible. Thus, in the early hours of 7 March, a never-to-be-forgotten day in Hardy's life, he set out on the tedious journey to Cornwall, 'armed with sketch-book, measuring-tape and rule'. He reached Launceston at about four in the afternoon and hired a conveyance to take him the remaining sixteen or so miles to St Juliot Rectory. Arriving in darkness he was met by Emma

Gifford, the sister-in-law of the Rector who was living with her married sister and helping where she could with the work of the parish. Four years later she was to become his wife.

Many years later, in 1911, not long before she died, Emma wrote, unknown to her husband, an account of her growing-up in Plymouth, her days at St Juliot, and her meeting with Hardy. She called it *Some Recollections* and Hardy read it soon after her death, intended at one time to publish it, but never did so. It was finally published in 1954. Here is her description (the English uncorrected) of that first meeting:

It was a lovely Monday evening in March [1870] after a wild winter we were on the *qui-vive* for the stranger, who would have a tedious journey, his home being two counties off changing trains many times and waiting at stations – a sort of cross jump-journey – like a chess-knight's move. The only damper to our gladness was the sudden laying up of my brother-in-law by gout, and he who was the chief person could not be present on the arrival of our guest. The dinner cloth was laid, my sister had gone to her husband, who required the constant attention of his wife. At that very moment the front-door bell rang and he was ushered in. I had to receive him alone, and felt a curious uneasy embarrassment at receiving anyone, especially so necessary a person as the Architect. I was immediately arrested by his familiar appearance, as if I had seen him in a dream – his slightly different accent, his soft voice; also I noticed a blue paper sticking out of his pocket. I was explaining who I was – as I saw that he took me for the parson's daughter, or wife – when my sister appeared to my great relief, and he went up to Mr Holder's room with her. So I met my husband or rather he met me.

I thought him much older than he was. He had a beard and a rather shabby great coat, and had quite a business appearance. Afterwards he seemed younger, and by daylight especially. . . . the 'blue paper' proved to be the MS. of a poem, and not a plan of the Church, he informed me, to my surprise. (*Some Recollections*, 1979, pp. 33–4)

The feelings of Hardy about his meeting with Emma are caught in one of his most successful lyrics, 'When I Set out for Lyonnesse' (*C.P.*, 254). It is dated 1870.

When I set out for Lyonnesse,
  A hundred miles away,
  The rime was on the spray,
And starlight lit my lonesomeness
When I set out for Lyonnesse
  A hundred miles away.

What would bechance at Lyonnesse
  While I should sojourn there
  No prophet durst declare,
Nor did the wisest wizard guess
What would bechance at Lyonnesse
  While I should sojourn there.

When I came back from Lyonnesse
  With magic in my eyes,
  All marked with mute surmise
My radiance rare and fathomless,
When I came back from Lyonnesse
  With magic in my eyes!

Lyonnesse is the name he used for Cornwall and the poem beautifully captures the lonely early-morning departure from Bockhampton, the strange and magical chance that brought the lovers together and the radiant way in which he returned. It is typical of Hardy's love of the enigmatic that we are not told what did 'bechance at Lyonnesse' or why he returned so changed. Nor does it really matter. The poem allows us to share the rare and memorable expression of love's first fine careless rapture. His notes in more prosaic terms about his short stay in St Juliot read:

March 7. The dreary yet poetical drive over the hills. Arrived at St Juliot Rectory between 6 and 7 [somewhat later probably]. Received by young lady in brown, (Miss Gifford, the rector's sister-in-law). Mr Holder gout. Saw Mrs Holder. The meal. Talk. To Mr. Holder's room. Returned downstairs. Music.

March 8. Austere grey view of hills from bedroom window. A funeral. Man tolled the bell (which stood inverted on the ground in the neglected transept) by lifting the clapper and letting it fall against the side. Five bells stood thus in a row (having been taken down from the cracked tower for safety). Stayed there drawing and measuring all day, with intervals for meals at rectory.

March 9. Drove with Mrs Holder and Miss Gifford to Boscastle, and on to Tintagel and Penpethy slate-quarries, with a view to the church roofing. . . .

March 10th. Went with E. L. G. to Beeny Cliff. She on horse-back-. . . . On the cliff. . . . 'The tender grace of a day', etc. The run down to the edge. The coming home. . . .

In the afternoon I walked to Boscastle, Mrs H. and E. L. G. accompanying me three-quarters of the way: the overshot mill: E. provokingly reading as she walked; evening in garden; music later in evening.

March 11. Dawn. Adieu. E. L. G. had struck a light six times in her anxiety to call the servants early enough for me. The journey home. (*Life*, pp. 77–8)

The two lovers-to-be were not young, both being in their thirtieth year, and Michael Millgate is probably right when he says 'There can be little doubt that Hardy's engagement and eventual marriage to Emma Gifford were in some measure the calculated outcome of a conspiracy – if only of discretion – involving the entire rectory household' (Millgate, p. 123). Hardy says that 'he was soon, if not immediately, struck by the nature and appearance of' Emma. 'She was so *living*, he used to say. Though her features were not regular her complexion at this date was perfect in hue, her figure and move-ment graceful, and her corn-coloured hair abundant in its coils' (*Life*, p. 76). In *Desperate Remedies* Cytherea's hair is 'of a shining corn yellow in the high lights deepening to a definite nut-brown as each curl wound round into the shade'. Seen in the magical sur-roundings of a remote romantic Cornwall it is not surprising that he had soon lost his heart and it seems probable that the poem 'At the Word "Farewell" ' (*C.P.*, 360) beautifully conveys the moment of parting of a couple who have begun to realise their feelings of affec-tion for each other.

'I am leaving you . . . Farewell!' I said,
    As I followed her on
By an alley bare boughs overspread;
    'I soon must be gone!'
Even then the scale might have been turned
    Against love by a feather,

> – But crimson one cheek of hers burned
>   When we came in together.

Her feelings about their meeting may not have been as romantic as his. In *Some Recollections* there is not much enthusiasm about Hardy's beard, his shabby great-coat and business appearance and she thought him 'older than he was'. There is something very human in Hardy's addition of 'he being tired' after these words in her MS, an addition he subsequently tried to erase, probably realising that 'all is vanity'. She was, too, very conscious of being genteel and is capable of writing 'I have never liked the Cornish working-orders as I do Devonshire folk.' There was no doubt that she was a snob and that for a long while she had no idea how lowly was Hardy's background or how sensitive he was to the whole class issue. There were rocks ahead, but for the moment they were happy with their Cornish romance. The poems that Hardy was to write more than forty years later about the beauty and happiness of the four years of their 'Cornish Romance' cannot have been entirely the result of a nostalgic imagination.

There was much correspondence between them but none of this has survived. He was back again in Cornwall in August and Emma was able to discuss literature with him and help him by writing out the fair copy of *Desperate Remedies*. It was on this occasion that Hardy drew a picture of Emma searching for a glass which had fallen into a little waterfall in the river Valency. Years later he wrote a poem, 'Under the Waterfall' (*C.P.*, 276), about this. There were further meetings in 1871 and 1872 and in August of 1872 Hardy asked Emma's father, a haughty, retired, penurious solicitor, then living near Bodmin and given to drunken bouts, for his daughter's hand in marriage. He was contemptuously rejected and, it is said, referred to as a 'low-born churl who has presumed to marry into *my* family'. The poor man and the lady indeed! Hardy must have been intrigued by the repeated patterns and the multiplying ironies of his personal life. However, Hardy, undeterred, went on to St Juliot where the atmosphere was more genial and spent about a month with Emma and the Holders, visiting the local places of interest, especially Tintagel which had a special romantic appeal for the lovers, and on his last Sunday in Cornwall reading the lesson at the afternoon service in the now-restored church, remembered later in his poem 'Quid hic Agis' (*C.P.*, 371). He may have spent Christmas there and his meetings with Emma in 1873 included a stay in Bath which enabled them to visit Bristol and Tintern Abbey. There was another visit to Emma at St Juliot at Christmas and then in 1874, with his growing success as a writer, marriage became financially possible. Emma was very proud of her uncle, Dr Edwin Hamilton Gifford, the headmaster of King Edward's School, Birmingham, and later Archdeacon of London, and it was arranged that he would conduct the wedding at the recently built St Peter's Church, Paddington. That the wedding was attended by no more than Hardy and Emma, Dr Gifford and two witnesses may be a reflection of the hostility felt not only by Emma's father but also on Hardy's side of the family where his mother had not taken kindly to Emma's middle-class airs, quite apart from the fact that she was a threat to the Hardy family solidarity which meant so much to Jemima. It is, again, ironic that Emma probably thought that she was a good match for Hardy, while Jemima thought Emma wasn't good enough for her son. Hardy's announcement of the marriage in the *Dorset County Chronicle* read as follows:

HARDY–GIFFORD. Sept. 17, at St. Peter's Church, Paddington, by the Rev. E. H. Gifford, D. D., hon. canon of Worcester, uncle of the bride, Thomas Hardy, of Celbridge-place, Westbourne Park, London, son of Mr. T. Hardy, of Bockhampton, to Emma Lavinia, younger daughter of J. A. Gifford, Esq., of Kirland, Cornwall.

That Hardy felt his own class inferiority comes out in 'J. A. Gifford, Esq.' but 'Mr. T. Hardy'.

The first few nights of their marriage were passed in a hotel in Brighton and then they went on a honeymoon which took them to Dieppe, Rouen and Paris. One hopes that Emma did not read during it the September instalment of the serialisation of *Far from the Madding Crowd* in which Troy says 'All romances end at marriage.' The diary Emma kept at that time has now been published as a book meticulously edited by Richard Taylor. Although it tells us little about her relationship with her husband there are interesting details of her travel described in a simple if occasionally naive way.

Hardy seems not to have been so discouraged by the harsh criticisms of *Desperate Remedies* and the fact that it was remaindered and that he lost some of the money he had been forced to advance towards publication costs, as to abandon novel-writing even if a certain bitterness is observable in a note he made at that time: 'Strictly, we should resent wrongs, be placid at justice, and grateful

for favours. But I know one who is placid at a wrong, and would
be grateful for a simple justice; while a favour, if he ever gained
one, would turn his brain' (*Life*, p. 87). In the summer of 1871 he
finished *Under the Greenwood Tree: A Rural Painting of the Dutch
School*, which seems to have had its genesis in the praise he received
for the country scenes in *The Poor Man and the Lady*, and to have
used some of the material from it. In choosing as his title a well-
known literary quotation he followed a fashion of the time but
allusions to *As You Like It* in the text show that Shakespeare's play
was much in his mind during the period of writing. The MS was
again sent to Macmillan whose reader, John Morley, described it as
'extremely careful, natural, and delicate, and the writer deserves
more than common credit for the pains which he has taken with
his style and with the harmony of his construction and treatment.
It is a simple and uneventful sketch of a rural courtship. . . . I don't
prophesy a large market for it, because the work is so delicate as
not to hit every taste. . . . But it is good work, and would please
people whose taste is not ruined by novels of exaggerated action
or forced ingenuity' (*The House of Macmillan*, pp. 96–7).

In spite of these words of praise, Alexander Macmillan did not
agree to an immediate acceptance of the book and Hardy, either
through a misunderstanding or impatience, offered it to Tinsley
who had almost certainly done better out of *Desperate Remedies* than
had Hardy. Tinsley agreed in April to publish it and offered him
£30 for the copyright. Inexperienced in these financial matters as he
was at that time and anxious to be published, Hardy accepted this
wholly inadequate payment (two years later Tinsley refused to sell
the copyright back to him for less than £300) and lost control of the
novel for very many years. Tinsley's business was eventually bought
up by Chatto and Windus and this is the reason for the many
editions of *Under the Greenwood Tree* which bear the Chatto imprint
long after Macmillan had become his recognised publisher in 1902.

By May 1872 Hardy, who had returned to London and was helping to design schools for the new London School Board set up as
the result of the 1870 Education Act, was reading the proofs of
Under the Greenwood Tree, and it was published in two volumes
in June with a speed which makes most modern book-publishing
look snail-like. Hardy was still unable to face giving his name to the
book, and the title-page said no more than that it was 'By the author
of *Desperate Remedies*'. These must have been particularly worrying
years for Hardy, desperately anxious to be a writer but lacking the

secure income to abandon architecture, wanting to marry Emma but lacking the means to do so. However, there were the visits to St Juliot and a great deal of letter-writing between them. In one letter he announced his intention to give up novel-writing and concentrate on architecture but she 'with no great opportunity of reasoning on the matter, yet, as Hardy used to think and say – truly or not – with that rapid instinct which serves women in such good stead, and may almost be called preternatural vision, wrote back instantly her desire that he should adhere to authorship, which she felt sure would be his true vocation' (*Life*, p. 89).

They must both have been encouraged by the reviews of *Under the Greenwood Tree* which were mostly favourable although there was some patronising and damning with faint praise. *The Athenaeum* deplored the anonymity, but applauded his decision to work 'principally that vein of his genius which yields the best produce and wherein his labours result in more satisfaction to his readers than did his explorations into the dark ways of human crime and folly'. The love story had held the reviewer's interest and Hardy was 'not destitute of humour'. Horace Moule in *The Saturday Review* thought it was 'the best prose idyll that we have seen for a long while past . . . the author has produced a series of rural pictures full of life and genuine colouring'. However, no one would have guessed from the reviews that the book under discussion would still be widely read more than a century later and that it would become such a favourite of the ordinary reader. By 1894 Annie MacDonell in her *Thomas Hardy* (p. 32) was describing it as being 'All but flawless in workmanship' and saying that 'To not a few the book appears as Mr Hardy's surest claim to recognition in another age, inasmuch as it is least coloured by the dusty complexion of ours.'

It does, indeed, avoid the 'dusty' as if Hardy was determined that this should be before all else a light-weight 'entertainment'. He is deliberately concentrating for the moment on that aspect of his writing which had most impressed the publishers' readers of his novels – his ability to portray with authenticity and humour the life of the country-folk he knows so well. There is an authority about the writing which comes from mastery of his subject, and no matter what he might say about his novels not being autobiographical this one draws heavily on his own early life. Like so many of his novels, it deals with a time two or three decades earlier and he relies heavily on what he had learned from his family about the early days at Bockhampton.

The story has two strands: that of the village choir with its instrumentalists which Mr Maybold, the new young vicar, has decided to replace with a fashionable organ, and that of the new young schoolmistress, Fancy Day, whose hand is sought by three men – Dick, the son of Reuben Dewy the tranter, Farmer Shiner, and the vicar himself. Hardy's first plan seems to have been to make the love interest subsidiary but it grew in importance during the writing. He locates his story in Mellstock which is a scarcely disguised Bockhampton; Reuben and his wife have many of the characteristics of his own parents; he makes extensive use of the stories of the old Stinsford church choir which had been imparted to him by his father and uncle; and he draws heavily on his own experience of country dances, of folk and religious music, and of the countryside and its varied seasons and occupations.

It would be wrong to look upon this as apprentice work because it is all so accomplished. No sensitive reader opening this new novel in 1872 could have failed to realise that there was a new voice in the land, that this was the work of a craftsman who knew and loved his subject. The first paragraph tells the reader so:

> To dwellers in a wood almost every species of tree has its voice as well as its feature. At the passing of the breeze the fir-trees sob and moan no less distinctly than they rock; the holly whistles as it battles with itself; the ash hisses amid its quiverings; the beech rustles while its flat boughs rise and fall. And winter, which modifies the note of such trees as shed their leaves, does not destroy its individuality. (*N.W.E.*, p. 33)

The influence of Hardy's architectural studies may already be seen in the structuring of his first two novels. *Desperate Remedies* is seen in terms of blocks of time – 'The Events of Thirty Years', 'The Events of One Day', 'The Events of Three Days'. The seasons of the year dictate the structure of *Under the Greenwood Tree*. It is divided into five parts – 'Winter', 'Spring', 'Summer', 'Autumn' and 'Conclusion'. This enables Hardy to show relationships between the seasonal activities of the country-folk in their work and the actions of his characters in the story, a technique which becomes ever more powerful in his later work.

Under the Greenwood Tree is redolent of Hardy's own childhood, a warm and affectionate picture of a community which has changed little with the years and is apparently secure from those outside

influences and developments which will eventually sound its death-
knell. It bubbles with good humour and joy in living and with
'Great Things' – the country-drinks like cider and mead, country-
dancing and romance. This is the Hardy novel to be read when one
is young and meeting him for the first time, it is a walk through
fields and wood where nature is still comparatively benevolent and
'all's right with the world'. But not completely. Irony is always present in the novels and the humour here is sometimes undercut with
it, while the lightness of touch does not completely conceal those
serious aspects of life which will become ever more dominant in the
later novels. Even in this gentle pastoral all does not go smoothly.
There is conflict for Fancy's hand and she nearly betrays Dick. Her
father is against her marriage to Dick and has to be won over by a
deceit. The choir is replaced by an 'isolated organ' and a valuable
feature of community life disappears for ever. The new vicar lacks
the easy-going casualness of his predecessor and does not quite fit
in to the rural life. He is an 'outsider' threatening to destroy an
important aspect of village life with his new ideas. And Nature is
not entirely benevolent. As Dick waits to have his request for Fancy's
hand rejected by her father (another echo of Hardy's own life), 'the
stillness was disturbed only by some small bird that was being
killed by an owl in the adjoining wood, whose cry passed into the
silence without mingling with it'. Even the happy ending, so conventional at that time and almost to disappear in Hardy's later
novels, is stained by Fancy's evasion when she is questioned by her
husband about their having no secrets between them. We see in this
underlying seriousness the shape of things to come. Fancy keeps her
secret: Tess does not.

There was much about Hardy that was secretive and in almost all
his novels there is a secret which is concealed from some of the
characters and the readers. In *Desperate Remedies* the relationship
between Aeneas Manston and Miss Aldclyffe is kept secret – even
if we may guess it – until the book is well-advanced: there is, as we
have seen, a secret in *Under the Greenwood Tree*.

His third published novel begins with a concealment and ends
with one. *A Pair of Blue Eyes* was the third and last of Hardy's novels
to be published by Tinsley, and the first of his novels to be serialised. Tinsley, pleased with the financial results of *Under the Greenwood Tree*, had asked Hardy for another novel and this time Hardy,
who soon became well able to look after his own business interests,
was not to be caught again. He read his way through *Copinger on*

Copyright and insisted that Tinsley's rights would be limited to the serial only. The serialisation was an important breakthrough because there was a great demand for serials which were the television soap-operas of that time. Literacy for men increased from 67.3 per cent in 1841 to 97.2 per cent in 1900, and for women from 51.1 per cent in 1841 to 96.8 per cent in 1900, and this, together with improvements in printing and transport which meant that newspapers and magazines could be marketed more cheaply and distributed more efficiently, led to a rapidly growing demand for fiction either as short stories or serialised novels. Very large sums of money could be earned by successful writers of serials and Hardy must have been pleased when Tinsley suggested serialisation in *Tinsley's Magazine*. It meant more money and a larger audience.

A Pair of Blue Eyes has been described as one of Hardy's neglected novels, and it does not deserve to be so. After the 'socialistic' satire of *The Poor Man and the Lady*, the murder and mystery of *Desperate Remedies* and the pastoral romance of *Under the Greenwood Tree*, *A Pair of Blue Eyes* widens his range and reveals a rapidly maturing sensibility. The serial version was published from September 1872 to July 1873 (the three-volume first edition in May 1873), and it was obviously written at speed, Hardy admitting that at the time of submitting the manuscript of the first number 'he had shaped nothing of what the later chapters were to be like'. The first five chapters appear to have been written, printed and published between 27 July and 15 August 1872. Working with such rapidity it was inevitable that Hardy would draw largely on his own experience and although he repeatedly denied that the novel was in any way autobiographical, it is inescapable that it is, and that not only does his life tell us something about the novel, the novel tells us something about his life. Much of the action takes place (just as much of the novel was written) in Cornwall near Castle Boterel (Boscastle). The heroine, Elfride Swancourt, is the daughter of the Rector and has many of the characteristics and some of the physical qualities of Emma Gifford and she lives in Endelstow Rectory which is very like St Juliot Rectory. Stephen Smith, a young architect, who is the son of a master-mason of humble background, arrives to plan the restoration of the church and falls in love with Elfride, as she does with him. Her snobbish father rejects Stephen when he discovers that his parents are humble folk from the neighbourhood. All this is closely related to Hardy's experiences in Cornwall and his personal involvement with the story could not be concealed when in 1920, when Hardy was 80, Macmillan published the de-luxe Mellstock Edition of his works and in 1920 reprinted some of the 1912 Wessex Edition novels, and almost the only changes in the texts which Hardy requested were to *A Pair of Blue Eyes*. These involved, significantly, changing 'vicarage' to 'rectory' throughout, locating more exactly the church and the rectory so that they are more easily identified as those of St Juliot, and identifying the song sung by Elfride in Chapter 3 as a popular song of the time called 'Should He Upbraid'. This was one of Hardy's favourite songs, described by him in *The Life* as 'the most marvellous old song in English music in its power of touching an audience' (p. 122), and it seems almost certain that this was one of the songs Emma sang to him during that never-to-be-forgotten first visit to St Juliot in March 1870. Fifty years later, with Emma no more than a memory, this meant so much to him that he meticulously excised a line-and-a-half of the earlier text and replaced it with

Next she took 'Should He Upbraid', which suited her exquisitely both in voice and mien.

Interestingly enough, at the same time he realised the ambiguity of having Knight 'speak between his pants' in Chapter 21 and removed the offending words! As if all the aspects of the novel's location and story which obviously draw on his own experience were not enough, there is evidence from the Rector of St Juliot who was visited by Hardy after Emma's death and wrote to a friend in 1936:

Mr Hardy on both his visits talked freely about his first wife and his novel *A Pair of Blue Eyes*, and told us that the heroine of that book was indeed Miss Emma Gifford. He also said that nearly all the incidents in the story were true, as *inventing fiction was too much trouble*. (my italics)

And Hardy could have added that Stephen's voluble, proud and characterful mother had, like Mrs Dewey in *Under the Greenwood Tree*, much in common with his own mother.

A Pair of Blue Eyes is, then, an intriguing mixture of the real and the imagined, with Elfride obviously modelled to some extent on Emma, Stephen Smith based loosely upon Hardy himself and Smith's rival for Elfride's hand, Henry Knight, a man of culture and education and of higher social class than Smith, having a good deal in

common with Horace Moule. These obvious influences of the life in
the novel must not, however, lead the reader to think that Stephen
Smith is Hardy or Elfride is Emma. Hardy made whatever changes
happen to be required by his creative needs. Thus both Elfride and
Stephen are portrayed as being about ten years younger than Hardy
and Emma were when they first met, almost certainly because Hardy
wanted to emphasise the youthful innocence, and inexperience of
the lovers at that time. Elfride's immaturity and ingenuousness were
a vital element in the story and may well reflect Emma's own immature and fey qualities. If so, it is no wonder that until after her
death Hardy was so anxious to deny the autobiographical nature of
his story.

A Pair of Blue Eyes has much to recommend it and had a very
close place in Hardy's heart because it reminded him of those intoxi-
cating romantic days in Cornwall. It was the first of his novels to
bear his name on the title-page and was a favourite novel of Tennyson and Coventry Patmore. Proust, who had read several Hardy
novels, said that 'of all books the one which he would himself most
gladly have written' was *A Pair of Blue Eyes* (Harold Nicolson's diary,
21 June 1933). When the concept of 'Hardy the Wessex novelist'
came to Hardy a year or two later he must have realised that Cornwall could hardly be called Wessex, and he tried to overcome this
little local difficulty in his 1895 Preface to the Osgood, McIlvaine
edition by describing 'Castle Boterel' as lying 'near to, or no great
way beyond, the vague border of the Wessex kingdom . . .'. Not that
it matters. He goes on to say:

> The place is pre-eminently (for one person at least) the region of
> dream and mystery. The ghostly birds, the pall-like sea, the frothy
> wind, the eternal soliloquy of the waters, the bloom of dark purple
> cast that seems to exhale from the shoreward precipices, in them-
> selves lend to the scene an atmosphere like the twilight of a night
> vision.

The magic in his eyes which he brought back from Lyonesse was
to last a life-time and something of that magic is found in *A Pair of
Blue Eyes*. Its isolated setting in what was at that time a very remote
part of a distant county, the description of the wild, lone hills and
the windows of Endelstow House 'transfigured to squares of light
on the general dark body of the night landscape as it absorbed the
outlines of the edifice into its gloomy monochrome', the bare black

lonely edifice which is St Juliot church, and the 'haggard' cliffs of the coast, all these contribute to a background which seems to have some mysterious power over the imagination, and it is surely in this sense that Hardy uses the word 'magic'.

Against this background the story is acted out and once again we have an attractive young woman wooed by a number of men of different class and character, and subjected by Hardy to a penetrating psychological analysis. Elfride, she of the blue eyes, 'blue as autumn distance', is a remarkable study of someone who is betrayed by her own character, by a man who claims to love her, and by fate. Like Tess, Elfride has the President of the Immortals playing with her, and if she were a stronger, more characterful person she might have attained tragic stature. But at this early stage of his career Hardy cannot write tragedy. That will come later. Elfride's rejection by Knight because she had already been kissed by a man seems contrived compared with Tess's rejection by Angel because she has been seduced and had a child, and although there is much that is intriguing about the capricious, immature Elfride, she is no Tess, although one suspects that she is very much Emma.

Elfride is singularly unlucky in the men in her life. Her father is a snobbish, hypocritical, lazy, unfeeling clergyman, her first lover, Felix Jethway, dies, and Stephen is charming but still much of a boy in his behaviour. It is perhaps relevant that on one occasion Hardy described himself as being a boy until he was 25. Knight, a writer and lecturer like Hardy's friend and mentor Horace Moule, is described by his young friend Stephen as the noblest man in the world and is certainly nothing of the kind. His pathological obsession about being unable to love a woman whose lips have been contaminated by the kisses of an earlier suitor reveals a sick man full of sexual inhibitions and frightened of physical contact. His treatment of the woman he claims to love is disgraceful even by Victorian standards of behaviour in such matters. Hardy has created in him an interesting study of male chauvinism, intellectual and social snobbery and emotional cruelty, a kind of Hamlet betrayed by an inner psychological sickness. His very unpleasantness makes the reader feel more sympathetic to poor Elfride. For her there is to be one more man in her life – the aristocratic Lord Luxellian – who is more aware of her physical charms than either Stephen or Knight, who marries her as soon as his own wife is dead, and is indirectly responsible for her death when she has a miscarriage.

Hardy's 'architectural' mind at work can been seen in *A Pair of*

Blue Eyes in its careful planning and a structural device he was fond of, parallelism. Both of Elfride's lovers play chess with her, both go with her to Windy Beak, both are involved with her ear-rings and both talk with her at Felix Jethway's tomb. This results in some interesting contrasts which throw light on the characters. Elfride could easily have beaten Stephen at chess but she allows him to win two out of their three games, whereas Knight has no mercy on her. Stephen's weakness and Knight's toughness are imaged in these parallel scenes, which may result from Hardy's meditating upon his relationship with Horace Moule.

There is much in *A Pair of Blue Eyes* which stamps it as an apprentice work but much that is reminiscent of the later, greater Hardy. We find it in the penetrating interest in man–woman relationships and characterisation, in a story full of memorable incidents (including what may be the first cliff-hanger in our literature), and in the pervasive irony with which the whole story is charged. Death, which is to be a recurrent theme in all of his great novels, is a strong motif here. Young Jethway has died before the novel begins, the first Lady Luxellian dies during it, and Elfride herself, so full of life at the beginning of the novel is dead at the end. The writing at times is as good as anything Hardy achieved later. Chapters 26 and 27, in which the vault is prepared for the dead Lady Luxellian and Knight and Elfride meet Stephen beside her coffin, are brilliantly conceived and powerfully executed. It is rich in resonance of what has happened in the past and prefigures ironically the future while being Shakespearian in its introduction of humour into the vaults of death itself.

> 'I suppose my lord will write to all the other lords anointed in the nation, to let 'em know that she that was is now no more?'
> ''Tis done and past. I see a bundle of letters go off an hour after the death. Sich wonderful black rims as they letters had – half an inch wide at the very least.'
> 'Too much,' observed Martin. 'In short, ''tis out of the question that a human being can be so mournful as black edges half an inch wide.' (*N.W.E.*, p. 274)

Shortly after the first edition of *A Pair of Blue Eyes* was published in May 1873 tragedy occurred in Hardy's own life. As we have seen, Horace Moule provided ideas for the character Knight and he wrote to Hardy in the same month saying 'You understand the *woman* infinitely better than the *lady* . . . how gloriously you have idealized here and there as far as I have got. Yr slips of taste, every now and then, I ought to say pointblank at once, are *Tinsleyan*.' That this was condescending and damning with faint praise would have been obvious to Hardy who would have seen an ironic parallel in the description of Knight in the novel regarding the lower-class Stephen Smith as a 'country lad whom he had patronized'. It is strange that Moule did not see himself in Knight – or perhaps he did. There have been suggestions that Moule met Emma during Hardy's courtship of her and fell in love with her. But whatever the relationships were between these three, and there is much evidence that in spite of differences of social class and age there was an affectionate friendship, we know that on 20 June, before visiting Emma in Bathy, Hardy travelled to Cambridge and stayed with Moule at Queens' College where Moule would almost certainly have shown him the comparatively new tiled and painted fireplace in the Hall. This was created by William Morris and depicted the twelve months of the year with central panels indicating the labours of each month, designed by such artists as Edward Burne-Jones, Ford Madox Brown and Morris himself. Hardy, with his great interest in art, would certainly have found them worth looking at and he might well have carried away in his visual memory pictures of such monthly events as the sending of valentines in February and a peculiarly realistic Morris painting of a pig having its throat cut in December. On 21 September Moule committed suicide by cutting his throat in his College rooms. A distinguished classical scholar, he was a victim of the vagaries of the Cambridge examination system which required him to be competent in Mathematics as well as Classics and he was unable to obtain his degree. Depression because of this and his drunken bouts and possible sexual problems had proved too much for him.

Hardy's respect and love for Moule had been great and he was never to forget him. Michael Millgate (p. 156) suggests that the poem 'Standing by the Mantelpiece: (H.M.M. 1873)' (*C.P.*, 874) possibly reveals a homosexual approach by Moule to Hardy which angered Hardy but led to poignant feelings when Moule shortly afterwards committed suicide. That the poem was intensely personal is almost certainly shown by Hardy's inability to expose it to public view in his own lifetime. It must have been written not long after Moule's death but it was not published until 1928 in Hardy's posthumous book of verse, *Winter Words*.

By the end of 1873 Hardy had three published novels to his credit and he was sufficiently encouraged by the minor success of *Under the Greenwood Tree* and *A Pair of Blue Eyes* to risk giving up almost all his architectural work and devote himself to writing. In this he was strongly supported by Emma, and many years later, talking to Eden Phillpotts he mentioned his everlasting gratitude to her for this. An important step along this road had taken place in December 1872 when he had received a letter from Leslie Stephen, the editor of the prestigious *Cornhill* magazine, inviting him to write a serial. He describes in *The Life* (p. 98) how the letter nearly went astray.

> Mr Stephen's request for a story had been picked up in the muck of the lane by a labouring man, the schoolchildren to whom it had been entrusted having dropped it on the way.

Stephen thought the descriptions in *Under the Greenwood Tree* 'admirable' and this remark from such a distinguished man of letters must have done a great deal for Hardy's morale, as must the request from the American publisher, Henry Holt, that he be allowed to produce editions of Hardy's novels in the States. With the completion of the writing of *A Pair of Blue Eyes* in March 1873 Hardy, who had previously told Leslie Stephen that it would be some months before he could begin a new story, started planning his next novel. He was now living again in his parents' cottage at Bockhampton and it was natural that, as the story grew in his imagination, its centre, Weatherbury, should be based upon Puddletown, only a few miles from the Bockhampton cottage and one-time home of many of his relations, including Tryphena Sparks. He knew it well and many years later was to point out to Hermann Lea, his official topographer, the houses he imagined as the farms of Boldwood and Bathsheba, the Puddletown church which is a central feature of the story, and the actual sheep-wash described in Chapter 19: 'a perfectly circular basin of brickwork in the meadows, full of the clearest water. To birds on the wing its glassy surface, reflecting the light sky, must have been visible for miles around as a glistening Cyclops' eye in a green face.' In September he walked to Woodbury Hill Fair, near Bere Regis and about ten miles from his home, in order to get material for his description of 'Greenhill Fair' in his new novel.

Far from the Madding Crowd is the first of Hardy's great novels. It is not the greatest, but it is certainly the favourite of many, and has remained a bestseller for more than a century. Leslie Stephen's invitation could not have come at a better time. Hardy was as happily in love as he was ever going to be, and he was living in the cottage of his birth, looked after by his mother and surrounded by the people and country he knew and loved. If in his previous novels he had been 'feeling his way towards a method', he had now found it. *Far from the Madding Crowd* is the harvest of the previous novels. In all three of these first novels can be seen emerging those qualities which are to come together so successfully in *Far from the Madding Crowd*; his passionate interest in humankind; his liking for a strong story; his wise exploration of serious issues; his intimate knowledge of country life; his ability to blend, like Shakespeare, the comic and tragic elements of life; and a sorrowful awareness of life's transience and suffering which makes him profoundly responsive to the beauty and yet sadness of our human existence.

To compare Hardy's treatment of the Elfride–Stephen Smith– Henry Knight relationship with that of Bathsheba and Gabriel Oak, Sergeant Troy and Boldwood, is to see how rapidly Hardy is developing as a novelist. Bathsheba is exposed to three different kinds of amatory experience: the steady, enduring though unexciting, love of Gabriel; the obsessive, frustrated, insanely self-centred doting of Boldwood; and the exciting, romantic, physical attractions of the flattering and mendacious Troy. All three of the men in her life are more credible, more interesting and more memorable than are the men that poor Elfride attracts to her and there is a stronger narrative line with less reliance on coincidence. *Far from the Madding Crowd*, too, is marked by a wider range of involvement with life. The insight into sexual relationships is deeper and more comprehensive and, in the words of Lord David Cecil, Hardy's dominating theme is becoming 'mankind's predicament in the universe'. Love is 'the strongest passion known to humanity' but it can destroy as well as create. What Bathsheba has finally to face is reality and Hardy, like George Eliot whose writings he knew so well, is once again intrigued by the clash between the ideal and the real, a clash he must have been aware of in his own life. It becomes a recurring Hardy motif and in *Far from the Madding Crowd* Bathsheba refuses to face the truth about Troy, Boldwood the truth about Bathsheba. The rustic chorus with its earthy realism provides a contrast with the illusory world of the lovers, as does Gabriel who loves Bathsheba for what she is and has no illusions.

Life has taught Gabriel the folly of illusion and he is realistic in his attitude towards nature because he knows that for all her occasional beauty she can be stormy and cruel. His knowledge and acceptance of nature in all her moods means that he is able to work with her. He shares a fatalistic attitude with the workfolk (as Hardy liked to call them), and with Hardy's father whom Hardy compared to Horatio in *Hamlet*. Like Hardy's father Gabriel is a 'man that fortune's buffets and rewards/ Hast ta'en with equal thanks'.

A great deal of the strength of the novel comes from the influences upon him of his first thirty years. His knowledge and appreciation of architecture are seen in his descriptions of Bathsheba's farm and of the old tithe barn (based upon two he knew at Abbotsbury and Cerne Abbas):

> The vast porches at the sides, lofty enough to admit a waggon laden to its highest with corn in the sheaf, were spanned by heavy-pointed arches of stone, broadly and boldly cut, whose very simplicity was the origin of a grandeur not apparent in erections where more ornament has been attempted. The dusky, filmed, chestnut roof, braced and tied in by huge collars, curves, and diagonals, was far nobler in design, because more wealthy in material, than nine-tenths of those in our modern churches. (*N.W.E.*, p. 138)

His interest in music and his ability to make use of it in his novels are revealed in his naming of the actual folk-songs played by Gabriel on his flute and sung at the sheep-shearing supper. These are chosen carefully so that they have a greater significance than may appear at first. Thus Bathsheba's song 'The Banks of Allan Water'

> For his bride a soldier sought her,
>   And a winning tongue had he,
> On the banks of Allan Water
>   None was gay as she!

prefigures her wooing by Sergeant Troy. Hardy uses music in such a way that we can date the action by the reference to the hymn 'Lead Kindly Light' in Chapter 56. We are told that it was a new hymn, and it was first heard in 1868. Even his studies in art in London are used to add richness to the texture of his story. Gabriel's dog, George, has a coat 'approximating in colour to white and slaty

grey; but the grey, after years of sun and rain, had been scorched
and worked out of the more prominent locks, leaving them of a
reddish brown, as if the blue component of the grey had faded, like
the indigo from the same kind of colour in Turner's pictures' (*N.W.E.*,
p. 52). It is probable, too, that in addition to the famous painting of
'The Light of the World', already mentioned, another of Holman
Hunt's paintings, 'The Strayed Sheep' was in his mind when he
describes the death of Gabriel's sheep in Chapter 5.

But the most powerful influence of all was his own upbringing
in the Dorset countryside. It meant that having carefully structured
his story so that the lives of the characters have as background the
lives of the sheep, he is able to write with authority about lamb-
ing, sheep-washing, sheep-shearing, sheep ailments and Greenwood
Fair where the sheep are taken to be sold for slaughtering. Into the
scenes in Warren's Malthouse he pours the anecdotes and humour
he has heard from his mother and grandmother and while fiddling
away at parties in his youth. The sense of community in *Far from the
Madding Crowd* is powerfully felt. The rustics share a tradition, a
common stock of stories of the past, of folk-songs, ballads and jokes.
We see them at work in the fields and at leisure in the malthouse.
We may laugh when the reply to the news that Tompkin's old
apple-tree has been taken out by the roots is 'Ah! stirring times
we live in – stirring times', but by such deft touches Hardy makes
us aware that these people are a closely-knit community. In the
later novels a major theme is to be the break-up of that community
but in *Far from the Madding Crowd* the community and its culture
are not yet under threat.

Although Hardy, never accustomed to bragging, was writing
about this time to Leslie Stephen that he wished 'merely to be
considered a good hand at a serial', he must surely have been
delighted with *Far from the Madding Crowd* and have recognised his
own rare qualities as a novelist. It is the first of his novels in which
we are repeatedly conscious of what have been called his 'Moments
of Vision'. Of these moments of greatness Virginia Woolf, Leslie
Stephen's daughter, wrote in her essay on Hardy's novels:

'moments of vision' exactly describes those passages of astonishing beauty and force. . . . With a sudden quickening of power
which we cannot foretell, nor he, it seems, control, a single scene
breaks off from the rest. We see, as if it existed alone and for
all time, the waggon with Fanny's dead body inside travelling

along the road under the dripping trees; we see the bloated sheep struggling among the clover; we see Troy flashing his sword round Bathsheba where she stands motionless, cutting the lock off her head and spitting the caterpillar on her breast. Vivid to the eye, but not to the eye alone, for every sense participates, such scenes dawn upon us and their splendour remains. (*The Second Common Reader*, London, 1944, pp. 188–9)

The writing of his new novel occupied him for most of the late summer and autumn of 1873 and on 30 September he sent off to Leslie Stephen about ten to twelve of the opening chapters. Stephen was so impressed that he warned Hardy that the first instalment of the story was likely to be published in the following January – and it was. Even so Hardy was pleasantly surprised when on New Year's Eve he bought a copy of the January *Cornhill* on Plymouth Station on his way home from a visit to St Juliot and saw his story placed at the beginning of the magazine, with a striking illustration, by Helen Paterson, known better today by her married name of Helen Allingham. Her marriage took place in September 1874, the same month as Hardy's, and many years later he was to say of this 'charming young lady' that he should have married her rather than Emma 'but for a stupid blunder of God Almighty'. Little could he have foreseen in 1874 that his hopes of happiness in marriage would come to this! All of Hardy's published novels except the first two were serialised and all the serials except *Two on a Tower* were illustrated. Of the illustrators Helen Allingham was one of the best, Ruskin regarding her as successful in making serial illustration 'forever lovely'. Hardy was not so much concerned with the loveliness as the accuracy, and as with almost all subsequent illustrators, he sent to Helen Allingham precise details and sketches of such items as 'smock-frocks', 'gaiters', and 'sheep-crooks'. Writing to Stephen in October 1873 he expressed 'a hope that the rustics, although *quaint*, may be made to appear intelligent, and not boorish at all'. Arlene Jackson's *Illustration and the Novels of Thomas Hardy* is well worth reading on this subject. Hardy's interest in the work of his illustrators is further evidence of his strong visual awareness.

His growing confidence in himself as a novelist is shown by the fact that the first edition of *A Pair of Blue Eyes*, published in May 1873, bore his name on the title-page. Serials in *The Cornhill* were customarily anonymous and one of the very first reviewers of the first instalment of *Far from the Madding Crowd* in *The Spectator* even seemed to believe that it might possibly be written by George Eliot. This was praise indeed although Hardy did point out with some asperity that 'she had never touched the life of the fields'. He had not finished writing his story when the first instalment appeared and he worked away at it in Bockhampton and completed it 'at a gallop', as he said, in the middle of July. It was published in two volumes in November and the reviews were better than anything he had so far experienced, *The Saturday Review* commenting that if only he would 'throw aside his mannerism and eccentricity' he might 'rise to a high position among English novelists', while for *The Examiner* 'This last work of Mr Hardy at once lifts his name above the crowd, and gives him a position among the eminent few.' Other indications of his rise in authority as a novelist could be seen in the attention he received in the American press, in a request for a German translation, and in invitations to go to London and meet such distinguished people as Leslie Stephen and Mrs Procter, the poet and acquaintance of many well-known writers and artists, and – more important – publishers and editors who might commission further work from him. But even so, there must have been some regrets as he left Dorset in July and took up residence once again in London. Upward mobility exacts a price and, with his marriage approaching in September, he could no longer think of the cottage in Bockhampton as his home.

LONDON AND DORSET (1874–85): 'THE WAYFARER'

It was to be eleven years before Hardy and Emma after their September wedding had a really settled home. During that time they moved from one lodging to another. After their honeymoon abroad they took rooms in Surbiton for about six months. From 1875 until 1878 they were in lodgings in Swanage, Yeovil and Sturminster Newton in Dorset, but then it was back to Tooting in London for two years before yet another and final return to Dorset in 1881. It was as if Hardy was torn between the deep instinctual call of his home county where he was little recognised, and the rather more glamorous, if superficial, call of a London where he was being increasingly acknowledged as a novelist of importance. There is significance, however, in his remark that 'I find it a great advantage to be actually among the people described at the time of describing them' and in the fact that what must certainly be seen as his two

least successful novels – *The Hand of Ethelberta* and *A Laodicean* – were
conceived and written in part or in the whole while he was living
in London where he had no roots.

Leslie Stephen was so impressed by the quality and success of
Far from the Madding Crowd that in December 1874 Hardy was asked
to write a new serial to begin in the middle of 1875. He was still not
earning large sums of money for his work but there was steady
progress. He was paid £700 by the well-known publisher Smith,
Elder for the serial rights and the right to publish the first volume
edition of the new story, say about £15 000 in present money. He
might have no security of residence, but he did now have security
of income, the more so as he signed a contract with *The New York
Times* which would give him £1250 for the serial rights. He submitted a draft of the new story, to be called *The Hand of Ethelberta*, in
January and it began its life as a serial in *The Cornhill* in the following July, running for eleven monthly instalments. But in March the
publishers on seeing the manuscript of the opening chapters complained that they were not getting what they expected, which was
another story like *Far from the Madding Crowd*. Hardy had, indeed,
changed his direction. Irritated by reviewers who thought that he
was imitating George Eliot, and by comments such as Henry James's
'the only things we believe in are the sheep and the dogs', and
embarrassed possibly by his own sensitivity to his humble rustic
background, he determined to show that he was capable of writing
something other than pastoral fiction, and he embarked on what
he was later to call a 'somewhat frivolous narrative'. It is a tale of
a quite exceptional woman, Ethelberta, who finds herself as a result
of a marriage moving in aristocratic circles although she is herself
from a poor family. Left a widow, she shows remarkable energy
and initiative in earning a living and providing work for her father,
her numerous brothers and her sister while concealing their relationship to her. It is an over-ingenious situation but it enables Hardy
to 'excite interest in a drama . . . wherein servants were as, or more
important than, their masters', as he says in his 1895 Preface to the
novel. Although too contrived in its plot, it does provide Hardy
with opportunities of satirising Ethelberta's aristocratic friends
and some of the satirical humour is very well done. Once again
the emphasis is on class-distinction and snobbery and Hardy is as
merciless in his criticism of the 'nobility' as he must have been in
The Poor Man and the Lady. The inverted Cinderella theme which
was the basis of that novel now becomes the Cinderella theme but,

sadly, the prince is dissolute and elderly. Here is Ethelberta considering the necessity of marrying into the aristocracy:

> I must get a Herald to invent an escutcheon of my family, and throw a genealogical tree into the bargain in consideration of my taking a few second-hand heirlooms of a pawnbroking friend of his. I must get up sham ancestors, and find out some notorious name to start my pedigree from. It does not matter what his character was; either villain or martyr will do, provided that he lived five hundred years ago. (*N.W.E.*, p. 127)

Hardy was to use this situation again in *Tess* where the wealthy 'Stoke' family take over the name 'd'Urberville'. The basic idea behind the story of a woman from a poor working-class family moving in aristocratic, upper-class circles gives Hardy superb opportunities of exposing shallowness, smugness and hypocrisy. Epigrammatic sayings abound: 'But nothing is so easy as to seem clever when you have money'; 'Mediocrity stamped "London" fetches more than talent marked "provincial"'; 'Poverty in the country is a sadness, but poverty in town is a horror'; 'A half-knowledge of another's life mostly does injustice to the life half known.' Some of these quotations are autobiographical, all are designed to impress. Hardy is determined to show that he is not just a provincial and can write social comedy as well as any Londoner.

To dismiss *Ethelberta* as a minor novel is unfair. It must be judged by what it is and what Hardy intended it to be; that is, a critical examination of the class structure, of the relation between town and country attitudes, and of love among the aristocracy. It provided him with a very necessary catharsis and showed that he was a master of satiric as well as of bucolic humour. And it has one other distinction; in Ethelberta he has created one of the finest, strongest, most self-sacrificing women in nineteenth-century literature. She is fascinating in herself but especially interesting because she has so much of Hardy about her. She comes from a poor country family, goes to London, finds herself mixing with a higher social class, supports her relatives, and is a poet and storyteller. She is a realist with no room for idealism because her main purpose in life is to earn a living which will help her to look after her parents and her brothers and sister. The hand of Ethelberta is sought by four men, only one of whom she loves, and him she lets go to her sister, in an act of self-sacrifice, marrying herself a disreputable old viscount with vast wealth and large estates. We feel sorry for her and in the farcical closing scenes of the book hope that she will escape the clutches of this unpleasant old roué, but in vain. However in a neat twist in a final chapter headed 'Sequel' we find Ethelberta with a hand in everything, ruling the Lord Mountclere and his estate with a rod of iron. As her mother nicely puts it, 'And it is wonderful what can be done with an old man when you are his darling.' D. H. Lawrence in his essay on Hardy perceptively sees *Ethelberta* as 'the one almost cynical comedy. It marks the zenith of a certain feeling in the Wessex novels, the zenith of the feeling that the best thing to do is kick out the craving for *Love* and substitute commonsense, leaving sentiment to the minor characters.' In his introduction to the New Wessex edition of *The Hand of Ethelberta* Robert Gittings finds the source of Hardy's intimate knowledge of the life of servants in London to be his close association with his maternal cousin of the Sparks family, Martha. It is possible that in the early 1860s Hardy had been in love with Martha who was a lady's maid in London, and she would have talked to him about life 'upstairs and downstairs'. And as so often in his novels he uses locations close to him at the time of writing – London where he began writing the story, Rouen which he had visited on his recent honeymoon, and Swanage (Knollsea) to which he moved in July 1875.

No one would claim for *The Hand of Ethelberta* that it is a great novel. Hardy himself in a note of 1875 highlighted his problem when he said 'Yet he took no interest in manners, but in the substance of life only' (*Life*, p. 107). In 1912 he put it among his 'Novels of Ingenuity', of which he said they 'show a not infrequent disregard of the probable in the chain of events, and depend for their interest mainly on the incidents themselves'. It is far too contrived, artificial and dependent on one character, and tries too hard to impress, becoming at times tiresome in its ingenuity. In its division of mankind into 'them', the stereotyped upper class who are all bad, and 'us', the working class who are all good, it is naive and unbalanced but it is a very good example of its particular literary genre and tells us a great deal about Hardy's own predicament and his feelings of growing away from the class into which he had been born in such passages as 'It was that old sense of disloyalty to her class and kin by feeling as she felt now which caused the pain, and there was no escaping it.'

The novel was not, however, what Leslie Stephen and his publisher wanted and the latter complained that the new serial had nothing in common with anything he had written before. The reviews were lukewarm and comments like 'scrappiness', 'an unworthy theme', 'little emotional excitement', 'a lack of grasp or organised plot' and 'an improbable story' confirmed the publisher's disappointment, and he was never again to write a novel for *The Cornhill*. But any disappointment he himself may have felt at the reception of *Ethelberta* would have been mitigated by the growing recognition of him as a writer to be respected. In the spring of 1875 he had joined The Copyright Association and in May he was part of a deputation which met Disraeli in order to call for an enquiry into the state of the copyright law. It was in 1874 that he first met Edmund Gosse and a friendship began that lasted for the rest of his life. He had begun a correspondence in June with R. D. Blackmore, the well-known author of *Lorna Doone* and invitations to dine were reaching him as were invitations to write short stories. In November there was another success. His humorous poem 'The Fire at Tranter Sweatley's' was published in *The Gentleman's Magazine*. It was one of the poems he had written in the mid-1860s but failed to get published, and it is another sign of his growing reputation that the magazine editor had written to him in September requesting 'a short sketch, or brief story, or an article on some literary, art or social subject'. It is a very funny, farcical poem and Hardy's irritation when critics of some eminence took it seriously can be imagined. It is no wonder that he was to write later 'Hardy had a born sense of humour, even a too keen sense occasionally: but his poetry was in general placed by editors in the hands of reviewers well meaning enough, yet who had not a spark of that quality' (*Life*, p. 324).

Part of the history which Hardy absorbed as a child was that of the Napoleonic War, which had ended with the Battle of Waterloo only twenty-five years before his birth. In his Preface to *The Trumpet-Major* Hardy writes of local survivals which remind him of that period, 'an outhouse door riddled with bullet-holes' which had been used for target practice, and of 'heaps of bricks and clods' on the top of a beacon-hill which had once formed the walls of the hut of the man who was to light the beacon if Napoleon's invasion took place. He was fascinated by this particular chapter of the past and in June 1875 he paid the first of several visits he was to make to Chelsea Hospital on the anniversary of Waterloo. Here he met survivors from the fighting and listened to them talking of their memories of sixty years earlier. The way in which ideas gestated in

Hardy's mind over long periods is illustrated by the following note
he made just after that visit to Chelsea: 'Mem: A Ballad of The Hundred Days. Then another of Moscow. Others of earlier campaigns –
forming altogether an *Iliad* of Europe from 1789 to 1815' (*Life*, p. 110).
It was to be nearly another thirty years before *The Dynasts* was born.

From Surbiton, Hardy and Emma moved into London in March
1875 and then to Swanage in July. While looking for lodgings in
Dorset they had a short stay in Bournemouth and some evidence
of early difficulties in their married life may be contained in the
poem 'We Sat at the Window' (*C.P.*, 355) which has under the title
'(*Bournemouth, 1875*)'. It is a picture of boredom and frustration,
ending with

> Wasted were two souls in their prime,
> And great was the waste, that July time
> When the rain came down.

The fact that it was St Swithin's Day could reflect Hardy's sadly
prophetic view about their future relationship.

They travelled from Bournemouth to Swanage by boat and 'found
lodgings at the house of an invalided captain of smacks and ketches'
where, Hardy tells us, he suspended his house-hunting and 'settled
down there for the autumn and winter to finish *The Hand of Ethelberta*'
(*Life*, p. 110). The cottage Ethelberta finds for her family at Knollsea
is based upon these lodgings. The retired seaman, Captain Masters,
talked a good deal about his experiences as a mariner and it is likely
that the description of the rough seas in Chapter 43 owes something
to him. Whatever happened at Bournemouth, their months at Swanage seem to have been happier and Hardy's poem 'Once at Swanage'
(*C.P.*, 753) ends 'and there we two stood, hands clasped; I and She!'

While at Swanage they were visited by Hardy's sisters and had
a breakfast picnic at Corfe Castle. In January of the following year
he completed his writing of the new novel and it was published in
two volumes in April 1876. In May he and Emma had a second holiday on the Continent. They crossed from Harwich by night to Rotter-
dam and then visited the Rhine Valley and a number of German
towns before staying in Brussels. Here Hardy spent a day inspect-
ing the battlefield of Waterloo, and, shortly after his return to England he was once again at Chelsea Hospital on the anniversary of
the battle. It is not surprising that at this time Hardy's Dorset
relatives are said to have described them as 'wandering about like

two tramps'. A more settled period was ahead, however, when in
July, after a short stay in Yeovil, they moved into an unfurnished
house in Sturminster Newton overlooking the river Stour, and spent
£100 on furniture in Bristol, a considerable sum in those days. It
was to be what Hardy later called their 'happiest time'. He was back
in Dorset, living in an attractive market-town of great antiquity,
surrounded by walks to villages and places he would make use of
later in his writings. It was a busy productive period in their lives.
Emma had writing ambitions like her husband. She had begun a
novel called 'The Maid on the Shore' while at St Juliot and work
on this went on from time to time. She had also begun to organise
Hardy's literary notes. He had for several years made hundreds of
extracts from books and newspapers of items which interested him
and might be used in his novels.

1876 was the beginning of a period when he felt it necessary to
cease writing novels for a few months, to reflect and take stock of
his literary position and experience, and, as he put it at that time
in a letter to a publisher, to take time off 'until I can learn the best
line to take for the future.' In the spring he wrote to Leslie Stephen
asking for recommendations of literary criticism he should read
and, to quote Lennart A. Björk, the editor of *The Literary Notebooks
of Thomas Hardy*, 'he embarked on a planned and determined course
of study and note-taking'. There is something touching in the picture
of this man, who had already written one great novel, so worried
by the strictures of reviewers and so insecure because of his own
lowly background that he reads his way through dozens of books
copying out – or getting Emma to copy out – passages which might
possibly be introduced into his future writings in order to impress
readers. And, ironically, some of these often over-erudite passages
are now regarded as blots on his work. In his next novel, *The Return
of the Native*, Hardy made use of no fewer than twenty of these
literary notes.

Emma and Hardy would have been brought together by such
shared activities but, as Denys Kay-Robinson points out in his
balanced and informative *The First Mrs Thomas Hardy*, Hardy had
shown her little sympathy when she experienced 'great fatigue' on
the visit to the field of Waterloo and he frequently left her alone
at Sturminster Newton, and their stay there may not have been
so idyllic for her as he later imagined it was for him. One poem,
'Overlooking the River Stour' (*C.P.*, 424), describes the swallows
flying above the river, a moorhen, and the kingcups but ends with

the suggestion that in his close attention to nature he was neglecting his wife:

> And never I turned my head, alack,
>   While these things met my gaze
>   Through the pane's drop-drenched glaze,
> To see the more behind my back. . . .
> O never I turned, but let, alack,
>   These less things hold my gaze!

How easy it is to see with hindsight where we went wrong, and how human! They were not helped either in their marital relationship by their failure to produce a child, a failure emphasised by an incident which occurred at Sturminster Newton. Late one night they discovered their maid-servant letting her lover into the house:

> Before I had thought what to do E. had run downstairs, and met her, and ordered her to bed. The man disappeared. Found that the bolts of the back-door had been oiled. He had evidently often stayed in the house. She remained quiet till between four and five, when she got out of the dining-room window and vanished. (*Life*, p. 118)

The epilogue to this incident is ironic in the extreme. Six weeks later appears the note, 'Aug. 13. We hear that Jane, our late servant is soon to have a baby. Yet never a sign of one is there for us.' Could there be, one wonders, any connection between that incident and a note made by Hardy a month earlier: 'The sudden disappointment of a hope leaves a scar which the ultimate fulfilment of that hope never entirely removes'?

Disappointment plays a large part in *The Return of the Native*, which he began writing during the winter of 1876–7 at Sturminster Newton and finished in the following November. After his foray into the world of London Society, Hardy returned to his roots and the action is almost entirely confined to an area within a mile or two of the Bockhampton cottage. He hoped that once again *The Cornhill* would publish his new novel but Leslie Stephen had not recovered from his disappointment over *The Hand of Ethelberta* and 'though he liked the opening, he feared that the relationship between Eustacia, Wildeve and Thomasin, might develop into something "dangerous" for a family magazine', and he would not consider publication until he could see the complete manuscript. This was the first, but not the last, serious trouble Hardy had with a publisher for what might be called moral and sexual reasons. Stephen had been worried by one or two aspects of *Far from the Madding Crowd*, and deleted 'a line or two in the last batch of proofs from an excessive prudery of wh. I am ashamed. . . . May I suggest that Troy's seduction of the young woman will require to be treated in a gingerly fashion . . .'. Now Hardy was faced with a complete rejection of his work by the magazine editors because of their fear of Mrs Grundy and desire not to publish anything which 'would bring a blush into the cheek of the young person'.

In writing *Far from the Madding Crowd* he managed to avoid giving offence by the use of subtle erotic imagery in the scenes where Troy traps Bathsheba with his spur and impresses her with his masculinity in the fencing display. He uses this device so cleverly that he makes a virtue out of necessity; some of the best writing in his novels uses symbolism and imagery to convey powerful sexual feelings. In the novels that followed *Far from the Madding Crowd* he was increasingly to use a second method of dealing with the susceptibilities of his prudish editors and readers – the provision after the serial edition of alternative, unbowdlerised versions of the novels, and, as we shall see later, the volume forms of *Tess* and *Jude* are markedly different from those of the serials.

Having received what was tantamount to a rejection from *The Cornhill*, Hardy, probably somewhat short of money as he had had nothing published for some time, submitted what was written of the manuscript to *Blackwood's Magazine* but it was again declined, on this occasion because the opening chapters were too static. A further rejection followed and it was finally accepted by Chatto's magazine *The Belgravia*, and published in monthly instalments in 1878 and in novel form in November of that year. In his book *The Making of 'The Return of the Native'* John Paterson indicates the extent to which changes were forced on Hardy. Eustacia suffers most because Hardy's problem is to write a story about a deeply sensual woman without too obviously mentioning her sensuality. Using the device of suggestive imagery he repeatedly associates her with fire and heat. She stands by a bonfire which lights the darkness of the heath. The fire is a signal for Wildeve, her lover, who describes himself as suffering from 'the curse of inflammability'. If we could have seen the colour of her soul it would have been 'flame-like'. And at the end of the novel all this warmth and passion is extinguished in the cold waters of Shadwater Weir.

To turn from *Far from the Madding Crowd* to *The Return of the Native* is, in many ways, to turn from light to dark, and its opening chapter is like the overture to a tragic opera. The deservedly famous description of Egdon Heath has a gaunt but majestic sombreness; it provides the setting on which the protagonists will act out their sad tale of wildness and primitive passions and sets the mood. This is a different Hardy from the one who wrote *The Hand of Ethelberta*. He has returned to his roots and writes about places he has known intimately since childhood. The descriptions of the heath and its natural life at different times of the year are the result of genuine knowledge, detailed observation and a sensitive response. We learn of the rare birds and see a heron flying, 'the edges and lining of his wings, his thighs and his breast . . . so caught by the bright sunbeams that he appeared as if formed of burnished silver', and we see the wasps 'rolling drunk with the juice of apples'. The setting is one in which Hardy is completely at home and this gives it a rich authenticity.

Clym, the returned native, has something of Hardy about him. Hardy denied this, saying 'I think Clym is the nicest of all my heroes, and *not a bit* like me', but Hardy, after a period of wandering, has returned to his native Dorset. Like Clym, he has given up a good and steady job in a large town, for a career which was much less secure and certain. Did Hardy's mother, one speculates, regret his giving up architecture for the career of a writer, and did she, like Clym's mother (and Hardy acknowledged a similarity between them), want him 'to do well'? Clym replies, 'Mother, what is doing well?' and in doing so, Hardy questions his own undoubted ambition and desire to succeed. Here we begin to see that ambivalence which is so much a strength of his later writing. When Hardy describes Clym's knowledge of the heath, 'He was permeated with its scenes, with its substance, and with its odours. . . . His eyes had first opened thereon: with its appearance all the first images of his memory were mingled . . .' he might well be describing himself. So strong is the sense of place that, for the first edition, he drew a map of the region in which the action of the story takes place. Sadly, it has been omitted by the publishers in almost every subsequent edition.

The Return of the Native was Hardy's first attempt to write a great tragic novel which would establish him as one of England's great novelists. Its structure is that of a five-act play with an epilogue, it keeps close to the unities of time and place, and its tragic vision is seen in the awe-inspiring timelessness of the heath on which the little lives of men are acted out. The heath, Hardy writes 'had a lonely face, suggesting tragical possibilities' and in later novels there is to be an increasing emphasis on the loneliness so painfully described in the lives of Boldwood and Fanny in *Far from the Madding Crowd*. Is Hardy, one wonders, portraying his awareness of the loneliness which, in spite of his marriage and growing success as a writer, was almost certainly an element in his own life? Writing is always a solitary and a lonely occupation, and tragic characters are almost always tragic in their loneliness. Eustacia's loneliness is apparent throughout and is emphasised just before her death by her 'isolation from all of humanity'. She is another of Hardy's fascinating heroines and she grows in interest as the novel proceeds but sadly she is not big enough to carry the tragedy and *The Return of the Native* can now be seen as a noble failure but an important milestone in Hardy's career.

On 18 March 1878 Hardy and Emma moved from Sturminster Newton to a large house in Tooting which they had taken on a three-year lease. It was the end of what he was later to call their 'Sturminster Newton idyll', a happy time in which he wrote a very unhappy novel. We must beware of assuming that the mood of his life must *always* have a close correlation with the mood of the piece of writing occupying him at the time. London cut him off from his roots but it did enable him to take part in its life, to visit its theatres, concerts and galleries and to make yet more literary and publisher friends, among whom was Alexander Macmillan, head of London's most prestigious publishing house. Hardy became a member of the Savile Club and applied to the British Museum for a reader's ticket. He met fellow-author Walter Besant who had founded the Incorporated Society of Authors, and his support for Besant showed how aware he already was of the need for authors to fight for their rights. Such was his standing now that he did not just go to Sir Henry Irving's last night at the Lyceum Theatre, he was invited to drink champagne in the dressing-room afterwards.

In November *The Return of the Native* was published in volume form and had a mixed reception from the reviewers. 'Inferior to his other work', 'impossibly Elizabethan peasants', 'not ill conceived but clumsily expressed', 'cold, intellectual and unnecessarily depressing', were some of the adverse comments. However, atmosphere, description, the vividness of individual scenes, the striking story were praised, and *The Return of the Native* drew from D. H. Lawrence an inspired comment:

This is the wonder of Hardy's novels, and gives them their beauty. The vast, unexplored morality of life itself, what we call the immorality of nature, surrounds us in its eternal incomprehensibility, and in its midst goes on the little human morality play, with its queer frame of morality and its mechanised movement; seriously, portentously, till some one of the protagonists chance to look out of the charmed circle, weary of the stage, to look into the wilderness raging around. Then he is lost. . . . (*Study of Thomas Hardy*, Cambridge, 1985, p. 29)

Lawrence has assuredly put his finger on the importance of *The Return of the Native* in Hardy's growth towards greatness as a tragic novelist, and it was becoming clear that the 'vast unexplored morality of life itself' would become an increasingly important factor in the novels.

Work had now begun on his next novel, *The Trumpet-Major*. Research was done in the library of the British Museum and there was another visit to the veterans at the Chelsea Hospital in October. He was also writing more short stories. 'The Impulsive Lady of Croome Castle' had been published in March and it was followed by 'An Indiscretion in the Life of an Heiress' in July. It tells us something about Hardy's methods of working that the latter makes use of a substantial part of *The Poor Man and the Lady*. As other bits of that unfortunate novel had been used in *Under the Greenwood Tree* and *A Pair of Blue Eyes*, Hardy had obviously been told by his mother that 'to waste not was to want not'. The native returned to his parents' home at Bockhampton early the next year partly in order to see his sick mother, but also to find material for the new novel. He got his father to talk to him about his grandfather's experiences as a volunteer in the years when it was expected that Napoleon would invade England, and he visited Portland, Weymouth and Sutton Poyntz, all of which he was to use as locations for the story.

That he did not completely abandon poetry-writing during these years is evidenced by his poem 'A January Night (1879)' (*C.P.*, 400). This with its 'hid dread' and its 'spirit astray' of the man in the coffin is both sombre and enigmatic, and it is made the more so by Hardy's drawing attention to it in *The Life* (p. 128) where he says the poem 'relates to an incident in the New Year (1879) which occurred here at Tooting, where they seemed to begin to feel that "there had past away a glory from the earth." And it was in this house that their troubles began.'

Tantalisingly, he does not tell us what the 'troubles' were. There had been a deterioration in his health but nothing serious so far. Professionally, *The Return of the Native* had not been the success he had hoped for and some of the reviews had been cruel but he had been able now for several years to earn a small if not spectacular income as a writer, and publishers were beginning to ask for his work. Such troubles as there were, then, seem likely to have been in his private life. He had been married for nearly five years and there were, sadly, no children, nor were there likely to be any now. They were both approaching middle-age and Hardy may have been realising that Emma was not the ideal wife for an up-and-coming writer in London. She had quickly lost her food looks and there may already have been signs of the mental instability that was to make her behaviour so unpredictable in later years. Robert Gittings thinks that 'the eye of the impressionable Hardy was beginning to rove at this precise time' and this may have added to their current difficulties but there is little evidence that he was more impressionable at that time than at others, nor does Gittings seem to have realised that the majority of men are impressionable and respond to the looks of a pretty woman. Hardy might have remarked wryly that it was all part of Nature's 'holy plan'!

1879 was largely taken up with the writing of *The Trumpet-Major* and negotiating for its publication. Hardy tried in February to interest *The Cornhill* again, but without success, and he was no luckier with Macmillan. However, by August a magazine called *Good Words* had agreed to take it as a serial and it appeared in monthly instalments throughout 1880 with a three-volume edition published in October. *Good Words* was edited by the Rev. Dr McLeod and printed, appropriately enough, by a firm with the name of Virtue & Co. But even so Hardy must have been surprised to be asked to change a lovers' meeting from a Sunday to a Saturday and there were to be no swear words even if this was a story about soldiers. There were to be no bad words in *Good Words*.

As had happened before, Hardy followed up a serious, sombre tragic novel with one that is much lighter in tone even if in *The Trumpet-Major* the blue sky has a background of very dark clouds. It grows out of his abiding interest in the Napoleonic War, an interest nurtured in him both by the anecdotes of his family and by his research in the British Museum Library where he had spent so many hours reading and compiling the 'Trumpet-Major Notebook'. But it was not just books, there were objects from the past to give reality to the imagination. As a boy at Bockhampton Hardy had been able to see the monument to Nelson's Hardy, Admiral Sir Thomas Masterman Hardy, the high tower on Blagdon Hill. He knew, too, the house in which the future Admiral was born at Portisham, west of Weymouth. Weymouth itself had been given status as a seaside resort by George III and during the year in which he had lived there Hardy would have certainly been very conscious of the King's influence on the town.

But, if a soldier is the main protagonist, the war is never more than a background. Hardy was shrewd enough to know that the description of battles was not for him. What is mainly a light romantic comedy in which, once again, an attractive young woman is being wooed by three men, is given deeper significance by such passages as the following which provides an elegy for Sergeant Stanner, a soldier who sings a song (written by Hardy for the occasion) during a very happy party given by the Miller for his son John, the Trumpet-Major:

> Poor Stanner! . . . he fell at the bloody battle of Albuera a few years after this pleasantly spent summer at the Georgian watering-place, being mortally wounded and trampled down by a French hussar when the brigade was deploying into line under Beresford. (*N.W.E.*, p. 50)

Having regard to the way in which by now Hardy's tragic vision was becoming dominant, it is not surprising that once again the heroine makes the wrong choice and marries John's brother, and the novel ended in *Good Words* with the words:

> The candle held by his father shed its waving light upon John's face and uniform as he turned with a farewell smile on the doorstone, backed by the black night; and in another moment he had plunged into the darkness, the ring of his smart step dying away upon the bridge as he joined his waiting companions-in-arms, and went off to blow his trumpet over the bloody battlefields of Spain.

The first edition is similar until we read that John 'went off to blow his trumpet till silenced for ever upon one of the bloody battlefields of Spain'. Hardy gave the serial readers what they wanted – a reasonably happy ending – as he had to, in fact, because he had offered the serial to an American magazine and told the editor that 'I may add that it is to be a cheerful, lively story, and is to end happily.' But is even the serial ending really happy? The connotations of 'black night', 'plunged into darkness' and 'dying away' make it inescapable to a sensitive reader that John is on his way to extinction. Hardy had to earn money and he had to conform to the demands of his magazine editors if he was to obtain the useful contribution to his income the serials provided, but he had learnt to make a virtue out of necessity by using language in poetic and imagistic ways of great power in order to convey his subtext to the less naive of his readers. Such moments as that when Anne, standing on Portland, sees the *Victory* heading down-Channel and taking Nelson to his death at Trafalgar, or when Hardy completes his description of the review of his troops on the downs near Weymouth with the words,

> but the King and his fifteen thousand armed men, the horses, the bands of music, the princesses . . . how entirely have they all passed and gone! – lying scattered about the world as military and other dust, some at Talavera, Albuera, Salamanca, Vittoria, Toulouse, and Waterloo; some in home churchyards; and a few small handfuls in royal vaults. (*N.W.E.*, p. 100)

such moments turn what would otherwise be just another entertaining historical romance into something with a touch of greatness. It deserves Barbara Hardy's tribute to it as a great historical novel and it is more highly regarded today than it was in 1880 although even then the reviews rated it as one of the best stories Hardy had so far written.

The income from the serials and from his short stories was vital to Hardy because in volume form his novels had not sold well. *The Hand of Ethelberta, The Return of the Native* and *The Trumpet-Major* first editions had all been remaindered and, although he was now becoming acknowledged by more discerning readers, he was still unknown to most middle-class readers of that time who devoured Dickens, Trollope, Thackeray, Mrs Henry Wood, William Black and Charlotte Yonge in such large quantities. However, his sense that the literary world was being slow to recognise him must have been weakened by the invitation in 1879 to join the newly-formed Rabelais Club with its aim to bring together the more 'virile' of writers, and, as 1880 passed, he met Matthew Arnold for the first time in February, and his friendship with Ann Procter led to his meeting Tennyson and Browning. He had lunch with Tennyson, who had 'a genial human face' and 'was very sociable', telling Hardy that he liked *A Pair of Blue Eyes* the best of his novels.

Hardy was now becoming known in America as a short-story writer. His American publisher, Harper, impressed by his writing, now asked him to contribute a serial to the new European edition of *Harper's Weekly*, and he began to plan his next novel, *A Laodicean*. A member of Harper's firm, R. R. Bowker, called on the Hardys in Tooting and described how he was 'received in a pretty parlour by Mrs Thomas Hardy with her Kensington-stitch work, and her pet cat; she is an agreeable youngish English lady, immensely interested in her husband's work.... Hardy presently came down, a quiet-mannered, pleasant, modest, little man, with sandyish short beard, entirely unaffected and direct...'. Harper had already published *The Return of the Native* as a serial in America, and as an indication of the growing interest in Hardy there was a short article about him published in *The Literary World* (Boston) in August 1878. This was almost certainly written by Hardy himself and it reveals very clearly once again Hardy's sensitivity about his lowly background. The humble cottage at Bockhampton is 'a lonely old-fashioned house on the margin of a wood' and his higher education was looked after 'by an able classical scholar and Fellow of Queens' College, Cambridge'. How ironic that at this stage of his life in order to earn 'an honest dime' he found it necessary because of the pressures on him of the class-ridden society in which he now moved to hide what was the main constituent of his genius, the Dorset background among ordinary working people. In 1880 with a living to earn, which of us would not have done the same? He had come a long way in the past decade but with little in the way of royalties to give him a steady income, he was still living on a hand-to-mouth basis.

The fragility of his financial situation was made all the more painfully obvious by an illness which seems to have developed slowly throughout that year. He was well enough to go to Epsom on Derby Day and to dine during the summer at a number of clubs where he met, among others, Lord Houghton, George du Maurier, Henry Irving and Alma-Tadema. In July he and Emma went abroad for a holiday, visiting Boulogne, Amiens, and other places in northern France. At one seaside resort he spent so much time in the water swimming, a recreation he loved, that he thought this might have triggered off his illness. In Trouville 'On a gloomy gusty afternoon ... they came upon a Calvary tottering to its fall; and as it rocked in the wind like a ship's mast Hardy thought that the crudely painted figure of Christ upon it seemed to writhe and cry in the twilight: "Yes, Yes! I agree that this travesty of me and my doctrines should totter and overturn in this modern world!" They hastened on from the strange and ghastly scene' (*Life*, p. 143). In October he and his wife spent a week in Cambridge during which he felt 'an indescribable weariness'. On return to London he was so unwell that a doctor was sent for and diagnosed internal bleeding. The Macmillans' own doctor was then called in and Hardy was informed that an operation could be avoided provided he could lie in bed for several months.

Work had begun on the new novel, *A Laodicean*, during the first half of the year. Harper's offer of £100 for each of thirteen instalments of the serial was generous and would make Hardy's future more secure. The eminent artist and writer George du Maurier had been asked to provide illustrations and work had to proceed on the new story because the first instalment was to appear in the first number of the European Edition of *Harper's New Monthly Magazine* in December. Knowing that he had to finish the serial 'so as not to ruin the new venture of the publishers and also in the interests of his wife, for whom as yet he had made but poor provision in the event of his own decease' (*Life*, p. 150), he dictated the remaining instalments to his wife while lying in bed in some pain. He pays a touching tribute to Emma in *The Life* for her brave devotion to him both as nurse and amanuensis, and what troubles there were in their marriage at that time must have been no more than occur in many marriages. Two of his notes from the six months of illness give some idea of the sombreness of his thoughts: 'Carlyle died last Saturday. Both he and George Eliot have vanished into nescience while I have been lying here' (*Life*, p. 152) and 'The emotions have no place in a world of defect, and it is a cruel injustice that they should have developed in it' (*Life*, p. 153).

A Laodicean was finished in May 1881 and in the same month Hardy made his first walk out alone. He stood on Wandsworth Common and recited verses from Gray's 'Ode on vicissitude' about the invalid who at length is able to 'breathe and walk again':

> The meanest flowret of the vale,
> The simplest note that swells the gale,
> The common sun, the air, the skies,
> To him are opening Paradise.

In that spring the call of Wessex to Hardy must have been strong. London had become at times a nightmarish 'monster whose body had four million heads and eight million eyes'. It had twice been associated with illness and he now knew that his best writing was not just about Wessex, it was done in Wessex. By the end of May, having decided that they would in future live in Dorset and take lodgings in London for the Season, they were looking for accommodation and on 25 June they moved into a detached house in Wimborne, about twenty miles from Dorchester. This had the advantage of being sufficiently near Hardy's parents for him to be able to visit them in a day and yet sufficiently far from them to avoid any problems in Emma's relationship with her mother-in-law. If, as seems probable, they did not get on well with one another, Emma could keep away and be kept away.

It has become customary to see *A Laodicean* as probably the weakest of Hardy's novels and, in fact J. I. M. Stewart dismisses it as Hardy's 'only unredeemed failure'. However, in his valuable *The Neglected Hardy* – a book which has itself been unduly neglected – Richard Taylor says of *A Laodicean*:

> *A Laodicean* deserves to be rescued as much as any, if only because it is usually so uncompromisingly written off as Hardy's worst novel. In fact it is by no means the least interesting, and it is a mistake to assume that, because for a long period it is laden with melodramatic devices, it is not a serious work. Its defects derive from the accident of its having been largely written under the stress of serious illness, and only this vitiated its early promise of being Hardy's most successful social comedy. (p. 179)

It has a special claim on our interest as students of Hardy's life because in 1900 Hardy told an American visitor that '*A Laodicean* contained more of the facts of his own life than anything else he had ever written.' Architecture is an important strand in the story, so much so that *The Architect and Building News* of 20 January 1928 found 'Hardy still trailing his professional past; the hero is an architect, the second villain is an architect . . . and curious dated discussions on architecture take place'. In the very first chapter we meet an architect 'measuring and copying the chevroned doorway' of an English village church as Hardy must so often have done himself in his student days. The architect, Somerset, had written verse in his twenties but had it rejected by the publishers, and he meets his wife because of his work. While studying architecture in Dorchester in the 1850s, Hardy had spent many hours with the two sons of the Baptist minister arguing about infant baptism. This subject is quickly introduced in the novel and is argued at length in Book First, Chapter 7, while the Baptist minister, Mr Woodwell, is based upon the Baptist minister in Dorchester. The storm which interrupted the garden-party reflects a similar occurrence at a garden-party given by the Macmillan family in July 1879, and Paula's journey on the Continent makes extensive use of Hardy's own recent holiday there. But as might be expected from the writing of a man dangerously ill and facing the possibility of early death, *A Laodicean* is a serious discussion of some of the many aspects of his life and career upon which his illness had given him time to meditate. His life had been a conflicting mixture of the old and the new, of Bockhampton and London, of studies of the past and of the present, of the Bible and of Darwin, of ancient and modern architecture, of those who were in favour of church restoration and those who were against. In 1881 he joined the Society for the Protection of Ancient Buildings and he read a paper to that Society in 1906 in which he discussed the conflict on the one hand between the wish to preserve the old and the need to restore it. He concluded, 'the opposing tendencies ... can find no satisfactory reconciliation'. These conflicts are symbolised in *A Laodicean* in which Somerset talks about 'A clash between ancient and modern'. Paula, rich heiress of the fortune made by her railway-building father, lives in an old castle bought with his money, and Hardy puts into her mouth some of his own thoughts: 'Do you think it a thing more to be proud of that one's father should have made a great tunnel and railway like that, than that one's remote ancestor should have built a great castle like this?' This leads Somerset to reply that 'From a modern point of view, railways are, no doubt, things more to be proud of than castles ... though perhaps I myself, from mere association, should decide in favour of the ancestor who built the castle' (*N.W.E.*, p. 119). Ambiguity of response is deepened when Somerset looks down at the railway tunnel and we are told that 'The popular commonplace that science, steam, and travel must always be unromantic and hideous, was not proven at this spot' while the castle is described as 'the hoary memorial of a stolid antagonism to the interchange of ideas, the monument of hard distinctions in blood and race, of deadly mistrust of one's neighbour ... and of a sublime unconsciousness of any other force than a brute one ...' (*N.W.E.*, p. 52).

Some of the antagonism to *A Laodicean* arises from its abandon-
ment of the successful formula, a novel about country people living and working in what Hardy called 'the part-real, part-dream'
world of Wessex. The name 'Wessex' had not been in general use
for many centuries when Hardy used it in *Far from the Madding
Crowd*, but it was picked up by the reviewers and he soon became
'the Wessex novelist'. Knowing, as he said, 'the pecuniary value of
a reputation for a speciality', he exploited the commercial value
of this by an increasing emphasis on the Wessex topography and
by such titles as *Wessex Tales, Wessex Poems*, the Wessex Novels and
the Wessex Edition. In *A Laodicean* it is as if he needed to break
away for at least one novel from the Wessex connection. The subtitle is 'A Story of Today' in itself a break-away from the historical
dimension which was a feature of the truly *Wessex* novels, and we
are concerned in this latest novel with scientific discovery, photo-
graphy, railway engineering and telegraphy. Today we can see it
as a brave attempt to tackle something different, and recent critics
with the exception of Robert Gittings, always so prone to see the
worst in Hardy, have found much to commend. Barbara Hardy
in her introduction to the New Wessex Edition saw it as offering
more than entertainment in its high moments of passion and idea,
and she thought its language interesting, and its action enlivened
by setting and feeling. For Richard Taylor it is 'a fascinating ex-
position of Hardy's social beliefs and his concern about the aes-
thetic and cultural implications of social revolution and technical
progress'.

Paula's laodiceanism echoes Hardy's. In reply to a question from
Somerset she says 'What I really am, so far as I know, is one of that
body to whom lukewarmth is not an accident but a provisional
necessity, until they see a little more clearly.' Havelock Ellis saw
Paula's attitude as one 'which we recognise as implicit throughout
Mr Hardy's novels', and the title inspires a sensitive summing-up
by Michael Millgate of one of the main qualities of Hardy's writing:

> Hardy seems to have been constantly drawn towards a 'Lao-
> diceanism' of his own – a reluctance to adopt absolute or even
> firm positions, a willingness to see virtue in all sides of a ques-
> tion, an insistence upon the provisionality of his opinions and the
> need to register them rather as a series of tentative impressions
> than as the systematic formulations of a philosopher. (Millgate,
> p. 220)

Part of Hardy's greatness lies in this ambivalence. It is not true that the best lack all conviction but it is true that they see life as being far more complex than the supporters of so many '-ist' movements with their simplistic panaceas for the troubles of humankind.

Hardy found much that was congenial about life in Wimborne, an attractive market-town on the river Stour with a fine minster. Their house had a pleasant garden and in it during September he corrected the proofs of *A Laodicean* for its issue in volume form, sitting under a vine 'which for want of training hangs in long arms over my head nearly to the ground. The sun tries to shine through the great leaves, making a green light on the paper, the tendrils twisting in every direction, in gymnastic endeavours to find something to lay hold of' (*Life*, p. 155). He made long walks through this eastern part of Dorset and in July went for a drive in a wagonette with his two sisters which took him past Charborough Park, seventeenth-century home of the aristocratic Erle-Drax family. On a hill in the grounds stands a high tower built as a folly, and the driver of the wagonette told his passengers that a certain Miss Drax had married a man much younger than herself. We see here the beginnings of his next novel. The social life was attractive, too. There was a Shakespeare reading group, a neighbour who was a county-court judge, and even an invitation to a ball at Lady Wimborne's Canford Manor. It was all a long way from life at the cottage at Bockhampton. Hardy was becoming socially acceptable. In August he and Emma went on a holiday in Scotland and he was delighted to meet someone who could remember Sir Walter Scott.

Refreshed in mind and body and anxious to earn some more money his thoughts were now turning to his next novel. In July he had jotted down some notes which tell us about his own writing:

> The real, if unavowed, purpose of fiction is to give pleasure by gratifying the love of the uncommon in human experience mental or corporeal. . . . The writer's problem is, how to strike the balance between the uncommon and the ordinary so as on the one hand to give interest, on the other to give reality. . . . The uncommonness must be in the events, not in the characters. (*Life*, p. 154)

His correspondence at this time shows Hardy dealing with an increasing number of requests for stories, translations, and foreign editions of his work with a professionalism and a commercial shrewdness of a high order. He has very rapidly learnt a great deal since his early transactions with Tinsley, and he is a strong supporter of attempts to bring writers together in an association which will look after their interests.

In September 1881 Hardy agreed to write a serial for the American magazine, *The Atlantic Monthly*, and it occupied him for most of 1882, the novel being published in book form in October. Hardy's interest in astronomy had begun when he was a boy and references to the stars and planets occur frequently in his earlier novels. The nearness of the tower at Charborough, the story of the aristocratic lady marrying a man younger than herself and his observation of a comet in June, all contributed to the choice of subject. With his usual thoroughness he prepared himself for his new novel by applying to inspect the Royal Observatory at Greenwich in November and by writing to a Professor of Mechanical Engineering about lenses. Writing to Edmund Gosse, he described the story as 'carefully thought out' even if it was 'lamentably hurried' because of the pressures of American serialisation. This careful thought manifests itself throughout the novel which is planned to be far more than just a romantic love story by its constant reminder of the insignificance of human lives when seen against the vastness of space and time. The story is full of surprises, coincidences and ironic circumstances, of, in fact, the 'uncommon' but the two protagonists are human, believable and appeal to our sympathy. *Two on a Tower* was chosen as a title not just because of Hardy's joy in alliteration but because it is a succinct symbol of the ideas in his mind at that time. The 'two are the two lovers who meet for the first time in the tower, fall in love there and act out most of their drama there'. It has a sexual significance and the fact that it was built on a prehistoric spot and commemorated a person now dead and completely forgotten is a reminder of the little lives of men. But it has another function. It is the observatory from which Swithin looks out into a space so vast that the mind cannot really comprehend it. Interested as he was in scientific philosophy, Hardy was painfully aware of the way in which sciences such as astronomy had challenged so much that had been taken for granted in his childhood. In Tennyson's *In Memoriam* he would have read

'The stars,' she whispers, 'blindly run;
    A web is woven across the sky;
    From out waste places comes a cry,
And murmurs from the dying sun:

and those great lines of Matthew Arnold in 'Dover Beach' were
well-known to him:

Ah, love, let us be true
To one another! for the world which seems
To lie before us like a land of dreams,
So various, so beautiful, so new,
Hath really neither joy, nor love, nor light,
Nor certitude, nor peace, nor help for pain;
And we are here as on a darkling plain
Swept with confused alarms of struggle and flight,
Where ignorant armies clash by night.

Swithin talks to Viviette, Lady Constantine, about the stars and
tells her that 'whatever the stars were made for, they were not
made to please our eyes . . . nothing is made for man . . . astronomy
is a bad study for you. It makes you feel human insignificance too
plainly.' But that is not all: 'the actual sky is a horror. . . . If you are
cheerful, and wish to remain so, leave the study of astronomy alone.
Of all the sciences, it alone deserves the character of the terrible'
(*N.W.E.*, pp. 56–8). In another letter to Gosse about *Two on a Tower*
Hardy says his aim was 'to make science, not the mere padding of
a romance, but the actual vehicle of romance' and there is no doubt
of his success in achieving what was an unusual and original idea.
The vastness and coldness of the astronomical world serves as a
contrast with the world of human beings and the warmth of human
love between men and women. One is reminded of an occasion in
the 1890s when Hardy had been visiting the young and precocious
Powys brothers. He listened to them talking abstract literary the-
ory, then they walked through the streets of Montacute and one of
the brothers pointed out the village beauty. 'And so we get back
to humanity', said Hardy. There is a good deal of Hardy in Swithin.
Swithin's grandmother 'gazing into the flames, with her hands upon
her knees, quietly re-enacting in her brain certain of the long chain
of episodes, pathetic, tragical, and humorous, which had constituted
the parish history for the last sixty years' (*N.W.E.*, p. 41) reminds us
of Hardy's grandmother. Swithin is from the same kind of humble
family background as Hardy and he shares Hardy's aspirations,
interest in science, and sense of detachment and isolation resulting
from the nature of his career. A writer spends long hours immured
in his study just as Swithin spends long hours in his tower and it

may be that at this stage of his life Hardy was beginning to feel his loneliness, torn as he must have been between the worlds of Wessex and London, between the homely warmth and basic living of the Bockhampton cottage and the brightness and luxury of the Savile Club.

Ironically it is only when Swithin overhears the down-to-earth rustics talking about his relationship with Lady Constantine that he responds to the appeal and charm of this woman who has so much more to offer him than astronomy ever can. It is part of Hardy's wisdom that for him the heart is always more important than the mind. Swithin and Viviette are two of Hardy's most appealing characters. The opening chapters describing their falling in love are delightfully written and Hardy soon wins our sympathy for Viviette who has been treated with such callous cruelty by her dominating husband. Bored, lonely and sexually frustrated, she is in a sense the first of Hardy's 'Noble Dames', most of them suffering because of their position as aristocratic women. Sadly, Hardy manipulates his plot too crudely in order that Lady Constantine shall also suffer because of her acceptance of class distinctions, and the tragic ending is gratuitous. *Two on a Tower* is another variation on the 'Poor Man and the Lady' theme.

In the story of Hardy's life it is interesting in yet another way. He contrives a plot which makes it clear that he is becoming ever more outspoken in his attack on Victorian proprieties. He now feels sufficiently established as an author to be able to say what he was not allowed to say in his first unpublished 'socialistic' novel. The Bishop, as ridiculous a suitor as Mr Collins in *Pride and Prejudice*, is not just a figure of fun, but is riddled with assumptions of male superiority, smug self-satisfaction and ecclesiastical arrogance. In ridiculing him as he does, Hardy is attacking a pillar of the Establishment in no uncertain way, and he adds insult to injury by the way in which Viviette deceives the Bishop into believing that Swithin's son is his own. This brought down on Hardy's head, as he must surely have expected, the wrath of many of his reviewers. This incident, thundered *The Saturday Review*, is 'an extremely repulsive element' in the book. The Boston *Literary World* thought it a 'bad novel, tasteless and outrageous', while *The Spectator* found the story 'as unpleasant as it is practically impossible' and 'objectionable without truth'. Hardy must have been both amused and irritated by all this critical blustering. 'The critics have been quite acid', he wrote in a letter. One reviewer of *A Laodicean* had made the classic remark 'Mr Hardy has a way of insisting on the physical attractions of a woman which, if imitated by weaker writers, may prove offensive'. Even the Editor of *The Atlantic* was worried and is reported to have said, 'I asked Hardy for a family story, and he has given me a story in the family way.' Hardy's battle with Mrs Grundy was really getting under way and it can only have been with his tongue in his cheek that in his Preface to the 1895 edition he wrote, 'I venture to think that those who care to read the story now will be quite astonished at the scrupulous propriety observed therein on the relations of the sexes ... there is hardly a single caress in the book outside loyal matrimony ...'. As he had so planned the dates in his novel that it was inescapable that the baby was conceived out of wedlock this is equivocation. Hardy's growing criticism of the clergy is evident here and his dislike of hypocrisy and dogmatism will be heard even more strongly in his later work.

In spite of the reviews *Two on a Tower* sold quite well, maybe because of the publicity about its morals, and as with all Hardy's minor novels it is now seen as interesting and important in Hardy's development. As early as 1915 one American critic was saying that it 'deserves far greater praise than it has ever won'. More recently Richard Taylor has seen it as 'a novel of poetic charm, unique conception and humane impulses' and for Frank Pinion it is one of Hardy's 'most readable and remarkable novels'. Lady Constantine is certainly one of his finest pieces of characterisation. Weighed down by the pressures of respectability and Victorian conventionality and afflicted with a villainous brother who regards her as a disposable asset, she meets life's buffets with courage and displays a warmth and altruism in her love for Swithin which endears her to us.

A Laodicean and *Two on a Tower* were the eighth and ninth novels to be published in a period of about twelve years – a remarkable tribute to Hardy's energy and creativity. All except the first two, *Desperate Remedies* and *Under the Greenwood Tree*, were published as serials and put extra pressure on the writer. These latest two novels may not have been among his greatest but they enabled him to try something new and we begin to see developing in them the main themes of the four great novels yet to come. He is not yet a famous writer but he is well-known and mixes among literary figures who matter. He knows that his work is in demand by publishers and this gives him a confidence that we feel very strongly in *Two on a Tower*. His last great novels will not just be of tragic proportions in their stories and characterisation, they will be a serious criticism of life, concerned with man's inhumanity to man – and particularly women – with the destructive nature of so much Victorian hypocrisy and Grundyism, and with the need for compassion and loving-kindness if humankind is to survive. *A Laodicean* and *Two on a Tower* have enabled him to explore the ache of modernism. He has looked at the impact of modern science and technology and, like his Swithin, had looked up at the heavens and seen not God but the sheer horrifying immensity of space. Like his Paula, the result was a laodiceanism, a kind of Keatsian negative capability which enabled him to develop an ambivalence which plays an ever larger part in his writing.

The ambivalence is seen in an essay he wrote during the early months of 1883 for *Longman's Magazine*. Writing to Mrs Oliphant the previous year he told her that he had 'often thought of taking the labouring poor of this my native county seriously' and writing a paper about them. In a letter to John Morley written on 25 June 1883 he mentions the essay which had just appeared and says 'Though a Liberal, I have endeavoured to describe the state of things without bias.' That he had been asked to write such an article is evidence of the impression his novels of rural life had made even if so many of his rustic chorus had been but minor figures in them. 'The Dorsetshire Labourer' opens with an attack on the commonly accepted view of Hodge as a pitiable figure of 'uncouth manner and aspect, stolid understanding, and snail-like movement' living in a cottage where 'Misery and fever' lurk. In fact, Hardy points out, these rural communities have an ability to enjoy life and there is a variety about their lives which undermines the whole concept of a typical Hodge. The Hodges are 'men of many minds, infinite in difference; some happy, many serene, a few depressed; some clever, even to genius, some stupid, some wanton, some austere'. Drudgery in the city is far harder to bear than drudgery in the country and Hardy has contempt for the 'philosophers who look down upon that class [the 'workfolk' as he calls them] from the Olympian heights of society'. But there are sad times, as for example, when the labourer is out of work and attends a hiring-fair, and Hardy paints a moving picture of an old shepherd 'bowed by hard work and years' standing waiting for work. There is a fine description of the migration which takes place on Lady Day as the farm-workers move with all their belongings from one farm to another and Hardy sees this migration, rapidly increasing at that time, as both good and bad. 'Change is also a certain sort of education. Many advantages accrue to the labourers from the varied experience it brings, apart from the discovery of the best market for their abilities. They have become shrewder and sharper men of the world . . .'. These migrants are 'more wide-awake and aware of what is going on'. But, as Hardy knows, all progress is at some kind of cost and 'the result of this increasing nomadic habit of the labourer is naturally a less intimate and kindly relation with the land he tills'. They are not so well-known to their employers, have no stability of tenancy and the education of their children is affected by this mobility. After a glowing tribute to Joseph Arch, who fought so hard for the rights of the agricultural labourer, Hardy concluded with a discussion of agricultural incomes and an expression of alarm at the depopulation which was affecting village life and robbing it of that 'interesting and better-informed class . . . the blacksmith, the carpenter, the shoemaker, the small higgler, the shopkeeper' (*Thomas Hardy's Personal Writings*, pp. 168–89). This was a class from which many of Hardy's own family had come and they had provided Hardy with many of his fictional characters. 'The Dorsetshire Labourer' is a balanced and informed essay and it provides further evidence of the tension in Hardy's life at that time between his love for the past and his realisation that 'change has marked the face of all things' and that much of that change was to be welcomed, even if some of it was to be deplored. He must have been very conscious of the weakening of his own roots because of the peregrinatory nature of his life from 1862 onwards, and those roots were showing themselves to be a vital part of his writing life. It was the memory of them that had drawn the native back to the county of his birth and would soon restore him to the locality in which he had been born and bred. Roots! To Hardy they were vital and the main protagonists of his last four great novels were all victims of deracination.

1883 was a busy year. The Dorset air had reinvigorated Hardy. In addition to 'The Dorsetshire Labourer', he wrote a long short story called 'The Romantic Adventures of a Milkmaid', and another called 'The Three Strangers' which is among his best. He also wrote a twenty-thousand-word story called 'Our Exploits at West Poley' for the Boston *Youth Companion*, his only attempt at writing a boys' story. It had a strange history. For some unknown reason it was not published by the *Youth Companion* in 1884 as planned but first appeared in an American magazine called *The Household* in 1893. It was then forgotten until discovered by Professor Purdy and published in book form by the Oxford University Press in 1952. It is an

excellent story and shows that Hardy could easily have been successful as a writer for the young. Two boys divert the course of a
stream and bring consternation to the villagers (Marcel Pagnol used
a similar plot in his novel *Manon des Sources*). Once again, as in the
sending of the valentine in *Far from the Madding Crowd*, a trivial,
thoughtless action brings devasting results. Writing about his story,
Hardy said 'In constructing the story I have been careful to avoid
making it a mere precept in narrative – a fatal defect, to my thinking,
in tales for the young, or for the old.' So much of the literature
written for children was at that time overtly didactic that Hardy
wisely refrained from preaching. He never forgot that the primary
purpose of literature was to entertain.

In June 1883 he and Emma moved from Wimborne to Dorchester
and moved into lodgings close to the prison in the very centre of
the town. Hardy was then 43 and almost exactly half-way through
his life and nearly ten years of wandering came to an end. Dorchester
was to be his home for the rest of his life. While in Wimborne the
previous year he had made enquiries about building sites in and
near Dorchester. He was now sufficiently comfortable financially to
think of having his own home and by October he had purchased a
plot of land from the Duchy of Cornwall. It was on the eastern out-
skirts of Dorchester in what was then a fairly lonely and exposed
part of the country. Bockhampton and his father and mother were
about two miles to the north and Stinsford church, so full of memories, was about a mile in the same direction. Both could be reached
by a pleasant walk across the water-meadows and the valley of the
river Frome. He was close to his old home but not so close that wife
and mother would be brought together frequently. He designed the
new house himself and called it Max Gate because it was close to
an old toll-gate known as 'Mack's Gate'. By October 1883 he was
able to mark out the spot where the well was to be dug and his
brother, Henry, who was to be the builder, began marking out the
site in November and they moved into their new house in June
1885. Emma may have had some worries about her husband's now
being so close to his powerful mother but she must have been
delighted at last to have a home of her own with a large garden and
several cats. To give them some protection from winds and prying
eyes Hardy personally planted 'some two or three thousand small
trees, mostly Austrian pines' which were later almost entirely to
hide the house from the road. Max Gate is a solidly-built Victorian
house of no great beauty but it makes a good home with a gracious

hall, staircase and drawing and dining rooms, and it will outlive many a house built in the twentieth century. Hardy showed an understandable caution in building it, because 'I was resolved' he said, 'not to ruin myself in building a great house as so many other literary men have done.' As he became wealthier he added extra rooms and a further half-acre of garden. Little did Hardy and his wife realise in 1885 that it was to become one of the most famous of all writers' houses and that it would become a place of pilgrimage for so many other great – and not-so-great – writers anxious to meet one who during the forty-three years of living there would become the Grand Old Man of English literature.

Hardy's next novel, *The Mayor of Casterbridge*, brings him back to Dorchester itself, the very centre of his 'part-real, part-dream' Wessex. The action of *A Laodicean* took place around Dunster, some hundred miles from Dorchester; that of *Two on a Tower* brought him back to within twenty miles, and as he himself returned to live in Dorchester it became – almost inevitably – the location for one of his greatest novels. Ideas for the new novel were clearly in his mind in the early months of 1884 when, with the opening of the new premises of the Dorset County Museum just around the corner from where he was living, he began to read his way through the back-numbers of the local newspaper, *The Dorset County Chronicle*, from about 1826. Here he would have read of skimmington rides, of a wife-selling that had occurred in Somerset, and of the corn trade and the way in which it was affected by uncertain harvests and the Corn Laws. The main action of *The Mayor of Casterbridge* takes place in the late 1840s, the time of Hardy's own childhood, and the memories came flooding back as in this description of Casterbridge. Susan and her daughter are entering the town from the east just as Hardy did every day when a boy on his way to school:

> Its squareness was, indeed, the characteristic which most struck the eye in this antiquated borough. . . . It was compact as a box of dominoes. It had no suburbs – in the ordinary sense. . . . Country and town met at a mathematical line. (*N.W.E.*, p. 46)

With his return to Dorchester Hardy was able to see a good deal more of his family, although it seems that his wife seldom joined him on his visits to the Bockhampton cottage. He was there on his birthday in 1884. 'Alone in the plantation at 9 o'clock. A weird hour: strange faces and figures formed by dying lights. Holm leaves shine like human eyes, and the sky glimpses between the trunks are like white phantoms and cloven tongues. It is so silent and still that a footstep on the dead leaves could be heard a quarter of a mile off' (*Life*, p. 172). Dr Fisher, the family doctor, describes the Hardys about this time in these words: 'The whole family, two sons and two daughters, could tell stories, and did so during the long winter evenings round the big fireplace, criticising one another's efforts very freely.' Possibly some of the stories of the past told then found their way into Hardy's current novel.

Everything seemed to come together to make *The Mayor of Casterbridge* one of Hardy's greatest novels. In the words of Rosemary Sumner in her *Thomas Hardy: Psychological Novelist*, 'we see Hardy exploring varieties of modes of being, making discoveries about ways of feeling and behaving, extending our awareness and our acceptance of human diversity. . . . Hardy had a far wider view of the nature of psychological problems than any single twentieth-century psychologist' (p. 57). It is Hardy's *King Lear*, the study of a man who makes a tragic mistake and has to pay for it. Henchard is a remarkable psychological analysis of a disturbed personality. He is a man of many virtues but also of some uncontrolled vices which finally destroy him. There is a classical concentration on the main character which is suggested in the novel's full title, *The Life and Death of the Mayor of Casterbridge, A Story of a Man of Character*. Michael Henchard is bad-tempered, impulsive, moody, tyrannical and cruel, and yet Hardy wins our sympathy for him because of his terrifying honesty about his own weaknesses, his warmth and kindness, and his poignant loneliness. 'For the sufferings of that night, engendered by his bitter disappointment, he might well have been pitied.' Of Hardy's compassion for his suffering character there can be no doubt and the closing chapters are emotionally very powerful as Henchard, once again down and out, returns to the place where, twenty years before, all his troubles began. Designed as it was for initial serial publication Hardy thought he might have damaged it by having too many 'events' but if these 'events' are such that they hold the reader's attention throughout they become a strength rather than a weakness. Great writers like Shakespeare and Hardy make a virtue out of necessity, and just as the lack of scenery in the Elizabethan theatre resulted in some of Shakespeare's finest descriptive verse so the need to write in instalments presented little difficulty to a born storyteller like Hardy. His story is superb in the cleverness of its plot and the successful use of surprise, suspense and irony. This can be seen in the classical proportion and structuring of *The Mayor of Casterbridge*. It begins with the *hamartia* or tragic error which is the result of Henchard's moral weakness. Henchard is out of work and feels burdened by his wife and child whom he treats like chattels and sells to an unknown stranger for five guineas. Eighteen years pass and in Chapter 3 we find him a successful businessman and Mayor of Casterbridge, at the top of the wheel of fortune. But *nemesis* comes with the return of his wife and the arrival of Farfrae, the outsider who plays such a large part in many of Hardy's novels. He represents the forces of modernism which will inevitably destroy the old world of Henchard. He brings efficient book-keeping and the new seed-drill and the novel is enriched by these symbolic means. The discovery of the trick played on him by his wife is the *anagnorisis* and it marks a stage in Henchard's fall. As he, a representative of a dying age, falls, Farfrae, a representative of a new materialistic and technological age, rises, taking from him his business, his home, his 'daughter' and his mayoralty, and we see Henchard fall from the top of the wheel of fortune to the bottom where he meets his lonely end on the heath with only Abel Whittle (Lear's fool – 'wittol' was a middle-English word for a fool) to help him. *The Return of the Native* was meant by Hardy to be a great tragic novel in the classical tradition: *The Mayor of Casterbridge* is. And it is remarkable that the tragic hero is not a king but a humble country-man, a hay-trusser.

Far from the Madding Crowd, *The Return of the Native* and *The Mayor of Casterbridge* are the three great successes out of the ten novels he had published so far, and they have in common their closeness to Hardy's own life. Weatherbury is the Puddletown he knew so well because it was only two or three miles from Bockhampton and many of his relatives lived there. Egdon Heath is the heath behind the cottage where he played as a boy, and Casterbridge is the Dorchester to and from which he walked almost every day during his years as a schoolboy and architectural apprentice. He changes its name to Casterbridge because, of course, there is a fictitious element in his descriptions, but essentially Dorchester and Casterbridge are the same and this gives the novel a satisfying authenticity. What we have is richly historical because it is not only the history of the Dorchester of Hardy's childhood, but we are constantly reminded of the age of Dorchester, of its connections with a remote past:

> The Ring at Casterbridge was merely the local name of one of the
> finest Roman Amphitheatres . . . remaining in Britain. Casterbridge
> announced old Rome in every street, alley, and precinct. It looked
> Roman, bespoke the art of Rome, concealed dead men of Rome.
> It was impossible to dig more than a foot or two deep about the
> town fields and gardens without coming upon some tall soldier
> or other of the Empire, who had lain there in his silent unobtrusive
> rest for a space of fifteen hundred years. (*N.W.E.*, p. 79)

In digging the well at Max Gate (about the time that Hardy began
to write *The Mayor of Casterbridge*), the workmen came upon Romano-
British urns and skeletons. He wrote a paper about these and other
remains found on the site and read it at a meeting of the Dorset
Natural History and Antiquarian Field Club in May 1884.

Some of Hardy's dominant motifs appear yet again in *The Mayor*:
the relationship of character and fate, remorse and regret for an
irretrievable unchangeable past, and the way in which 'our deeds
carry their terrible consequences', to use George Eliot's words. But
now these concerns are treated in an altogether more sophisticated,
intense, coherent and serious way. This may be partly because for
the first time Hardy was under no pressure from his publishers
while writing it. Much of it was written in 1884 and it was finished
by April 1885 but not published as a serial until January 1886 and
as a book until May of that year. A good many speculations have
been made about the reasons for its profoundly tragic note. Among
them are the staleness of his marriage and his increasing awareness of Emma's inadequacies, his loss of faith, his realisation of the
'non-rationality of the universe' and that he 'was living in a world
where nothing bears out in practice what it promises incipiently'
and the tension resulting from the gap between his two lives, that
of the Bockhampton boy with his working-class relations and that
of the London literary personality with his middle-class and aristocratic friends. No doubt they all contributed something, but there
must surely have been another reason – that of just growing older
and becoming ever more painfully aware of the tears of things, of
the vanity of human wishes.

Dickens in 1857 was about the same age as Hardy when he published *The Mayor* and he had just published *Little Dorrit*. He was
immensely wealthy, famous and successful, yet *Little Dorrit* is one
of his most bitter and sombre criticisms of Victorian life at that time
and one of the major themes is that our expectations are mostly

illusions which will never be fulfilled. The very first poem in Hardy's first book of verse, published in 1898, is called 'The Temporary the All' and it says precisely that. Of Elizabeth-Jane in *The Mayor*, a character Robert Gittings thinks has something of Hardy's sister Mary in her, Hardy says 'she had still that field-mouse fear of the coulter of destiny despite fair promise, which is common among the thoughtful who have suffered early from poverty and oppression' (*N.W.E.*, p. 93). Hardy speaks there for himself – and for Dickens. Published in book form on 10 May 1886, *The Mayor* had mixed reviews and some of the first edition had to be remaindered, no doubt justifying to the publishers their comment 'that the lack of gentry among the characters made it uninteresting'. When Hardy revised it for the Collected Edition of his novels in 1895 he made several changes. Some of these were topographical and designed to emphasise the Wessex setting, others were changes in Farfrae's dialect. The relationship between Lucetta and Henchard becomes a sexual liaison with no bigamous marriage. One change may reflect on Hardy's own marital relationship. In 1885, the description in Chapter 1 of Henchard and Susan as husband and wife goes on to say that

No other than such relationship would have accounted for the atmosphere of domesticity which the trio carried along with them.

By 1895 'domesticity' had been replaced by 'stale familiarity' an interesting hardening of his attitude towards marriage generally, and surely to his own relationship with Emma.

1884 and 1885 were busy years, for in addition to his writing *The Mayor* and two or three more short stories, he visited the Channel Isles in August 1884 with his brother Henry, was appointed to the bench of magistrates in Dorchester, was in London in December for a banquet at the Mansion House, spent April to June 1885 in London for the Season, and began work in November on his next novel. More and more Society ladies were 'taking him up' and he clearly enjoyed the company of lively, intelligent and frequently beautiful upper-class women. In March 1885 he made the first of a number of visits to the noble Portsmouth family who lived in Devon. Emma did not accompany him and, perhaps somewhat insensitively, he wrote to her about Lord Portsmouth's brougham waiting for him at the station, the very handsome house, the attentive young ladies (there were several attractive daughters) and the altogether 'delightful household'. Lord Portsmouth showed him 'a bridge over which bastards were thrown and drowned, even down to quite recent times' (*Life*, p. 177). Lady Portsmouth was the sister of the Earl of Carnarvon and in mid-May Hardy makes a note that he was at a party at Lady Carnarvon's for the second time that Season. It is easy to mock Hardy for this 'weakness' but which of us would have resisted such invitations? It was very much a love–hate affair. At Max Gate when he was not in London there began the arrival of the first of the multitude of visitors who were to call there – Robert Louis Stevenson and his wife. In a letter to a friend Fanny Stevenson wrote that Hardy was 'small, *very* pale, and scholarly looking, and at first sight most painfully shy' and that Emma was '*very* plain, quite underbred, and most tedious . . .'. Hardy and Emma might have wished for better luck with their first guests! Another visitor who with her brother Gordon was to spend many months at Max Gate during the next ten years was Lilian Gifford, Emma's niece. The kindness of the Hardys towards these young children should not be forgotten. Hardy may have been childless but he had Lilian and Gordon living with him for long periods and seems to have helped with the expense of their education, presumably 'to please his wife'.

In London during the autumn of 1884 he agreed with Macmillan to write a story to be published in twelve instalments in *Macmillan's Magazine* in 1886. Macmillan, who had rejected *The Poor Man and the Lady* nearly twenty years before, were now anxious to have Hardy writing for them. In *The House of Macmillan* Charles Morgan describes Hardy as a man who

> wrote his own business letters and had a keen eye for a percentage as he had for all else, but there is character – a mingling of firmness and gentleness and dignity – even in his negotiation of a contract, which proves him once more to have been what all men found him to be in other courses of life: the most lovable and least pretentious of great artists. (p. 152)

By November 1885, with *The Mayor* out of the way, Hardy was working away at *The Woodlanders* from 'half-past ten a.m. to twelve p.m. to get my mind made up on the details' (*Life*, p. 182). He talks at that time about being 'in a fit of depression' and on 31 December is sadder than he has been on many previous New Year's Eves. In 1886, reading philosophy in the British Museum Library, he came to the conclusion that 'These venerable philosophers seem to start wrong; they cannot get away from a prepossession that the world must somehow have been made to be a comfortable place for man' (*Life*, p. 185). In London in June and July they were 'dining and lunching out almost every day' and although Hardy goes on to tell us that 'he did not take much account of these functions', he enjoyed them enough to carry on this way of life for many years, keeping a careful note of all the distinguished people he met. In 1886 this included the Humphrey Wards, Walter Pater, Lord Lytton, J. A. Froude, J. R. Lowell, Dr Oliver Wendell Holmes, Henry James ('who has a ponderously warm manner of saying nothing in infinite sentences'), George Meredith, Whistler, Bret Harte (who described Hardy as 'a singularly unpretending-looking man, and indeed resembling anything but an author in manner and speech'), Sidney Colvin, R. L. Stevenson, Leslie Stephen, George Gissing (who asked him for advice about novel-writing), Browning and Oscar Wilde. No matter what he says, Hardy must have found much to interest him listening, perhaps rather than talking, to these people and even if they were not people about whom he wished to write, they were people who would read and talk about his books, and they included publishers like the Macmillans whom it was useful to know. One hostess with whom they frequently dined was Mrs Jeune and Emma was very proud of the fact that Mrs Jeune was married to the brother-in-law of her uncle. Her pride became even greater when in 1891 she became Lady Jeune. In her book *Memories of Fifty Years* (1909) Lady St Helier, as she became in 1905 when her husband was created Baron St Helier, described how Hardy used to stay at her house during some of his visits to London and they sat around the fire 'listening to the stories, theories, and ideals out of which all his novels had developed. I think he is the most modest person I ever came across, and he hated the publicity which necessarily surrounded him' (p. 240). He went regularly to concerts at the Imperial Institute where they were able to hear some of the famous bands of Europe, and on one occasion they listened to Wagner: 'It was', said Hardy, '*weather* and ghost-music – whistling of wind and storm . . .'. Discussing this some time later with the famous Norwegian composer, Grieg, the latter said, 'I would rather have the wind and rain myself' (*Life*, p. 188). Hardy's interest in folk and religious music is well-known but here is further evidence of his wide-ranging interest in classical music.

To return to his parents' home at Bockhampton – and now that he was living so close he tried to visit them once a week – was to be aware yet again of the dichotomy which existed between the two sides of his life, between the past and the present, the rural and the urban, the social background of the characters in his novels and that of the middle- and upper-class readers who bought them. *The Woodlanders* again drew deeply upon personal knowledge and family history. His father and mother had married in Melbury Osmund church and his mother's mother, Betsy Swetman, had experienced poverty there while bringing up her children. It was an area of coppice and woodland north-west of Dorchester, and Hardy's mother would often have talked to him about it. In 1912 Hardy wrote 'On taking up *The Woodlanders* and reading it after many years I think I like it, *as a story*, the best of all. Perhaps that is owing to the locality and scenery of the action, a part I am very fond of' (*C.L.*, 4, p. 212). In the very early editions of his story it was clear that Hintock House was based on Melbury House, the home of the noble Ilchester family, and Little Hintock was Melbury Osmund. However, about this time he was becoming acquainted with the Ilchesters and it must have occurred to him that they might be offended to think of the adulterous Mrs Charmond as the owner of their property. On further thought he must have realised, too, that to draw the attention of the world to the poverty of his mother's life in Melbury Osmund and her precipitate marriage to his father six months before his birth was the kind of exposure he was anxious to avoid. Thus, in later editions there is a discreet changing of names which would imply that the action of the novel took place several miles to the east, and in response to enquiries Hardy had his little joke, saying that he himself did not know precisely where Little Hintock was and that he had 'once spent several hours on a bicycle with a friend in a serious attempt to discover the real spot; but the search ended in failure'. Recent research by Ruth Skilling makes it probable that if Hintock House was originally Melbury House, then Little Hintock was Stockwood (*Thomas Hardy Journal*, Feb. 1993). There may be something of Hardy's sister, Mary, in the quiet and self-sacrificing Marty, and Hardy is again remembering helping his father with the cider-making when he describes Giles Winterborne:

> He looked and smelt like Autumn's very brother, his face being sunburnt to wheat-colour, his eyes blue as cornflowers, his sleeves and leggings dyed with fruit-stains, his hands clammy with the sweet juice of apples, his hat sprinkled with pips, and everywhere about him that atmosphere of cider which at its first return each

season has such an indescribable fascination for those who have been born and bred among the orchards. (*N.W.E.*, p. 191)

Hardy's novels are all different but have much in common. In *Far from the Madding Crowd* he makes use of his knowledge of sheep-farming, in *The Return of the Native* of furze-cutting, in *The Mayor of Casterbridge* of the corn business, and now in *The Woodlanders* of planting and felling trees, stripping the bark and making spars and cider. In *Tess of the d'Urbervilles* he will make his agricultural background that of the dairy-farm in summer and root-crop farming in winter. The locations of each novel, too, although within twenty-five miles of each other are all different. With the Bockhampton cottage as the centre, *Far from the Madding Crowd* mostly takes place about four miles to the east, *The Return* on the heath immediately behind, *The Mayor* in Dorchester two miles to the west, *The Wood-landers* near Melbury Osmund, some twelve miles to the north-west, and *Tess* in the Valley of the Great Dairies, two or three miles to the south-east and in the Blackmoor Vale, an 'engirdled and secluded region' about fifteen miles to the north. It is as if Hardy consciously set out to vary the region and the local occupation of each of these novels so that eventually they become a kind of Wessex epic of the nineteenth century because in time, too, they cover almost every decade of that century. *Jude the Obscure* is the odd one out, but more about that rootless novel later. What the major novels have in common is a compassionate, thoughtful and exploratory approach to mankind's problems in a world dominated by Nature which cares for little other than the survival of the species.

The Woodlanders lacks the tragic, almost epic, qualities which are present in *The Mayor*. We have moved from the town to the country, to a small village almost lost among the woodlands where so much of the action takes place. Just as the dominating town has gone, so has the dominating character. Henchard stands out a larger-than-life figure against a universal sky; the characters of *The Wood-landers*, although very human, seem at times almost lost against their background of trees. Hardy loves trees, Max Gate was surrounded by them, he wrote poems about them, and they are central to this novel. They provide passages of powerful description, mark out the seasons of the year, and play a significant part in the story. They even provide the story with much of its colour and imagery. Marty's hair is 'a rare and beautiful approximation to chestnut' and Grace's heart 'rose from its late sadness like a released bough'.

Hardy's remarkable descriptive powers have been there since the beginning but with *The Mayor* and *The Woodlanders* they come to maturity. In 1886 he had seen an exhibition of Impressionist pictures in London and had remarked that their style was 'even more suggestive in the direction of literature than in that of art', and Marty in Chapter 2, as has already been pointed out, is described as being an 'impression-picture of extremest type'.

A major reason for the novel's failure to acquire tragic status is its lack of a truly tragic figure with whom the reader can identify. Melbury, Fitzpiers, Giles and Marty are all drawn with great skill, but it is Grace who is the central character in so far as there is one, and her situation is full of pathos but no more. Whereas the major concern in *The Mayor* had been Henchard's character, in *The Woodlanders* Hardy uses his story as a means of exploring moral, social and educational problems which have in the 1880s become a major part of his thought. With his own marriage settling down into 'stale familiarity' his thoughts were on the reasons why the wrong man appropriated the woman, the wrong woman the man. Once again we have the outsider, Dr Fitzpiers, who comes into the rural community with his new ideas and his easy morals, and plays havoc. Not only does he cause distress to Grammer Oliver by wanting to buy her head after death for anatomical purposes, and accelerate the death of John South by his pseudo-psychological theories, but he is even more successful with the women than Sergeant Troy and he shows that sexual desires have no class barriers by having a sexual relationship with the working-class Suke Damson, the middle-class Grace, and the upper-class Mrs Charmond. Needless to say, in the serial version of the novel Hardy was forced by his editor to hide this fact, and it robs him of a moment of sad humour when Grace takes her two rivals to see the injured Fitzpiers with the words 'you have a perfect right to go into his bedroom. . . . Wives all, let's enter together.'

Hardy is again writing about class-distinctions and in *The Woodlanders* this becomes a serious theme. At its most ugly it is found in Fitzpiers' remark to Grace, 'but I do honestly confess to you that I feel as if I belonged to a different species from the people who are working in that yard'. It was an issue Hardy could never forget. Grace, who – to some extent like Hardy – has been given a good education, finds herself, like Hardy, torn between two worlds. She has lost her roots in the woodlands where she grew up and has not put down any new roots among the middle-class girls with whom she was educated. Her dilemma is seen at its most destructive in the conflicting appeals in her life between Giles, the primitive labourer among the trees and symbol of the traditional way of life so rapidly passing away, and the educated, sophisticated middle-class Fitzpiers, with his new ideas and his superficial appreciation of those whose lives he has disturbed. Once again we find ourselves asking the question Clym asked his mother in *The Return*, 'Mother, what is doing well?' But Hardy knows that there is no easy answer and in *The Woodlanders* much of the novel's quality comes from the constantly reiterated ambivalences. With the exception of *A Pair of Blue Eyes* the early novels end with marriages which at least offer hope of some happiness, and there is no attempt to examine what happens to those marriages. In the last four major novels – *The Mayor*, *The Woodlanders*, *Tess* and *Jude* – the marriage has taken place or takes place sufficiently early for the marriage itself to become the subject, another reflection of Hardy's own marital situation. Grace finds herself in *The Woodlanders* with a promiscuous husband who has married for his material gain and looks down on her family, who are helping to support him. When Grace realises the truth about her husband she ponders over the marriage vow and 'That particular sentence, beginning, "Whom God hath joined together" was a staggerer. . . . She wondered whether God did really join them together.' Fitzpiers' double adultery allows Hardy to introduce the subject of divorce and refer to an Act of 1857 which meant that divorces could be granted without the need for expensive Acts of Parliament. But the law was still heavily weighted against women, because they could be divorced for adultery while their husbands could not. Hardy's sense of fairness was revolted, and he draws attention to this injustice by letting his heroine find herself with a womanising husband and with no possibility of getting free of him. *The Woodlanders* is rich in themes, ideas, moods and tones, and one is conscious throughout of a wise man brooding over the problems of a suffering world. It has been described as Hardy's loveliest, if not his strongest, book and it contains passages of great beauty such as the often-quoted planting of the young pines by Giles and Marty, and the novel's closing lines spoken by Marty over the grave of Giles.

'Now, my own, own love,' she whispered, 'you are mine, and only mine; for she has forgot 'ee at last, although for her you died! But I – whenever I get up I'll think of 'ee, and whenever I

lie down I'll think of 'ee again. Whenever I plant the young larches
I'll think that none can plant as you planted; and whenever I split
a gad, and whenever I turn the cider wring, I'll say none could
do it like you. If ever I forget your name let me forget home and
heaven! . . . But no, no, my love, I never can forget 'ee; for you was
a good man, and did good things!' (*N.W.E.*, p. 323)

Hardy, like Dickens, knew how to wring the heart, and Marty's
elegy is his elegy for a rural way of life that is passing away.

The Woodlanders was the first of the four novels Hardy was to
write at Max Gate. It was not until February 1887, well over a year
since he had begun writing it, that he was able to write in his diary,
'8.20 p.m. Finished *The Woodlanders*. Thought I should feel glad, but
I do not particularly, – though relieved.' As serialisation had begun
the previous May and had reached Chapter 40 by February, his
relief must have been great indeed. So efficient were the publishers
that it appeared in volume form in March, less than six weeks after
the last lines were written. Most of the reviewers were as pleased
with the new novel as they had been with *The Mayor*. For *The
Athenaeum*, 'The Novel is distinctly not one for the "young person" of whom we have lately heard, but should be read by all who
can tell masterly work in fiction . . .'. *The Saturday Review* talked of
'the richness and humanity of the book', and *The Academy* described
it as 'the best and most powerful work Hardy has produced since *Far
from the Madding Crowd*', while *The Spectator* found it 'a very powerful book, and as disagreeable as it is powerful', and 'written with
an indifference to the moral effect it conveys'. Hardy's confidence
would have been strengthened by the overall tone of the reviews
but there were hints in the reviews such as that of *The Spectator* that,
as he changed the emphasis on his studies of mismatings from the
distress caused by the lovers' own failure to that caused to them by
the unsympathetic, unfair and cruel social and moral codes of the
time, the forces of Grundyism would become ever more strident
and vocal. There were storms ahead.

Hardy's practice of going to London each spring and summer for
the Season undoubtedly interfered with his writing and on more
than one occasion he complains that he cannot work while there.
A common practice was for him to go to London and stay at the
Savile Club or with friends while looking for lodgings, and then,
having found them, Emma was summoned to join him. They were
in London together for several months in both 1886 and 1887. On

14 March 1887 they left for a holiday in Italy, visiting Genoa and Pisa, Florence, Rome, Siena and Venice, and finally Milan, and wherever he went, Hardy remembered the literary associations – Shelley watching the sunset from one of the Arno bridges, and Browning and *The Ring and the Book* in Rome, where he also visited Shelley's grave and sent some violets from Keats's grave to Edmund Gosse. One of Hardy's favourite Browning poems, 'The Statue and the Bust', is set in Florence where they also visited Mrs Browning's grave. They went on to Venice and saw places associated with Shelley and Byron. Napoleon was not forgotten in Milan, and Hardy visited the bridge at Lodi, scene of an early victory, about which he was later to write a poem. He thought it possible that it was on this visit that he conceived the Milan Cathedral scene in *The Dynasts*. Several of the 'Poems of Pilgrimage' which were published in 1901 were inspired by this holiday, and *The Life* tells us much about Hardy's reaction to the many famous places they visited. It also has some interesting personal recollections. Hardy described an 'unpleasant occurrence' in Rome: it looked as if some men were about to rob him when 'Mrs Hardy . . . cried out to her husband to beware, and with her usual courage rushed across at the back of the men, who disappeared as if by magic' (*Life*, p. 196). It is not to Hardy's second wife's credit that in editing *The Life* after his death she deleted this incident.

The Season that year, 1887, was a particularly distinguished one because it was Queen Victoria's Golden Jubilee, and on return from their holiday they almost immediately rented lodgings in London and took part in numerous luncheons and dinners and other social events. He kept notes of these occasions not only because it obviously appealed to him that he had been entertained by such aristocratic hostesses as Lady Stanley and Lady Carnarvon, but just in case, he claimed, he might one day have to make these London experiences the matter of a story. And he clearly enjoyed the company of these young and attractive 'noble dames', writing in his notes such comments as that Lady Catherine Milnes-Gaskell was the prettiest of all Lady Portsmouth's daughters and had 'Round luminous enquiring eyes'. He was a man who used to notice such things! But his notes were not just about such pleasant matters. On 14 July he was writing 'It is the on-going – i.e. the "becoming" – of the world that produces its sadness. If the world stood still at a felicitous moment there would be no sadness in it' (*Life*, p. 210).

He returned to Max Gate at the end of July and got down to the

serious business of writing. Back in Wessex and in contact again
with his father and mother, his mind began turning towards his
next novel but, in the meantime, there was a growing number of
requests for short stories. On 3 September he records his mother
telling him of a woman who refused to be called by her married
name, and on 2 October he makes a note of a visit to Rushy Pond,
a childhood haunt of his, just behind the Bockhampton cottage.
'Looked at the thorn bushes by Rushy Pond. . . . In their wrath with
the gales their forms resemble men's in like mood.' Under the same
date in *The Life*, we read:

> A variant of the superstitions attached to pigeon's hearts is that,
> when the counteracting process is going on, the person who has
> bewitched the other *enters*. In the case of a woman in a village
> near here who was working the spell at midnight a neighbour
> knocked at the door and said: 'Do ye come and see my little
> maid. She is so ill that I don't like to bide with her alone!' (p. 211)

With such thoughts in mind he began writing 'The Withered Arm',
one of his best short stories, which has superstition as an important
part of its plot. It is a tragic story of love and hate which takes place
in the valley of the Frome, known to Hardy since his childhood,
and ends with a hanging in the very gaol where as a boy he had
himself witnessed a public execution. No short story written by
Hardy is more full of his own memories of the past, and of locations
he knew intimately. The illegitimate boy who is hanged is shown
by Hardy to be the product of an ill-fated relationship, ignored by
his father and a victim of his mother's lack of affection. He was
hanged for being 'present by chance' when a hay-rick was set on
fire, and here Hardy is yet again remembering something related to
him by his parents. He told his friend, Newman Flower, probably
about 1920,

> 'I have seen some awful things, but what impressed me more
> than all else is something my father once told me. My father saw
> four men hung for *being with* some others who had set fire to a
> rick. Among them was a stripling of a boy of eighteen. Skinny,
> half-starved. So frail, so underfed, that they had to put weights
> on his feet to break his neck. He had not fired the rick. But with
> a youth's excitement he had rushed to the scene to see the blaze
> . . . Nothing my father ever said to me so drove the tragedy of

Life so deeply into my mind. (*Just As It Happened* by Newman Flower, p. 85)

What is remarkable about 'The Withered Arm' is the way in which Hardy has built a story based on superstitions which were rife in his childhood but which we would be sceptical about today, and yet succeeds in making us suspend our disbelief because of the subtlety and interest of the characterisation and what Kristin Brady in her *The Short Stories of Thomas Hardy* calls the 'insistently realistic details' (p. 24).

Hardy was by now a highly professional writer and never one to miss an opportunity of advancing his own work. With a number of successful short stories to his credit, he submitted a proposal to Macmillan for what was to be the first of four books of his short stories. To further register his claim to be the *Wessex* writer, he proposed the title *Wessex Tales*, and when it was published in May 1888 it consisted of five short stories: 'The Three Strangers', 'The Withered Arm', 'Fellow-Townsmen', 'Interlopers at the Knap' and 'The Distracted Preacher'. In later editions he added 'A Tradition of Eighteen Hundred and Four' and 'The Melancholy Hussar of the German Legion'. The four best of these – 'The Three Strangers', 'The Withered Arm', 'The Distracted Preacher' and 'The Melancholy Hussar' – are all firmly rooted in the Dorset Hardy knew so well and are still frequently included in anthologies. 'The Distracted Preacher' is a humorous tale about smuggling in the early nineteenth century, an 'occupation' with which Hardy's ancestors were supposed to have been connected, while 'The Melancholy Hussar' is a tragic tale of the falling in love and then execution for desertion of one of the German soldiers, stationed on the downs near Weymouth, who made up so large a part of the English army at the beginning of the nineteenth century.

In March 1888 he was working in the British Museum Reading Room, one of his favourite places in London, where, he tells us in a note, 'In the great circle of the library Time is looking into Space.' A month later he is thinking of a short story of a young man – 'who could not go to Oxford' – His struggles and ultimate failure. Suicide', something he recognised as 'probably the germ of *Jude the Obscure*'. In May there was another trip to the Continent, this time to Paris, and then it was back to London for thinking and research in the British Museum Library, for meeting old and new friends so different from those in Dorset, and watching and noting, as in the comment of 14 July, 'at Walter Pater's. Met Miss____, an Amazon; more, an Atalanta; most, a Faustine. Smokes: Handsome girl: cruel small mouth: she's of the class of interesting woman one would be afraid to marry' (*Life*, p. 221).

Further conversations with his father took place on his return to Dorchester in July and he began to focus with ever greater intensity on the next novel. Several ideas to be used in *Tess* such as the blood coming through the ceiling and the collision which kills the family horse, result from his reading of newspapers and are based on actual incidents. *The Dorset Chronicle*, the local paper regularly read by Hardy, contained on 4 November 1886 a report headed 'A Horse Killed', which describes how a frightened horse went through a plate-glass window in the centre of Dorchester, 'the broken glass inflicting a frightful gash above the shoulders, the blood from the wound pouring out in torrents, and deluging the shop. . . . The services of a butcher were obtained and the throat of the poor beast was cut.' About a year earlier, on 3 June 1885, Hardy had been with the Dorset Natural History and Antiquarian Field Club to visit Bindon Abbey and the Manor House at Wool where he had heard a paper read about the Turberville family, many of whom had been buried at Bere Regis, only a mile or two away. Now in September 1888 he visited 'The Valley of the Great Dairies' and, later in the day, he travelled by train to Evershot and walked on to Bubb Down with its lovely views over the Blackmoor Vale, 'The Valley of the Little Dairies'. The locations for his next novel were beginning to fall into place. At Evershot, which was to become the 'Evershead' of *Tess*, he was not far from Melbury Osmund, where some of his ancestors had lived and he noted 'The decline and fall of the Hardys much in evidence hereabout'. In a letter to Norman McColl dated 9 February 1892, Hardy describes how the opening incident of *Tess* was suggested to him.

I was standing at the street corner of a little town in this county when a tipsy man staggered past me singing 'I've – got a – great family vault – over at –' . . . I inquired of some bystanders, and learnt that all he had sung was quite true – and that he represented one of the oldest of our Norman families. (*C.L.*, 1, p. 258)

But these were just the culminating events in a whole series of ideas and influences which were now coming to fruition. This road towards *Tess* can be traced in the books he had written. In *A Pair of Blue Eyes* Knight abandons the woman he claims to love because he discovers that she has been kissed by a previous admirer. Angel Clare may have slightly more reason for rejecting Tess but here we have another man showing priggish insensitivity to a woman. Fanny Robin in *Far from the Madding Crowd* is seduced and ill-treated by Sergeant Troy, and Tess suffers a similar fate at the hands of Angel Clare. With almost every novel after *Far from the Madding Crowd*, Hardy's sympathy with women is seen growing, with Ethelberta, Eustacia, Lady Constantine, Elizabeth-Jane and finally Grace in *The Woodlanders*. But Grace is not conceived as a great tragic heroine and Tess is, and Tess owes something to poor Martha Browne whom Hardy had seen hanged when he was at a most impressionable age. It is significant that in *The Life* he has included the following passage with an item from *The Times* on 10 September 1888:

> Destitution sometimes reaches the point of grandeur in its pathetic grimness: e.g. as shown in the statement of the lodging-house keeper in the Whitechapel murder: –
> He had seen her in the lodging-house as late as half-past one or two that morning. He knew her as an unfortunate, and that she generally frequented Stratford for a living. He asked her for her lodging-money, when she said, 'I have not got it. I am weak and ill, and have been in the infirmary.' He told her that she knew the rules, whereupon she went out to get some money.' (*Times* report)
> 'O richest City in the world! "She knew the rules".' (p. 223)

Other passages in *The Life* about this time also have a bearing on *Tess*. On 5 May 1889 he notes that 'That which, socially, is a great tragedy, may be in Nature no alarming circumstance' (*Life*, p. 228), and meeting Mrs Hamo Thornycroft, wife of the sculptor, in July, he recalled that 'Of the people I have met this summer, the lady whose mouth recalls more fully than any other beauty's the Elizabethan's metaphor "Her lips are roses full of snow" . . . is Mrs H.T___' (*Life*, p. 230). He was to use those very words in describing Tess. Meeting the lady again in March 1890 he talks about the 'great eyes' of the 'most beautiful woman present' but adds, 'But these women! If put into rough wrappers in a turnip-field, where would their beauty be?' (*Life*, p. 235)

The victimisation of a woman by a heartless Victorian code of morality and by a religion ruled by dogma rather than by loving-kindness is to be the driving force behind his new novel. He must have realised, or course, the dangers that were likely to confront him in handling with candour the kind of sexual relationship he was contemplating but, then, he had been fighting a running battle with Mrs Grundy throughout his career as a novelist, and he would carry on the fight by continually probing to see how far he could go. If, as he said, his art 'was to intensify the expression of things', then there would obviously be risks in writing candidly about sexual relationships. In January 1890 his essay 'Candour in English Fiction' was published in *The New Review* and his irritation with the censorship which forces the writer to 'belie his literary conscience, do despite to his best imaginative instincts by arranging a *dénouement* which he knows to be indescribably unreal and meretricious, but dear to the Grundyist . . .' reveals how strongly he felt about this. And well he might, for he was in serious trouble with *Tess*.

As we have seen, events and ideas for a new novel had been taking over Hardy and work on it may have begun as early as the autumn of 1888. He had received a commission from Tillotson's, a newspaper syndicate in Bolton, for a serial to begin at the end of 1889 with a title 'Too Late Beloved!' By August he was able to send the publishers 'a list of some scenes from the story' and on 9 September there followed the MS for about the first half of the story. Once again there were difficulties. Tillotson's, a firm run by good Christians, were aghast at what seemed to them far too explicit a book (Hardy's first title was 'The Body and Soul of Sue') and when Hardy refused to make the changes they wanted, it was amicably agreed that the contract should be cancelled. The unfinished novel was then offered to *Murray's Magazine* in October but refused because of its 'improper explicitness', and then to *Macmillan's Magazine* who also turned it down. Hardy describes what happened next:

> Hardy would now have much preferred to finish the story and bring it out in volume form only, but there were reasons why he could not afford to do this; and he adopted a plan till then, it is believed, unprecedented in the annals of fiction. This was not to offer the novel intact to the third editor on his list . . . but to send it up with some chapters or parts of chapters cut out, and instead of destroying these to publish them, or much of them, elsewhere, if practicable, as episodic adventures of anonymous personages . . . ; till they could be put back in their places at the printing of

the whole in volume form. In addition several passages were modified. Hardy had never the slightest respect for his own writing, particularly in prose, and he carried out this unceremonious concession to conventionality without compunction and with cynical amusement, knowing the novel was moral enough and to spare. (*Life*, p. 232)

Any comment of this kind made by Hardy about his writing needs to be taken with a grain or two of salt. If he only wanted 'to be considered a good hand at a serial', as he told Leslie Stephen in 1874 and had no respect for his own writing, as he says here, why did he write so concernedly and intelligently about the art of novel-writing and why did he spend so much time revising his books whenever the opportunity offered itself? And how do we reconcile this with the second Mrs Hardy's reference to 'Hardy's inability to rest content with anything that he wrote until he had brought the expression as near to his thought as language would allow'? (*Life*, p. 489) At times Hardy puts on a mask. He knows that the real reason he is publishing his books first as serials in magazines is that the financial rewards of so doing are substantial, and life has taught him to be shrewd about money matters. But his irritation at having to falsify and bowdlerise his story is so deeply felt that he pretends to indifference rather than let the general public be aware of his feelings.

The 'mutilated' version of *Tess*, as he called it, was accepted by *The Graphic* magazine which had done well out of *The Mayor of Casterbridge*, and work on completing the novel in its two versions went on throughout 1890 with the intention of its being published in *The Graphic* in twenty-four instalments during the second half of 1891. This was a remarkably productive period for Hardy and at the same time as he was writing *Tess* he was writing a group of short stories for the Christmas number of *The Graphic*, which with the addition of a further four stories was eventually published in book form as *A Group of Noble Dames* in May 1891 by Osgood McIlvaine – his main publisher for the next ten years. Like *Wessex Tales*, it is a collection of stories drawn from Wessex history, but a more distant history. He used as a main source for his stories Hutchins's *History and Antiquities of the County of Dorset*, and as his main characters are aristocratic ladies of the seventeenth and eighteenth centuries it is not surprising that the stories lack the rich texture of *Wessex Tales* which were about ordinary people of the recent past. To provide the stories with a framework he imagines them being told by individual members of the Wessex Field and Antiquarian Club of which he was himself a member. The stories are acted out in a world of arranged marriages in which the wishes of the woman are seldom paramount, of passionate love transcending class distinctions, of hatred, jealousy and even sadistic cruelty. Hardy's sympathies are with the oppressed, as always, and the reader is aware throughout of his interest in the women who were so often the innocent victims. It was no coincidence that he was working on *Tess* at the same time.

But all was not smooth sailing with this new collection of short stories as Hardy's note of 23 June 1890 makes clear:

> Called on Arthur Locker [editor] at The Graphic Office in answer to his letter. He says he does not object to the stories . . . but the Directors do. Here's a pretty job! Must smooth down those Directors somehow I suppose. (*Life*, p. 237)

This note, written at the time about his troubles with *Noble Dames*, rings far truer than his comment on his troubles with *Tess*, written much later, with its attempt to deny that he had any respect for his own work. Once again he settled down to produce two versions of *Noble Dames*, one for *The Graphic*, and one for book publication.

All this work did not prevent his making the annual visit to London for the Season in 1890 and he records meeting Kipling probably for the first time, dining at the Savile Club with someone whose sense of art had caused him to lose all sense of 'art's subsidiary relation to existence', going the round of the music-halls, seeing Bizet's *Carmen*, attending the ballet at the Alhambra, meeting Stanley the explorer, visiting the police courts ('being still compelled to get novel-padding'), and writing at very short notice some remarkably good lines for a charity performance on behalf of Mrs Jeune's Holiday Fund for Children. They were back in Dorset in August, and within a few days Hardy went with his brother, Henry, on a visit to Paris which he explains away as being 'solely on his brother's account' and which included a visit to the Moulin Rouge, something which one assumes would not have been possible if Emma had been with them. Hardy's ability to see the nearness of life and death is superbly illustrated by his description of himself standing 'somewhere in the building looking down at the young women dancing the *cancan*, and grimacing at the men' and then becoming aware that behind them he could see through the window Montmartre cemetery and that over the heads of the dancers was 'the last resting-place of so many similar gay Parisiens silent under the moonlight' (*Life*, p. 240).

Later in the year, having finished adapting *Tess* for the serial issue, he found time to dip 'into a good many books . . . including Horace, Martial, Lucian, "the Voltaire of Paganism", Voltaire himself, Cervantes, Le Sage, Molière, Dryden, Fielding, Smollett, Swift, Byron, Heine, Carlyle, Thackeray, *Satires and Profanities* by James Thomson, and Weismann's *Essays on Heredity*' (*Life*, p. 240). He was now 50 but his energy seemed greater than ever, and with the problems he was experiencing in publishing his novels he was beginning to cherish a hope that he might be able to return to poetry. In *The Life* he quotes the following from his friend, Edward Clodd: 'The attitude of man . . . at corresponding levels of culture, before like phenomena is pretty much the same, your Dorset peasants representing the persistence of the barbaric idea which confuses persons and things and founds wide generalisations on the slenderest analogies', and then adds wryly (this 'barbaric idea which confuses persons and things' is, by the way, also common to the highest imaginative genius – that of the poet) (*Life*, p. 241). This entry is immediately followed by 'Christmas Day. – While thinking of resuming "the viewless wings of poesy" before dawn this morning, new horizons seemed to open, and worrying pettinesses to disappear.'

It was almost certainly money that kept him writing novels for several more years. His success and reputation as a novelist had steadily grown but he was not yet a big 'seller'. While Hardy's novels sold in thousands, the novels of a contemporary writer like William Black, now almost forgotten, sold in tens of thousands. Hardy could not afford to take up the writing of poetry until his novels were selling well enough to free him from any financial worry. *Tess* and *Jude* did just that.

In August and the autumn of 1891 Hardy was busy correcting *Tess* for its publication in volume form in November. Meanwhile the story was appearing week by week in *The Graphic* and it seems to have caused little comment. Hardy's bowdlerisation included omitting Tess's seduction and the baby. Instead she is tricked into a bogus marriage by Alec. There was some difficulty in handling the closing chapters and Hardy attempted, somewhat unconvincingly, to remove any possibility that Tess might be living with Alec as his mistress by referring to their separate rooms. The Editor of *The Graphic* even objected to Angel's carrying the milkmaids across the flooded road and Hardy resolved that little local difficulty by a wheelbarrow *ex machina* in which the girls were transported without the need for any physical contact.

Most, but not all, of the deletions were restored in the three-volume first edition which was given a subtitle 'A PURE WOMAN/ FAITHFULLY PRESENTED BY/ THOMAS HARDY' almost as a challenge to the opposition which Hardy was expecting. Later he was to say 'I may add that it was appended at the last moment, after reading the final proofs, as being the estimate left in a candid mind of the heroine's character – an estimate that nobody would be likely to dispute. It was disputed more than anything else in the book.' At first the reviews were generally favourable and Hardy was able to talk about ' "Tess" having been fairly received so far', but the Establishment then brought up its big guns and George Saintsbury in *The Saturday Review* rubbished the story, found the sexual suggestions of Tess's 'luxuriance of aspect' disagreeable, and ended with 'Mr Hardy, it must be conceded, tells an unpleasant story in a very unpleasant way.' R. H. Hutton in *The Spectator* questioned Tess's 'purity', and found it 'a story which, in spite of its almost unrivalled power, it is very difficult to read, because in almost every page the mind rebels against the steady assumptions of the author, and shrinks from the untrue picture of a world so blank and godless.' One might have hoped for more understanding from a woman novelist and critic, but Mrs Oliphant in *Blackwood's*, while finding much to admire, kept on protesting that Tess wouldn't have done this or that as if Tess was a real person and not a character created by Hardy. Mowbray Morris in *The Quarterly Review* was cutting: 'We are required to read the story of Tess . . . as the story of "A Pure Woman faithfully presented by Thomas Hardy." Compliance with this request entails something of a strain upon the English language. . . . Mr Hardy has told an extremely disagreeable story in an extremely disagreeable manner. . . . Poor Tess's sensual qualifications . . . are paraded over and over again with a persistence like that of . . . a slave dealer appraising his wares to some full-blooded pasha.'

Even though there was the consolation of some very good reviews – Richard le Gallienne in *The Star* described it as one of Mr Hardy's best novels – perhaps it is his very best': *The Athenaeum* thought that 'Mr Hardy has written a novel that is not only good, but great', while Clementina Black in *The Illustrated London News* thought that it was 'in many respects the finest work which he has yet produced, and its superiority is largely due to a profound moral earnestness...' – Hardy was deeply hurt by the attacks on him. The letters he wrote in the early part of 1892 reveal this: 'As to my choice of such a character after such a fall, it has been borne in upon my mind for many years that justice has never been done to such women in fiction' (*C.L.*, 1, p. 251) 'I may tell you that the review is an absolute misrepresentation by which I am made to say and suggest all sorts of things that I do not say or suggest' (*C.L.*, 1, p. 252) and 'On re-reading the reviews of *Tess* in *The Quarterly* I am struck more than I was at first with its mendacity' (*C.L.*, 1, p. 265). There is also a note about the *Quarterly* review in *The Life*, where Hardy describes it as 'smart and amusing...but it is easy to be smart and amusing if a man will forgo veracity and sincerity' (p. 259). There follows, 'Well, if this sort of thing continues no more novel-writing for me. A man must be a fool to deliberately stand up to be shot at.' It is a pity that Hardy could not have been present at the Hardy Society Conference church service in 1990 when the Bishop of Salisbury described *Tess* as 'surely one of the greatest novels in all world literature' and as 'one of the most truly and profoundly Christian novels'. The Church had come a long way, since as late as 1943 an Archbishop of Canterbury fulminated against *Tess* and described it as one of the worst books ever written. Hardy must have been wondering as he read the attacks on him in 1892 whether the fight against injustice, intolerance and hypocrisy would ever be won.

There were, however, material consolations. The first edition was sold out within a month, a second printing was sold almost as quickly, and *Tess* continued to earn large sums of money for its writer (and his publishers) throughout his life. A paperback edition sold 100 000 copies at sixpence between June 1900 and June 1901 with Hardy receiving one penny a copy, or more than £400 (about £12 000 in modern money) for that one edition of one of his novels. And it has continued to be a bestseller ever since. It has twice been made into a film, has had several stage adaptations including one by Hardy himself, and even inspired an opera, the first night of which in Naples in 1906 was unexpectedly eventful. 'Mount Vesuvius picked that very evening to start a volcanic eruption. Hot ash and fearful rumblings filled the air ... and next morning the authorities ordered the theatre to close to the public as a precaution against the possible collapse of the building' (Desmond Hawkins: 'The Tess Opera', pp. 5–6). No doubt there were some who saw this as a sign of the President of the Immortals' disapproval.

In addition to wealth, *Tess* brought Hardy fame on a scale he could never have dreamt of. More and more society hostesses, unaware that this was a man who had satirised the 'upper classes' in his first novel and would satirise them in his last, were anxious to show him off at their dinners and crushes even if they had, as one such lady put it, to divide their guests into those who loved the novel and those who hated it. Hardy's love–hate relationship with all this socialising continued. *The Life* has many references to 'his adventures in the world of fashion at dinner-parties, crushes, and other social functions, which Hardy himself did not think worth recording' but which 'have been obtained from diaries kept by the late Mrs Hardy' (p. 257). He goes on to describe himself as 'vibrating at a swing between the artificial gaieties of a London season and the quaintnesses of a primitive rustic life', which doesn't ring quite true. Of course, the second Mrs Hardy excised from her version of *The Life* many of these accounts of the 'artificial gaieties'. The 'scandalous notoriety', as Hardy called it, which some critics tried to pin on him also led to articles about him in the press and in magazines and even to his inclusion among the great who had had a 'Spy' cartoon devoted to them. Hardy, a modest man but always a good publicist for his own work, may even have contributed to this by ghosting articles about himself. Thus 'A Representative Man at Home', which appeared anonymously in *Cassell's Saturday Journal* (25 June 1892), was almost certainly largely written by him. It contains much of interest, including the admission that a good many of his characters are taken from life and that he always liked 'to have a real place in my mind for every scene in a novel. Before writing about it I generally go and see each place.' In an interview entitled 'A Chat with the Author of *Tess*' in *Black and White* (27 August 1892) he claims in *Tess* 'to have adhered to *human nature*. . . . I only try to give an artistic shape to standing facts', and he goes on 'I do feel very strongly that the position of man and woman in nature, things which everyone is thinking and nobody saying, may be taken up and treated frankly.' In a later interview with Frederick Dolman which appeared in *The Young Man* (March 1894) he says, almost prophetically, 'I don't believe in that idea of a man's imaginative powers becoming naturally exhausted; I believe that, if he liked, a man could go on writing till his physical strength gave out.' There is also in this interview an unusually revealing comment about the frankness of *Tess* and of the earlier novels:

Yes, but the frankness of the book (*Tess*) has brought me some asperities. . . . There have been very few objectors really, in their secret hearts people know there is nothing honestly to object to. As a matter of fact, my tone has been the same in regard to moral questions for the twenty years or more I have been writing. From the very beginning I resolved to speak out. I remember that in the very first edition of *Desperate Remedies* there were many passages exhibiting a similar plainness to *Tess*. Some of these were eliminated in the one-volume edition, in deference to my publishers; but I am sorry now that I did so, and if ever the book is included in the uniform edition of my works the old passages shall be restored.

One of the problems faced by editors of Hardy's prose and verse is which of a number of different texts is to be preferred: manuscript, serial, first edition or subsequent editions in volume form? We should be wary in such a situation of calling any edition 'definitive', but in view of what is above and of Hardy's letter to the publisher of *Under the Greenwood Tree* of 24 October 1875 (*C.L.*, 1, p. 38) in which he says that he 'sees many sentences that I should re-write or revise, supposing I had the opportunity', there does seem to be good reason for preferring the later editions to the earlier and accepting Hardy's description of the American Wessex Edition, called the Autograph Edition, that 'this is the authorised and definitive edition of my books'. What is impressive is the assiduity with which Hardy revised his work.

It is not easy to write about Hardy's marital relationship with Emma. In such affairs the outsider cannot know even half of what is happening and the pair themselves often do not understand. Hardy was intensely loyal to both his wives and said not a word in open criticism of them, whereas both Emma and Florence voiced their criticisms of him. By the time of *Tess* the first marriage had run into difficulties. They had failed to have children, Emma had become ever more religious as her husband became ever more agnostic. She was unwilling to recognise the demands made on him by his genius and career, and in her fifties she had so lost her looks that one visitor to Max Gate in 1885 said of her that 'ugly is no word for it!', while another in 1889 described her as an 'excessively plain, dowdy, high-stomached woman'. Christine Wood Homer, whose home near Puddletown the Hardys often visited in the 1890s, said that they had not been a happy couple for a good many years before Emma's death and describes her as 'a peculiar woman in many ways like a little child. . . . She was an increasing embarrassment to her husband' to whom it 'had been a burdensome grief . . . that (she) had not cared for any of his family' (Toucan Press Monograph No. 18). He for his part seemed at times strangely insensitive to her feelings and she could hardly have failed to be aware of his growing interest in other women. In 1889 he was impressed by the gift of a book of verse written by a young lady of considerable beauty called Rosamund Tomson and meeting her a year later, asked for her portrait, exchanged 'rhymes' with her and asked to be seated near to her at the dinner of the Society of Authors in July. His letters to her have that slightly arch and waggish tone which is so often the prelude to flirtation. In fact, as Hardy was to learn again and again, younger women were attracted to him by his fame and the possibility that he might be able to advance their literary careers rather than by physical appeal. He was to them no Sergeant Troy. It was not long before he realised that Rosamund Tomson was exploiting him and he was hurt by an article she wrote about him in *The Independent* (New York, 22 November 1892) which was incorrect in several of its facts. Not even her statement that he was a man of 'singular modesty' and with a 'still intensity of observation' who talked about his books with 'unaffected frankness and an absence of self-consciousness that is positively charming' could restore her to favour.

Hardy's sexual longings and frustrations become increasingly obvious during this period. In a note in *The Life* (p. 240) he sees 'A Cleopatra in the railway carriage . . . a good-natured amative creature by her voice, and her heavy moist lips.' A year later in 1891 he is at a lunch in London and he 'sat between a pair of beauties. – Mrs A. G. – with her violet eyes was the more seductive; Mrs R. C. – the more vivacious. The latter in yellow: the former in pale brown, and more venust and warm-blooded . . .' (*Life*, p. 249). In 1892 he 'called on "Lucas Malet". A striking woman: full, slightly voluptuous mouth, red lips, black hair and eyes' (*Life*, p. 258). But, as he was to show later, he could love the dead woman as much, perhaps even more, than he could the live. The only reference to Tryphena Sparks in *The Life* is this, dated March 1890:

In the train on the way to London. Wrote the first four or six lines of 'Not a line of her writing have I'. It was a curious instance of sympathetic telepathy. The woman whom I was thinking of – a cousin – was dying at the time, and I quite in ignorance of it. She died six days later. (p. 234)

The cousin was, of course, Tryphena and Hardy must have wondered whether he might have been happier if he had been able to marry her rather than Emma. He completed the poem, and with the title 'Thoughts of Ph-a/ At news of her death', published it in *Wessex Poems* in 1898. Did he really think that Emma would fail to see the connection and would not be hurt by the reference to Tryphena as 'my lost prize'? And just a few pages earlier in that book is a poem called 'The Ivy Wife' which she might well have seen as a bitter allusion to herself. How could the supremely sensitive Hardy have been so insensitive? Some three months after Tryphena's death Hardy and his brother cycled to Topsham, near Exeter, about fifty miles from Dorchester in order to visit the grave of the 'lost prize'. It was yet another case of 'Too Late Beloved'. There can be little doubt that the last twenty years or so of the Hardy's marriage lacked happiness, but they did share many things together, not least the past and their love of animals.

Sir George Douglas, whom Hardy had first met in 1881 in Wimborne, put together some recollections of his long friendship with Hardy after Hardy's death in 1928, and his article in *The Hibbert Journal* (April 1928) is informed and balanced. Speaking of their visit to his estate at Kelso in the summer of 1892, he says,

It would have been impossible, I fancy, to find pleasanter visitors than the Hardys proved to be.... Absorption in creative work puts a sore strain on human ties. But then, in an affectionate nature such as his, deep sorrow readily assumes some of the features of remorse. My own impression was that for Hardy custom had never staled the charm of the sweetheart in his first wife.... Each had sacrificed something to the other, but their attachment was strong enough for each to be resigned to that sacrifice.

What is so impressive about Hardy as a novelist is that more than almost any other writer of that time he saw and tried to express the power of nature expressing itself through human sexuality. At its rawest we see it in Arabella's physical attraction for poor Jude as his ideals of educational advancement disappear in a moment 'in commonplace obedience to conjunctive orders from headquarters' and he responds to 'the unvoiced call of woman to man'. In his 1895 Preface Hardy sees *Jude* as attempting 'to deal unaffectedly with the fret and the fever, derision and disaster, that may press in the wake of the strongest passion known to humanity'. In expressing Jude's agonising sexual frustration in his relationship with Sue, Hardy is expressing his own 'fret and fever' as in those 1890 years he sought in vain for a sexual satisfaction in an amorous relationship which was always to be denied him. But before *Jude* there was to be *The Well-Beloved*.

As a compensation to Tillotson's for his failure to provide them in *Tess* with a story they could safely publish in their magazines, he agreed in February 1890 to give them a new, less serious, serial. Because of the demands of *Tess*, work on the new novel, to be called *The Pursuit of the Well-Beloved*, did not commence until well into 1891. In December of that year he was assuring Tillotson's that the new story would have his full attention and be finished 'within the time specified – though probably not until the end of the time – 31 March 1892 – owing to my wish to verify some of the scenes' (C.L., 1, p. 249). In a prospectus submitted to the publishers he describes the scenes as shifting 'backwards and forwards from London studios and drawing-rooms of fashion to the cottages and cliffs of a remote isle in the English Channel, and a little town on the same.' That island, called in the novel the Isle of Slingers, is the Isle of Portland, more accurately a bare and stony peninsula, a rugged block of limestone, jutting out into the sea for nearly four miles and joined to the mainland near Weymouth by a narrow road with the sea on both sides. Its attraction for Hardy as a setting would have been that he knew it well, it had not already been used by him as the main setting for a novel, and it had a remoteness and 'foreignness' which suited his subject. He described the islanders as a 'curious and well-nigh distinct people, cherishing strange beliefs and singular customs, now for the most part obsolescent'. An added appeal for Hardy was that its great quarries had provided stone for building for hundreds of years, Wren using it for his new St Paul's. A home in *The Well-Beloved* is described: 'Like the island it was all of stone, not only in walls but in window frames, roofs, chimneys, fence, stile, pigsty and stable', and as a boy Hardy would often have seen his father, a practising stone-mason, working on Portland stone.

The Well-Beloved has more than once been called a strange novel, and it can now be regarded as in the nature of an experiment. This can be seen in the fact that it exists in two different published versions, first as a serial in *The Illustrated London News* between 1 October and 17 December 1892 and then, after substantial revision, in volume form in 1897. That gap of five years during which *Jude the Obscure* was written and published is evidence of Hardy's uncertainty about his aims and methods. Hardy himself described it as a 'fanciful, tragi-comic, half allegorical tale of a poor Visionary pursuing a Vision' (C.L., 2, p. 154) and in 1912 placed it among those of his novels he designated 'Romances and Fantasies'. His expressed desire to get 'nearer the heart and meaning of things' was one reason for his deliberate use of fantasy, a fantasy that was necessary for the expression of his main theme – the pursuit of the well-beloved, and certainly Jocelyn Pierston's life-long pursuit of that well-beloved does seem at first to have much that is bizarre about it. He falls in love with the first Avice when he is about 20, her daughter, Avice the second, when he is about 40, and her granddaughter, Avice the third, when he is 60. A recurring theme in his novels has been the need to view the well-beloved realistically. Men, he believed, are often looking for the unattainable, hoping to find in the woman they think they love the perfection of their ideal. The risk to happiness in loving a woman for what the lover wants her to be rather than for what she is played an ever larger part in Hardy's mind as he matured as a novelist. As he noted in 1891 when thinking about *The Well-Beloved*, 'It is the incompleteness which is loved when love is sterling and true.' This idea now received its most powerful statement, and, as he cogently remarked in his preface to the book in its 1912 Wessex Edition,

> As for the story itself, it may be worth while to remark that, differing from all or most others of the series in that the interest aimed at is of an ideal or subjective nature, and frankly imaginative, verisimilitude in the sequence of events has been subordinated to the said aim.

As with his remarkable retentive memory he looked back on his own life and loves, he may well have pondered on his own luckless pursuit of the well-beloved. He was now in his fifties and time was running out. Tryphena might have been the ideal but she had married someone else and was now dead. Emma had seemed the ideal in the 1870s but was certainly not so in the 1890s. And to what extent was he responsible for his own loneliness? To what extent was all this Shelleyan talk about the pursuit of the ideal woman no more than an attempt to rationalise and humanise the polygamous yearnings imposed on man by 'nature's holy plan'? As in almost every one of his novels, there is much that is autobiographical in *The Well-Beloved* and, in his portrayal of Pierston, Hardy is once again drawing heavily on his own thoughts and feelings and experiences. This can be seen too in another of the novel's themes. Hardy must have been continually aware of the close relationship between his own emotions and his creative work. He would have realised as he wrote *The Mayor, The Woodlanders, Tess* and *Jude* that his emotional concern over his own marital relationship with Emma was influencing his subject and producing what may be seen as a 'Marriage Quartet'. In so doing his writing became a kind of emotional relief, a catharsis. This relationship between life and art, the examination of the well-springs of artistic creation, is a major theme in *The Well-Beloved*, in which both Hardy and Pierston are conscious of the paradox that it is frustration and incompleteness in their personal lives which lead to their artistic creations. Their artistic temperament depends, that is to say, to a large extent upon the constant search for the ideal in life and art.

The Well-Beloved was greatly admired by Proust but dismissed by D. H. Lawrence as 'sheer rubbish, fatuity'. Today it can be seen as one of the most experimental and autobiographical of the novels. The plot is far-fetched, but it never strays so far from reality as to become unbelievable. The fantasy is continually leavened by the physical presence of the Isle of Slingers, that 'peninsula carved by Time out of a single stone', which is so firmly part of the earth. The natural life of its inhabitants is pointedly contrasted with the superficialities of life in London, something Hardy must have been so sensitive to in his own life at that time, and he makes good use of his by-now intimate knowledge of life among London's wealthy, high-born society. It is a subjective novel in that its writer is inextricably caught up emotionally with his own creation, but there is at the same time a measure of objectivity in its humour and tone of consistent irony. We see this in Hardy's ability to distance himself from his own deeply personal involvement and to laugh at himself by seeing the ambivalent ironies inherent in his own position. This situation will be even more strongly felt in his last novel, *Jude*.

In the prospectus about *The Well-Beloved* which Hardy had sent Tillotson's in December 1891 he had told them, 'There is not a word or scene in the tale which can offend the most fastidious taste; and it is equally suited for the reading of young people, and for that of persons of maturer years.' This was so manifestly untrue that one can only assume that he was once again deliberately deceiving the publishers in order to see just how much he could get away with before they shouted 'stop'. A story which begins with the Island custom of having sex before marriage, in which Pierston falls in love with a woman while she is drying her underclothes in a room he is sharing with her in a London hotel before they marry, and then agrees that either of them could remarry without bothering about a divorce, hardly fulfils the description of the story in the prospectus. Hardy himself must have had some worries about the book because he described it in 1892 as 'short and slight, and written entirely with a view to serial publication' and it was more than four years later that on 16 March 1897 he published it, much altered, in volume form. Hardy's 'notoriety' was by then such that it sold well, helped no doubt by the fulminations of the puritanical critics. Although most of the reviews were favourable, he was hurt by a review in *The World* on 24 March 1897 which contained the sentence, 'Of all forms of sex-mania in fiction we have no hesitation in pronouncing the most unpleasant to be the Wessex-mania of Thomas Hardy'. In a letter to Sir George Douglas on the following day, he is appalled that his story 'should be stigmatized as sexual and disgusting' and finds that criticism 'a piece of mendacity hard to beat in the annals of the press' (*C.L.*, 2, p. 154). It was surely a consolation to him to know that there would be no more novels and no more of this particular kind of unpleasantness.

The years between the serial publication of *The Well-Beloved* in 1892 and its appearance as a book in 1897 were among the busiest and most eventful of his life. As is inevitable when we find ourselves on the wrong side of 50, life becomes saddened by the deaths of relatives and friends. Tryphena's death in 1890 was followed by the death of his friend and publisher, James Osgood in May 1892 and that of his father in July 1892. Thomas the Second had lived his whole life of eighty years in the Bockhampton cottage, and Hardy's poem, 'On One who Lived and Died Where He Was Born' (*C.P.*, 621), is a moving tribute to this 'Wise child of November . . . Who saw quick in time/ As a vain pantomime/ Life's tending, its ending,/ The worth of its fame'. In *The Life* Hardy expresses his regret that he was not present at the death, and we are told that 'Almost the last thing his father had asked for was water fresh drawn from the well – which was brought and given him; he tasted it and said, "Yes – that's our well-water. Now I know I am at home' (*Life*, p. 262).

On 12 October Hardy attended Tennyson's funeral. The contrasts in Hardy's life between his professional and social and his family life could not have been more sharply illustrated than by the two contrasting funerals, one in Westminster Abbey, the other in Stinsford church. His own funeral was to repeat these contrasts. Another sadness was to see Stinsford House, linked with so many memories of the past, almost completely destroyed by fire in September 1892: 'a bruising of tender memories for me. . . . When it grew dark the flames entered the drawing and dining-rooms, lighting up the chambers of so much romance' (*Life*, p. 264).

It was romance that he hoped he might find when he met Mrs Arthur Henniker at the Vice-Regal Lodge in Dublin in May 1893. The invitation had come from Lord Houghton, her brother, the then Lord-Lieutenant of Ireland. They were the children of Richard Monckton Milnes, the first Lord Houghton, a distinguished statesman, poet and editor of Keats's poems and letters whom Hardy had met on several occasions before his death in 1885. The Honourable Florence Ellen Hungerford Milnes was born in December 1855 and named Florence after her godmother, Florence Nightingale. She was a precocious child, very interested in human nature, and a lover of literature who even as a child enjoyed writing. In 1882 she married the Honourable Arthur Henry Henniker-Major who, being a younger son with little money to inherit, joined the Coldstream Guards and after distinguished service in the Boer War worked his way up to the rank of Major-General. In spite of his almost complete lack of interest in literature the marriage seems to have been successful, he occupied with his military duties, she surrounded by her literary friends and trying to make a name for herself by writing novels and short stories. She was an attractive, good-looking woman and the contrast between her and Emma when they met in Dublin was striking. Hardy describes his meeting with her in *The Life* with tactful brevity: 'We were received by Mrs Arthur Henniker, the Lord-Lieutenant's sister. A charming, *intuitive* woman apparently' (p. 270). She immediately showed an interest in him because here was one of the great novelists of the day. No doubt she saw him as someone who could help her to advance her career, but although there was mutual attraction because of shared interests, there is no evidence that she felt any sexual love for this rather ordinary-looking 53-year-old countryman. For him Florence Henniker would have seemed the 'ideal', the 'well-beloved', and for a few months he obviously hoped for some kind of consummation. She was, after all, one of the 'new' women who seemed liberal and advanced in her views.

Once again it was not to be. Within a few days of returning to England he was writing on 3 June to her in his warm and arch manner. Further letters followed on the 7, 10, 20, 29 and 30 June, and *One Rare Fair Woman*, which is a book of Hardy's letters to her, has another sixteen written in the next six months, and this at a time when he was intensely busy with his own writing. Mrs Henniker was not disappointed in her hopes that he would help to advance her literary career. He gave her advice about her stories, helped her with their publication, and even collaborated with her in writing a story called 'The Spectre of the Real' which was published in a magazine in November 1894. Hardy was sadly disappointed in his hopes of an affair. In spite of all his literary advice and an offer of a guide to architecture which would take the form of 'oral instruction in actual buildings', and in spite of her teasing him by sending photographs and romantic translations of romantic verses, she was no more in love with him than Bathsheba was with Boldwood. On 8 August they met and visited Winchester together and it was almost certainly on that day that she told him that their relationship could never be more than that of friends. Friends indeed they remained, united by shared literary interests, and when she died in 1923, widowed, lonely and impoverished, he made the following note: 'April 5. In today's *Times*: "Henniker.-on the 4th April 1923 of heart failure, the Honourable Mrs Arthur Henniker. R.I.P." After a friendship of 30 years!' (*Life*, p. 452). J. I. M. Stewart has the Hardy–Henniker relationship well summed-up when in his *Thomas Hardy* he says, 'To me, at least, the Henniker affair suggests itself as being compounded out of middle-aged sentiment and a little sex in the head. But set a poet brooding on such an episode, and then rhyming on it, and the result may be the opening up of subterraneous channels of communication between it and matters of far deeper emotional involvement. So the poetry comes' (p. 30).

Once again Hardy used his life as material for his writing, and the poems 'At an Inn' (*C.P.*, 45), 'A Thunderstorm in Town' (*C.P.*, 255), 'The Division' (*C.P.*, 169) and 'A Broken Appointment' (*C.P.*, 99) are a moving commentary on his feelings about yet another 'lost prize'. Here is 'A Broken Appointment':

> You did not come,
> And marching Time drew on, and wore me numb. –

Yet less for loss of your dear presence there
Than that I thus found lacking in your make
That high compassion which can overbear
Reluctance for pure lovingkindness' sake
Grieved I, when, as the hope-hour stroked its sum,
　　　　You did not come.

　　　　You love not me,
And love alone can lend you loyalty;
– I know and knew it. But, unto the store
Of human deeds divine in all but name,
Was it not worth a little hour or more
To add yet this: Once you, a woman, came
To soothe a time-torn man; even though it be
　　　　You love not me?

There has been no better poem written about the disappointment of
what is today known as being stood-up, and the four short lines
mark the striking of the quarters of the hour on a clock as the 'time-
torn' man waits in vain. The source of this poem is obvious in his
letter to her of 28 June 1898.

　My dear friend:
　　　I am much disappointed at you not having a spare mo-
　ment till Thursday evening, as it again prevents my seeing you,
　for though I have been keeping all today & tomorrow for you, I
　have to leave Thursday morning . . . Hoping I may be more for-
　tunate next time I am
　　　　　　　　　Ever your affecte. friend
　　　　　　　　　　　Tho H.
　　　　　　　　　　　(*C.L.*, 2, p. 195)

His poem 'Wessex Heights' (*C.P.*, 261), dated 1896, contains a stanza
which is known to refer to Florence Henniker:

As for one rare fair woman, I am now but a thought of hers,
I enter her mind and another thought succeeds me that she prefers;
Yet my love for her in its fulness she herself even did not know;
Well, time cures hearts of tenderness, and now I can let her go.

He can't, of course, and as with Yeats and Maud Gonne the tenderness never died. A significant and bitter note in *The Life* of July 1893 reads: 'His last call this summer was on Lady Londonderry who remained his friend through the ensuing years. A beautiful woman still ... and very glad to see me which beautiful women are not always' (p. 273).

Echoes of the relationship with Mrs Henniker are also found in Hardy's short story 'An Imaginative Woman', which he wrote mainly during the summer and autumn of the year of his first meeting with the 'rare fair woman'. The imaginative woman, Ella Marchmill, is married to an armaments manufacturer and on holiday in Solentsea. Florence Ellen Henniker was married to a soldier and was that year at Southsea. Ella falls in love with a poet who has certain resemblances to Hardy, 'he was a pessimist in so far as that character applies to a man who looks at the worst contingencies as well as the best in the human condition'. His name is Robert Trewe but in the manuscript this had been 'Crewe', and Mrs Henniker's grandfather was Lord Crewe. Ella, a poet herself, but not as good and successful as Trewe, never meets him, partly because of her own limitations. The similarities to his own relationship with Mrs Henniker are clear. But her greatest literary influence on him is to be seen in the character of Sue in *Jude the Obscure*, Hardy's final novel and the end of his career as a novelist. Like *Tess*, *Jude* had been germinating in Hardy's mind for several years, and he would certainly have been aware of what had been called 'the Fiction of Sex and Women'. In the early 1890s a great many novels about sex and marriage, many of them written by women, had been published, and he had certainly read two of the most important of these, Sarah Grand's *The Heavenly Twins* (1893) and George Egerton's (Mary Bright's) *Keynotes* (1893). Such writers, with their criticism of Victorian marriage and their outspoken demands for equality with men, were the cause of much controversy and were bitterly attacked for undermining the stability of society. But Hardy said that they had more courage than the men and admired the frank way in which they dealt with sexual relationships.

The scheme of the novel, Hardy tells us in the Preface,

was jotted down in 1890, from notes made in 1887 and onwards, some of the circumstances being suggested by the death of a woman in the former year. The scenes were revisited in October 1892; the narrative was written in outline in 1892 and the spring

of 1893, and at full length . . . from August 1893 onwards into the
next year; the whole, with the exception of a few chapters being
in the hands of the publisher by the end of 1894. (*N.W.E.*, p. xxviii)

The reference to Tryphena's death in 1890 shows that Sue is not just
based upon Florence Henniker, and warns us against making over-
simple relationships between life and fiction. Just as Casterbridge
is and is not Dorchester, so Sue is and is not one single woman.
She is a highly complex personality, a composite character if ever
there was one. Her experiences at the teacher Training College at
Melchester were based to some extent on what he had learnt about
life there from his two sisters who had both trained as teachers at
the Training College at Salisbury. Kate had found the discipline there
hard to accept and must have discussed this with her brother. In
June 1891 he visited Stockwell Training College as part of his preparation for *Jude* and because it was the Training College Tryphena
had attended. Writing to Edmund Gosse on 20 November 1895
Hardy described Sue as 'a type of woman who has always had an
attraction for me . . . there is nothing perverted or depraved in Sue's
nature . . . her sexual instinct being healthy so far as it goes, but
unusually weak and fastidious' (*C.L.*, 2, p. 99). One wonders to what
extent Mrs Henniker saw herself in Sue. It is significant that writing
to her on 10 November 1895 he says, 'My hesitating to send "Jude"
was not because I thought you narrow' (*C.L.*, 2, p. 94). That is, of
course, exactly what he did think of her, and he found it difficult
to reconcile her liberal outlook and advanced views in certain areas
of life with her conservatism in moral matters and with what he
called her 'ritualistic ecclesiasticism'.

As has already been mentioned, one of Hardy's most important
friends in London, and one with whom he frequently stayed, was
Lady Jeune. She was the wife of a distinguished lawyer and divorce-
court judge and Hardy had discussed the divorce laws with him. I
am indebted to Professor William A. Davies for the information
that Lady Jeune in the 1880s and 1890s had written a number of
articles about women and that 'there was something of an ideolo-
gical battle over women's nature and roles in society, with Lady
Jeune taking the traditionalists' view that the "New Woman" is an
"excrescence" and Hardy taking the side of women's independence
while clearly showing the costs associated with the women's movement.' Hardy would certainly have discussed all this with her and
in creating Sue he gives his own impression of the difficulties faced

by the 'New Woman' having to live in a society dominated by an oppressive and hypocritical moral code and a religion of sin, sacrifice and punishment.

Love between men and women, 'the strongest passion known to humanity', is once again Hardy's major theme, but an important minor theme is the class-ridden educational system of the time. Hardy cannot get away from his sensitivity to the class distinction which he saw all around him. Jude, like Hardy, is a boy from a humble background who is anxious to better himself. Jude's rejection by the Christminster colleges is an angry comment on the higher educational system of his time, even if ironically the education on offer at Christminster is the result of 'four centuries of gloom, bigotry and decay'. Jude, even more than Hardy, is a self-educated man and, like Hardy, he moves from religious belief to doubt and to strong criticism of an intolerant Church. Jude saw himself as an 'outsider' in Christminster, and Hardy must have seen himself as still an 'outsider' even while he was being entertained by the rich and famous, and exploited by beautiful high-born women who would never take him to their beds.

Jude, a sensationally outspoken novel for its time, is thought by some to be the greatest of his novels and dismissed by others as a bitter, gloomy and pessimistic book which suffers from its inability to provide what T. S. Eliot called a satisfactory objective correlative for its author's feelings. Each to his choice, but what is undeniable is that in reading it we are brought into contact with a mind which is seething with ideas. In *Jude* chance plays its part as in all Hardy's novels (and in life), but the emphasis is now on men and women 'subject to the inexorable laws of nature' and in conflict with an unfeeling and dogmatic social code. *Jude* brings up important questions of culpability and responsibility, but whereas in the early novels Hardy seemed reasonably certain of what is right and what is wrong, *Jude* is written by a man whose painfully personal experiences have made him aware of life's complexity. He now broods over such questions as who is the moral man and who the moral woman. Sue's cry of 'O why should Nature's law be mutual butchery?' is followed by Jude's cry that they are fighting 'only against man and senseless circumstance' and we feel in these two cries Hardy's own despair and his inner loneliness as, in his mid-fifties, he surveys the life around him. Such is the despair, based to some extent upon Hardy's sexual frustration and his sense of life passing away, that many find the book too gloomy to read, and it is difficult to accept the unrelieved iconoclasm that deprives Jude of one ideal after another. Hardy resolves the clash between the ideal and the real firmly in favour of a very sordid reality. In *Jude* the stable, unchanging community life he had depicted in *Far from the Madding Crowd* has become a restless, rootless existence, dominated by change and by a *fin-de-siècle* hopelessness. Hardy the writer of the 1890s is a very different writer from the Hardy of the 1870s.

But if it is a difficult novel to like there is much in *Jude* to admire. There is the courage with which it handles the marriage question and suggests that it is better to live together in harmony and love without being married than to be married and living 'in the antipathetic, recrimatory mood of the average husband and wife in Christendom'; the brilliant structuring and planning, with its contrasts between Jude's religiosity and Sue's paganism, Sue's religiosity and Jude's paganism, Christminster gown and town, and living in marriage and living in 'sin'; the fascinating, subtle and deeply psychological characterisation; and finally the sparse description which is so powerful because it works both at the literal and metaphorical levels.

There were the usual Grundyan difficulties over the serial version and, as it appeared in *Harper's New Monthly Magazine*, it was more mauled by the need not to 'bring a blush into the cheek of the young person' than any other of his novels. In the serial the important fact that Jude is tricked into marriage by Arabella's telling him that he had made her pregnant is changed to her inventing another young man who will marry her if Jude doesn't. The chicken's egg concealed in Arabella's 'capacious bosom' and their going upstairs in her house are omitted, and another serious cut is that of the night which Jude and Arabella spend together in the hotel at Aldbrickham which is so important, in showing her sexual hold over him. Its publication in book form in its uncensored state caused even more of a fuss than did that of *Tess*. One bishop burnt a copy and got Smith's Circulating Library to withdraw the offending article from sale. Mrs Oliphant accused Hardy of trying to establish 'an anti-marriage league', described the book as 'a novel of lubricity' and dismissed it as 'one of the most objectionable books ever written'. But there were powerful voices speaking up in its defence. *The Illustrated London News* hailed it as 'manifestly a work of genius', *The Westminster Review* thought it 'the best English novel which has appeared since *Tess*' and H. G. Wells in *The Saturday Review* began 'It is doubtful, considering not only the greatness of the work but also the greatness of the author's reputation, whether for many years any book has received quite so foolish a reception as has been accorded the last and most splendid of all the books Mr Hardy has given the world.' It is a book 'that alone will make 1895 a memorable year in the history of literature', and Hardy's is 'the voice of the educated proletarian, speaking more distinctly than it has spoken before in English literature.'

In *The Life* Hardy entered a note a week after *Jude*'s appearance as a book, 'The Reviews begin to howl at *Jude*.' Shortly after, he mentions that 'he was called by opprobious names, the criticisms being outrageously personal, unfair, and untrue. . . . The onslaught started by the vituperative section of the press . . . was taken up by the anonymous writers of libellous letters and post-cards and other such gentry' (*Life*, pp. 287–8). Just how upset Hardy was by all this it is difficult to say, although he claimed in a letter to Sir George Douglas of 5 January 1896 that 'I have really not been much upset by the missiles heaved at the poor book', and he continues with the perceptive observation, 'Somehow I feel that the critics are not sincere: everybody knows that silence is the remedy in the case of immoral works. But they advertise it with sensational headings, because that advertises their newspapers' (*C.L.*, 2, p. 105). After his experiences with *Tess* he must have known that what Michael Millgate calls 'the final comprehensive challenge' of *Jude* would flutter the dovecotes. However, *Jude* had sold 20 000 copies within four months and he found on his return to London in the spring of 1896 'that people there seemed not to be at all concerned at his having been excommunicated by the press, or by at least a noisy section of it, and received him just the same as ever' and in no time at all he was 'attending a most amusing masked ball . . . where he and Henry James were the only two not in dominos, and were reck- lessly flirted with by the women in consequence' (*Life*, p. 292). It is not easy to reconcile such goings-on with the three 'In Tenebris' poems which are dated 1895 and 1896, and were first entitled 'De Profundis' and contain such lines as,

> Black is night's cope;
> But death will not appal
> One who, past doubtings all,
> Waits in unhope.

and

Let him in whose ears the low-voiced Best is killed by the clash
of the First,
Who holds that if way to the Better there be, it exacts a full look
at the Worst,
Who feels that delight is a delicate growth cramped by crooked-
ness, custom, and fear,
Get him up and be gone as one shaped awry; he disturbs the
order here.

(*C.P.*, 136–8)

Could the man who had written *Jude* and the 'In Tenebris' poem
really be the same man as the one who clearly enjoyed each year
his months in London being entertained by people he affected to
despise? He could, and it was partly because of that wide range of
human experience and the ambivalence that results from this that
he is the great writer he is. In his poem 'So Various' (*C.P.*, 855) he
mentions what appear to be contradictions in his own character –
ardent young man and cold old man, dunce and 'learned seer', a
'man of sadness' and 'a man so glad/ You never could conceive
him sad' – and the poem ends

Now. . . . all these specimens of man,
So various in their pith and plan,
Curious to say
Were *one* man. Yea,
I was all they.

Hardy's life during the 1890s was not just varied, it was extraordinarily full. Osgood, McIlvaine, a London-based subsidiary of
the American house of Harper & Brothers had become his publishers in 1891 with the publication of *A Group of Noble Dames*,
and when Sampson, Low's rights in the earlier novels expired in
June 1894 they were taken over by Osgood, McIlvaine who immediately took advantage of all the publicity generated by *Tess* to pro-
pose the publication of the first uniform and complete edition of
Hardy's works. The first volume of what was shrewdly called 'The
Wessex Novels' was, naturally, *Tess*, published in April 1895, and
subsequent volumes followed at monthly intervals. Hardy took the
opportunity of doing a thorough revision of the novels, some of
which had been written twenty years or so earlier. Throughout 1895
and much of 1896, at a time when he was involved in *Jude*, he was

kept busy with this major revision of twelve novels and three books of short stories, and with the very arduous proofreading involved. In addition, he was working on the Macmillan Colonial series of the novels which was to use the Osgood, McIlvaine plates. He was delighted to have achieved a status as a writer sufficient to warrant a collected edition, and the evidence of his success as a writer, both at home and overseas, was overwhelming. For example, *Tess* by 1895 had already been translated into German, French, Russian, Dutch, Italian and several other languages. For the Wessex Novels edition he made a number of topographical changes which resulted in greater consistency and emphasised their Wessexness, he added prefaces containing information and comment on each of the novels, and there was much re-writing. Some of this was so that he could be more sexually explicit. Thus we learn for the first time that Eustacia and Wildeve in *The Return* have had a sexual relationship before he marries Thomasin. The volumes in this edition are illustrated by Henry MacBeth-Raeburn with fine frontispiece etchings of places associated with them, and by this means Hardy once again emphasises the Wessex topographical element in his work. He spent some time with the artist in 1894 and 1895 and made detailed suggestions about what might be suitable.

As if all this wasn't enough, he continued to help Mrs Henniker with her literary career, wrote several more short stories, and worked on a dramatisation of *Tess* which led to his being pestered by some of the most well-known actresses of the day who all wanted to be Tess. He and Emma were in London for several months during the Seasons of 1895 and 1896 and once again particularly enjoyed concerts given by the famous bands of Europe at the Imperial Institute. Hardy's acquaintance with the works of such classical composers as Mozart, Verdi and Grieg, in those days before radio, records and touring symphony orchestras, must have come mainly from such London concerts.

In August 1896 they somehow found time to have an eight-week holiday which began with visits to Malvern, Worcester, and Warwick where not only did he correct some proofs but he saw the coffin of the recently-dead Lord Warwick who some while before had invited him to stay at the Castle, an invitation Hardy had not been able to accept. It reminded him of the transitoriness of life and ' "Here I am at last," he said to the coffin . . . "and here are you to receive me!" It made an impression on Hardy which he never forgot' (*Life*, p. 299). After Warwick they visited Stratford where he read

King Lear, and then it was down to Dover and a visit to Bruges, Spa, and then to Brussels where they stayed at the same hotel they had stayed at twenty years before. Hardy again visited the site of the battle of Waterloo with the idea of *The Dynasts* very much in his mind. He had got as far as giving the epic-drama he was planning the provisional title 'Europe in Throes'.

With the arrival of 1897 the period of the novel drew to its close. After the publication of the volume form of *The Well-Beloved* in March Hardy was to write no more prose fiction apart from two or three short stories, which with several others not previously published in book form were collected together and published in 1913 with the title *A Changed Man*. As Desmond Hawkins points out in his introduction to Hardy's *Collected Short Stories*, Hardy's was 'a bountiful pen' and his total achievement as a writer of short stories was considerable. The four books in which they were collected contained forty-five stories, and there were a further three stories which remained uncollected, together with his outstandingly good long short story, 'Our Exploits at West Poley'.

And now it was to be back to his first and main love, poetry. He could afford to go back because the novels would earn more than enough to support him for the rest of his life, and the copyright law passed in the United States in 1892 now at last meant that English authors would earn royalties there. He was tired of the vilification of the novel reviewers, aware that the novel was exploring new areas into which he had no desire to enter and 'which had nothing to do with art', and confident that he could 'express more fully in verse ideas and emotions which run counter to the inert crystallized opinion – hard as a rock – which the vast body of men have vested interests in supporting. . . . If Galileo had said in verse that the world moved, the Inquisition might have let him alone' (*Life*, p. 302). Some of his unpublished poems of the 1860s had somehow survived and although he had hardly written a poem in the 1870s and 1880s, he had written several since 1890 and had begun to find inspiration everywhere. In 1897 he tells us that he had 'already for some time been getting together the poems which made up the first volume of verse . . . at first with some consternation he had found an awkwardness in getting back to an easy expression in numbers after abandoning it for so many years; but that soon wore off' (*Life*, p. 310). It was probably in 1897 that he began to look through those poems of the 1860s with the idea of adding to them some of the poems he had written with increasing fluency in the 1890s. With a little bit of revision and the addition of a few more he could easily put together a book of poems, and Hardy's professionalism as a literary man with a living to earn had not diminished. He and Emma did not take a house in London for the 1897 Season because it was the sixtieth anniversary of Victoria's accession to the throne, and they wanted to escape 'the racket' of the Diamond Jubilee celebrations. Instead they took a holiday in Switzerland and read about the London celebrations 'in the snowy presence of a greater Queen (the Jungfrau), the maiden-monarch that dominated the whole place' (*Life*, p. 311). It was on this holiday that the ideas for the poems 'The Schreckhorn: with Thoughts of Leslie Stephen' (*C.P.*, 73), about Gibbon entitled 'Lausanne' (*C.P.*, 72), and about the deaths on the Matterhorn in 1865, 'Zermatt: To the Matterhorn' (*C.P.*, 73) came to him. Michael Millgate tells us much about Hardy's greatness as a poet when he writes about 'the trenchant simplicity of his assumption that poetry was an entirely natural medium of human experience and, as such, entirely appropriate to almost any human situation' (Millgate, p. 474).

In August they were back in England and visiting Wells and Salisbury Cathedrals. Salisbury was a place, he said, 'in which he was never tired of sojourning, partly from personal associations and partly because its graceful cathedral pile was the most marked instance in England of an architectural intention carried out to the full' (*Life*, p. 314). He walked around the Close late at night and standing by the west front 'watched the moonlight creep round upon the statuary of the facade. . . . Upon the whole the Close of Salisbury is as beautiful a scene as any I know in England – or . . . elsewhere' (*Life*, p. 314). It inspired the poem 'The Cathedral Facade at Midnight' (*C.P.*, 667) and it may have been about this time that he wrote 'The Impercipient: At a Cathedral Service' (*C.P.*, 44). And in the Bible given him by Emma in 1899, so anxious to bring him back into the Church, he later wrote alongside Jeremiah 6:4 ('For the day goeth away, the shadows of the evening are stretched out') 'Salisbury Cathedral, E.L.H. and T.H. Aug. 1897' He was then 57 and the third phase of his life was about to begin. He had begun the second phase in 1870 an unknown; he ended it in 1897, after twenty-eight years of life packed with incident and hard work, a great and famous novelist. His rise to fame was slow but when it came with *Tess* almost as rapid as that of Dickens had been with *Pickwick*. Could he now establish himself as a great poet?

Phase the Third: The Poet
(1898–1928)

Hardy's first book of verse was published in December 1898 with a title which showed him still exploiting the Wessex connection, *Wessex Poems*. In fact, they are not particularly about Wessex (several of them are about the Napoleonic war) and the fifty-one poems are a strange assortment. Only four had been published previously. Sixteen of them had been written in the 1860s, had somehow survived the peregrinations of those early years of their marriage, and now appeared possibly with some revision. The remainder had been mostly written in the 1890s as Hardy slowly began to think again of himself as primarily a poet. One problem faced by an editor of Hardy's poems is his habit of sometimes sitting on a poem for years without publishing it. The poems of the 1860s were not published then because no one would publish them but this was not so from 1898 onwards, and yet Hardy still did not publish all those poems which had been accumulating in his bottom drawer. In his final posthumous book of verse of 1928 we find poems dated 'October 1866 (recopied)', 'November 1868', '1884', '19 November 1898' and '17 December 1901'. It is sometimes possible to guess at the reason for this delay. The joyful and lyrical 'When I set out for Lyonnesse' (*C.P.*, 254) is dated 1870 and was almost certainly written at that time, but it was not given to the public until 1914. Probably, as he looked at the poems available for the 1898 volume, he put it on one side because the first fine careless rapture of the meeting with Emma seemed to have died so completely, but with her death in 1912 the old love returned and he published it at the first opportunity. It is ironic to think that Emma may never have seen the poem she had inspired.

In his Preface to *Wessex Poems* Hardy referred to the 'pieces' as being 'in a large degree dramatic or personative in conception', and he provided more than thirty pen and ink drawings. In the Preface

138

these are described as 'rough sketches . . . recently made and . . . are inserted for personal and local reasons rather than for their intrinsic qualities.' Hardy's use of the word 'personal' is interesting because of its autobiographical connotations. There is, as we have seen, a great deal of Hardy in the novels, but there is even more in the poetry because for Hardy poetry was a very personal form of expression. In *The Life* he quotes Leslie Stephen's comment, 'The ultimate aim of the poet should be to touch our hearts by showing his own . . .' and adds, 'That Hardy adhered pretty closely to this principle when he resumed the writing of poetry cannot be denied' (p. 131). Certainly, no poet followed Sir Philip Sidney's Muse's instruction, 'look in thy heart and write' more than did Hardy. More than 150 of the poems in the *Complete Poems* begin with 'I' and he shares with his readers his deepest feelings and his wide experience of life. Often the event in his life which has led to the poem is identifiable (he liked to tell us where and when), but there are poems which are intensely personal and which leave us guessing about the autobiographical details. Some of these, like 'Wessex Heights', are deliberately enigmatic and biographers can guess but never be certain. So much of the material that would have answered our questions went up in flames in the bonfires on the Max Gate lawn before and after Hardy's death. At least one biographer, Robert Gittings, seemed unable to forgive Hardy for being so unhelpful, and he lambasted him for his 'clumsy writing of autobiography', 'ego-centricity', 'touchiness', 'perpetual adolescence', 'lack of confidence', 'secretiveness', 'close-fistedness', 'suspiciousness' and for being attracted to women! As very many of the hundreds of visitors to Max Gate described him as friendly, kind, hospitable, modest and with a sense of humour, one can only wonder why Gittings ignored this evidence. Here, for example, is just one of many appreciative accounts of visiting Max Gate. The American professor and critic, William Lyon Phelps, called on Hardy in 1900 without a previous appointment, was invited to tea and had a long talk. Hardy, he said, was 'exceedingly gracious, kindly, and sympathetic', and thought his poems far superior to any of his novels. Invited to return the next day for tea, he did so and found Hardy,

> almost covered with cats. Three or four cats were on various parts of his person, other cats were near at hand, and I noticed saucers of milk placed at strategic points in the shrubbery. 'Are all these your own cats?' 'Oh dear, no, some of them are, and

some are cats who come regularly to have tea, and some are still other cats, not invited by us, but which seem to find out about this time of day that tea will be going.'

He goes on, 'Mr Hardy was even more genial on this afternoon. . . . He was kindness itself, and seemed to be in almost radiant humour. We stayed two hours, and we shall never forget such kindness and hospitality' (*Autobiography*, pp. 389–95). Gittings quotes the piece about the cats but omits every other reference to the good side of Hardy's character.

Wessex Poems is a strange hotch-potch of a book, uneven in quality and covering a wide range of subject matter and mood, but it is inescapable that the best poems in it, and they are every bit as good as anything he was to write later, are all intensely personal. 'Neutral Tones' (*C.P.*, 9) is dated 1867. It is about the sorrows of love and ends,

> Since then, keen lessons that love deceives,
> And wrings with wrong, have shaped to me
> Your face, and the God-curst sun, and a tree,
>   And a pond edged with greyish leaves.

We don't know how much of this was written in 1867 and how much revision, if any, took place thirty years later. We don't know, although we can guess, who the couple are who stand 'by a pond that winter day'. But that does not matter. What does matter is that here we have a moving picture of disillusion expressed in terse and economic word and image. Hardy was to write nothing better. And 'The Impercipient' (*C.P.*, 44) is a painful exploration of his loss of religious faith and a criticism of the 'faithful' for *their* criticism of him when they should be showing him 'Christian charity' and sympathy in his loss. Stinsford (Mellstock) churchyard provides the location for one of his most anthologised poems, 'Friends Beyond' (*C.P.*, 36), and enables him to contemplate the midnight whisperings of both real characters like Lady Susan who had lived in Stinsford House and his own fictitious character from *Under the Greenwood Tree*, William Dewy. The real and the imaginary were always close to each other in Hardy's mind. At least one other poem is among his greatest – 'I Look into My Glass'. This is another of those short, powerful, economic poems in which he excelled, a lament for the ageing of the body while the emotions remain as strong as ever.

The loneliness of the line 'By friends grown cold to me' reveals something of his feelings in the late 1890s when this poem must have been written. Was one of these friends Mrs Henniker?

Hardy had not expected the reception of *Wessex Poems* to be good, and it wasn't. Writing to Gosse about a fortnight after publication he said:

> Well: the poems were lying about, and I did not quite know what to do with them. Considering that the Britisher resents a change of utterance, instrument, even of note, I do not expect a particularly gracious reception of them. It is difficult to let people who think I have made a fresh start know that to indulge in rhymes was my original weakness, and the prose only an afterthought. (*C.L.*, 2, p. 208)

For *The Saturday Review* (7 January 1899) this was 'a curious and wearisome volume' containing 'many slovenly, slipshod, uncouth verses, stilted in sentiment, poorly conceived and worse wrought', while in America the Chicago *Dial* (16 April 1899) saw the poems as no more than 'the literary diversion' of a novelist. Hardy spent a great deal of the rest of his life making the point that for him it was the novels which had been the diversion from what had been his true aim of being a poet. Thinking the book would lose money, he had told the publishers, Harper Bros, that he was willing to pay the cost of publication so that they would not be out of pocket. Harpers expressed themselves willing to take the risk, and risk it proved to be. The first edition of 500 copies seems to have taken three or four years to sell out, as a reprint was not required until 1903. Hardy was never to earn from his poetry even a modest living. With his gift for seeing parallels, one wonders whether he saw the similarity between the fate of his first published novel and that of *Wessex Poems*.

Although Hardy was not as upset by the reviews of *Wessex Poems* – and most of them had been friendly and respectful – as he was nearly thirty years earlier by the reviews of *Desperate Remedies*, he still thought it necessary to hit back at the obtuseness of some of his critics. The reviewers were obsessed by their assumption that 'novel-writing was Hardy's trade, and no other'. They had failed to realise the 'solidarity of all the arts' and completely overlooked his 'born sense of humour'. By not being 'imitative', by not being obviously influenced by poets like Wordsworth, Tennyson and Browning, he had forfeited his chance of being taken seriously. What had been regarded as ignorance of form or technical ability resulted from their inability to discern that 'the author loved the art of concealing art'. Hardy was to write nothing more important than this about his art as a poet, and it ends 'He had written his poems entirely because he liked doing them, without any ulterior thought; because he wanted to say the things they contained and would contain – mainly the philosophy of life afterwards developed in *The Dynasts* (*Life*, pp. 319–25).

The Hardys once again went to London for the 1898 Season and he spent some time at the British Museum Library reading about Napoleon and his wars in further preparation for his writing of *The Dynasts*. Listening to the orchestra of the Scala, Milan, at the Imperial Institute one afternoon, he wrote the note, 'Rain floating down in wayward drops. Not a soul except myself having tea in the gardens. The west sky begins to brighten. The red, blue, and white fairy lamps are like rubies, sapphires, turquoises, and pearls in the wet. The leaves of the trees, not yet of full size, are dripping, and the waiting-maids stand in a group with nothing to do. Band playing a "Contemplazione" by Luzzi' (*Life*, p. 317). In July, back in Max Gate, he became an ardent cyclist and either with Emma or his brother visited a great many places, including Bristol, Gloucester, Cheltenham, Sherborne, Poole and Weymouth.

The invaluable *Collected Letters of Thomas Hardy* show Hardy as writing an average of about thirty-four letters a year in the 1880s and about seventy-two letters a year in the 1890s. However, these figures must be handled with caution, because no one knows how many letters may have been destroyed or are still concealed in private hands. Moreover, with Hardy's growing fame the recipients of his letters, recognising their potential value, were more likely to preserve them. Hardy must have written many letters to his father and mother but not one survives. What we can say fairly certainly is that Hardy did have a large correspondence and that as almost all his letters are written by him in longhand, a considerable amount of his time was devoted to letter-writing. By the 1890s he was being pestered by letters asking him to autograph copies of his books, lecture, answer queries, serve on committees, and, most time-consuming of all, read and comment on other people's books. He told Middleton Murry in the 1920s that for a long time he had tried to answer every letter he received but he had had to give up. 'He was sorry, but it was impossible.' The *Collected Letters* show how professional he was in the last forty years of his life in defending himself against what would have been an insufferable burden. A typical reply thanks the donor for the book of verse, mentions one or two poems, and looks forward to reading the whole book later. Occasionally, one wonders whether that cold or sore throat which won't allow Hardy to accept an invitation is just an excuse of the kind that all busy writers have to make. The exploitation of him in the later years by hungry autograph hunters particularly annoyed him and he is reported at times to have agreed to sign his books only in return for a contribution to the local hospital. What better cause! James Stephens tells a story of W. B. Yeats asking Hardy what he did with books sent to him for autographing, and Hardy showed him an attic room packed to the ceiling with such books. 'Yeats,' said Hardy, 'these are the books that were sent to me for signature.' There was something of the Dorset countryman's toughness about Hardy which gave him some protection.

Hardy's fame also meant that more and more artists and photographers were anxious for him to sit for them. In 1894 William Strang had done the first of what were to be more than a dozen drawings, paintings and etchings of Hardy made by him during the following thirty years. That first drawing was the frontispiece of what was to be the first full-length book on Hardy's works – Lionel Johnson's *The Art of Thomas Hardy*. In the 1890s and early 1900s there were paintings of him by William Rothenstein and Jaques-Émile Blanche, and the best-known painting of all, that by Augustus John, was painted in 1923. Of this he is supposed to have said 'I don't know whether that is how I look or not – but that is how I *feel*' (*Life*, p. 471). Of the sculptors the most significant was Hamo Thornycroft who had met Hardy as early as 1883 and remained a firm friend for the rest of his life. His head of Hardy was made in 1915 and is now in the National Portrait Gallery. Hamo's beautiful wife, Agatha, was, as mentioned earlier, an inspiration to Hardy in his creation of Tess. Rothenstein described Hardy as modest and said that he 'commanded all one's affections'. He had, he said, much in common with painters like John Crome. Hardy had told him that he resented being called a pessimist and that 'had he told the truth about village life no-one would have believed him' (*Men and Memories*, 1932, p. 165). It is all very well for modern, Marxist critics in comfortable and secure academic posts to take Hardy to task for not depicting the poverty, hardship and cruelty of life among the agricultural workers of the period about which he was writing but to have concentrated

on this would have meant not being published and having to give
up his career as a writer. He had learnt a lesson from the rejection
of *The Poor Man and the Lady* and his approach to the problems of
the day was much more subtle.

In 1899 they were again in London for the Season where they
took a flat for about two months. While there he met A. E. Housman
whose *Shropshire Lad* he admired, and he visited Swinburne and
commented on his almost childlike manner. He greatly enjoyed a
midnight visit by lantern-light to Westminster Abbey which was
arranged for him and some friends by the Dean's daughter. On his
return from London there was a great deal of cycling and, often
accompanied by Emma, he would cover up to fifty miles a day.

About this time he met and became friendly with Hermann Lea
who shared his hatred of cruelty to animals, love of Dorset, and
compassion for humankind. He was an expert photographer and
Hardy's regard for him was such that several years later he worked
with him on a book which gave a great deal of the topographical
background to Hardy's works and was generously illustrated with
photographs. Called *Thomas Hardy's Wessex*, it was first published
in 1913. The object of the book, said Hermann Lea in his introduction,
was 'to depict the Wessex country of Thomas Hardy, with a view to
discovering the real places which served as bases for the descriptions of scenery and backgrounds given us in the novels and poems'.
Hermann Lea continually refers to Hardy's kindness of nature, his
comprehensive outlook on life, and his generosity. They cycled
together around Dorset and when Lea bought himself a car in 1914
he often took Hardy and his wife out with him, once going as
far as Torquay and back in a day. These outings lasted until 1916,
when petrol rationing brought them to a close. In 1915 they made
thirty-six tours in the car and Lea emphasised that Hardy always
insisted on paying all the expenses incurred.

On the outbreak of the Boer War in October 1899 Hardy deplored
the fact that so-called civilised countries still had to resort to such bar-
barous means to settle disputes. However, he was caught up in the
excitement to such an extent that on 20 October he cycled to Southampton to see the troops embark and the troopships sail. He also
witnessed the departure of the Battery of Artillery from Dorchester
Barracks in November, and from these events came several poems,
'Embarcation' and 'The Going of the Battery' being among them.
Hardy's attitude to war was a strange mixture of horror and sadness,
fascination and repulsion. He wrote to Mrs Henniker's husband,

who was about to leave for South Africa in command of a battalion of the Guards, an effusive letter saying that 'I have long thought you the most perfect type of practical soldier' (*C.L.*, 2, p. 233), at the same time as he was writing one of his greatest poems 'Drummer Hodge', a poem which transcends the blimpishness of war and is suffused with a cosmic compassion. The war was forecast to last three months: Hardy thought, correctly, that it would last three years. In 1914 he thought, contrary to public opinion, that the war would last for several years and be 'an untold disaster', and again he was right. No doubt there were those who thought he was a pessimist. A realist would be a more accurate description.

Emma's annoyance with her husband grew throughout the 1890s and was aggravated by his friendship with yet another aristocratic beauty anxious to make a name for herself as a writer. She was Mrs (later Lady) Agnes Grove, the daughter of the remarkable archaeologist General Pitt-Rivers. He met her at an open-air dance in the gardens of her father's estate in 1895, and he was never to forget the occasion and how he started the country-dances with Lady Agnes as his partner. It was, he said, the last occasion 'he ever trod a measure'. She was anxious to succeed in journalism and Hardy was soon helping his 'good little pupil' to write and get published. A woman of powerful personality, she appealed particularly to Hardy not only because of her looks but because she was a suffragette, a political Liberal and in sympathy with his own views. She was, like Mrs Henniker, happily married and she had three children but this did nothing to quell Hardy's enthusiasm. Volume 2 of the *Collected Letters* shows him writing her thirty letters between November 1895 and April 1900, and when she died in 1926 he wrote a poem 'Concerning Agnes', and the letters and the poem reveal a strong emotional attachment. Remembering the past, he wrote

> I could not, though I should wish, have over again
>   That old romance,
> And sit apart in the shade as we sat then
>   After the dance
> The while I held her hand . . . (*C.P.*, 862).

In his biography of Agnes, Desmond Hawkins concludes that 'Hardy, with his exceptional susceptibility to the latent powers in woman, responded to the wayward streak of originality in her, the panache, the restless striving' (*Concerning Agnes*, p. 140). There is little evidence that any of Hardy's 'pupils' responded to the restless strivings in *him*.

Poor Hardy – and poor Emma! Now approaching sixty she must have been aware of Hardy's interest in these beautiful, younger women and of his interest in their writing when he showed so little interest in hers. But no matter how jealous she was, it is difficult to excuse her constant criticism of her husband to other people. When Kenneth Grahame's wife, Elspeth, wrote to Emma in 1899 asking for advice about her marriage, Emma responded with a letter which included the following:

> I can scarcely think that love proper and enduring, is in the nature of man . . . and at fifty a man's feelings too often take a new course altogether Eastern ideas of matrimony secretly pervade his thoughts, and he wearies of the most perfect, and suitable, wife chosen in his earlier life . . . Keeping separate a good deal is a wise plan in crises – and being both free – and *expecting little* neither gratitude, nor attentions, love, nor *justice* . . . If he belongs to the public in any way, years of devotion count for nothing. (Bodleian MS, Eng. Misc. d.530. English uncorrected)

This sad mixture of bitterness, jealousy and stupidity – and visitors to Max Gate had described her as 'not remarkable for intelligence' and 'absurd, inconsequent' and 'rambling' – indicates how remarkably patient and long-suffering Hardy had to be during the final years of her life. She must at times have seemed like a child to him and, indeed, she had never really grown up.

Undeterred by the poor reception of *Wessex Poems*, Hardy published his second book of verse with the title *Poems of the Past and the Present* in November 1901. It contained ninety-nine poems, many of which had been written in the three-year interval. Two are dated in the 1860s and thirteen had been published previously in newspapers and journals, an indication of a rising interest in his work as a poet. One of these had been written for *The Times* on the death of Queen Victoria in January 1901 and was the first of about a dozen of his poems which were to appear there later. There is a group of eleven 'War Poems' written by him about the Boer War, and another eleven are grouped together with the title 'Poems of Pilgrimage'. These mainly result from his visit to Italy in 1887 and to Switzerland in 1897, but it is not clear just when they were written, and one is left asking the question, why, if they were written before 1898, didn't he publish them in *Wessex Poems*? Most of the poems come under the title 'Miscellaneous' and this is just what they are, ranging from philosophic poems about such matters as God's failure to look after the world he had created, to poems about women in his life like Lizbie Brown, the girl he had fallen madly in love with as an adolescent, and Mrs Henniker with whom he had fallen in love in his fifties. There are several poems about the suffering of animals and a number of ballad-like, storytelling pieces of verse which are, except for a few lines, little better than potboilers. There is little humour except for that in 'The Ruined Maid', quite undeservedly the most quoted of all Hardy's poems. In it Hardy cleverly mocks the accepted view that all prostitutes end in the Thames, and as he places it in the volume after 'The Levelled Churchyard' with its 'We late-lamented, resting here/ Are mixed to human jam' and before 'The Respectable Burgher' which mocks a great deal of Biblical belief, Hardy really is enjoying himself. And as there was no outcry from the keepers of the nation's morals about such outrageous comments Hardy was proved to be correct when he claimed that you could say in verse what you could not easily say in prose. The reviews were, in fact, quite good. Sir George Douglas in *The Bookman* thought that it very much surpassed its predecessor. *The Academy* described it as a very remarkable book, and *The Saturday Review*, although it echoed complaints that Hardy's verse was harsh and unmusical, thought that almost every poem had something to say with an 'arresting quality'. There was now more interest in Hardy as a poet and the first edition of 500 copies was soon sold out and followed by a second printing of the same size within a few weeks.

It is a sombre view of life which emerges from *Poems of the Past and the Present*, with the greatest of its poems – 'Drummer Hodge', 'To an Unborn Pauper Child', 'A Broken Appointment', 'The Superseded', 'The Darkling Thrush', 'Tess's Lament', and the three *In Tenebris* poems – marked by a sad melancholy. Hardy to some extent protected himself against the expected cries of 'pessimist' by his line in *In Tenebris II*, 'Who holds that if way to the Better there be, it exacts a full look at the Worst', and he made a note in January 1902 which reads 'Pessimism (or rather what is called such) is, in brief, playing the sure game. You cannot lose at it; you may gain. It is the only view of life in which you can never be disappointed' (*Life*, p. 333). In February 1901 he had given a long interview to William Archer and once again he defended himself against criticism of his pessimism. 'But my pessimism, if pessimism it be, does not involve the assumption that the world is going to the dogs. . . . On the contrary, my practical philosophy is distinctly meliorist. What are my books but one plea against "man's inhumanity to man" – to woman – and to the lower animals? Whatever may be the inherent good or evil of life, it is certain that man makes it much worse than it need be' (Wm Archer, *Real Conversations*).

That he was beginning serious work about now on *The Dynasts* may be evidenced by his writing of the poem 'One We Knew' in May 1902, with its reference to his grandmother's recollection of the Napoleonic wars. He was contemplating breaking his connection with Harper Brothers, the American publishers who had taken over Osgood, McIlvaine's business, and the sale of all Hardy's books except *Under the Greenwood Tree*, the copyright of which was still owned by Chatto. It was now more than thirty years since *The Poor Man and the Lady* had been rejected by Macmillan, and he must have had a feeling of triumph when it became clear that Macmillan would be honoured to become his main publisher. They took over the plates which had been used for the Osgood, McIlvaine Wessex Novels Edition, which they had already made use of for their Colonial Library edition of some of the novels, and, allowing Hardy to make a small number of revisions provided there was no repagination, began the publication in 1903 of what they called the Uniform Edition.

Hardy's problems with Mrs Grundy were still not quite over and at the end of April 1903 *The Cornhill* rejected the poem 'A Tramp-woman's Tragedy' because it was too outspoken. He was in London again that summer and one evening he and Clement Shorter and Clodd made a late-night visit to Madame Tussaud's waxworks as guests of the proprietor and 'pranced about' with Hardy wearing 'the Waterloo cocked hat'. Hardy was now a member of two exclusive London clubs, the Savile and the Athenaeum and met many of his friends there. He took Emma's niece, Lilian, to the Royal Academy *soirée*, a function he went to almost every year. Emma was not at all well and that year spent very little time in London. Later in the year, accompanied by Lilian and leaving Hardy at Max Gate, Emma made the first of several trips to France, perhaps her attempt to show her independence. His letters to her are friendly, even paternal in their kindly instructions to avoid catching cold and keep enough money for the return journey.

Hardy finished what was to be the first part of *The Dynasts* in September and it was in print by December and published early in

1904. The reviews were generally unfavourable. In *The Saturday Review* Max Beerbohm thought that Hardy should have written it in prose, John Buchan in *The Spectator* described it as 'the work of a poet, but rarely poetry', Harold Child in *The Times Literary Supplement* couldn't understand the concept of a play intended only for reading, and the New York *Tribune* described it as 'a fearsome hybrid, lacking all unity and charm'. Hardy expressed some doubt about continuing with the project but underneath the diffidence there was a determined man and for the next four years he worked away steadily at what he called his 'epic-drama'. Part II was published in 1906 to somewhat more favourable reviews, and when Part III came out in 1908 it was received with enthusiasm, Harold Child in a front-page article in the *Times Literary Supplement* now seeing it as 'A great work of art': 'Mr Hardy has achieved a work of art by doing violence to a form, and has sublimated a vast and infinitely various material into a single shapely whole. For a like achievement we can only go back to one thing – the historical plays of Shakespeare'. Hardy was delighted with the acclaim he received on the completion of his vast work 'in three parts, nineteen acts and one hundred and thirty scenes'. It established him as a major poet and it sold extremely well. Hardy was already receiving a 25 per cent royalty on his novels in the Uniform Edition and for *The Dynasts* he even asked Macmillan for a 33 per cent royalty if sales reached 8000. He would have been delighted, too, that a work, which could be said to have been begun in his childhood fifty years before with his reading of *A History of the Wars*, 'a periodical in loose numbers of the war with Napoleon, which his grandfather had subscribed to at the time' (*Life*, p. 21), had come to a successful conclusion.

Harold Orel in his valuable introduction to the New Wessex edition of *The Dynasts* calls it 'an extraordinary work'. 'It took,' he says, 'more time to prepare for, and to write, than any other work in Hardy's career. It was undoubtedly his most ambitious undertaking. Its thirty separate rhyme schemes illustrate his command of prosody on a very generous scale. It contains the most explicit statement of his philosophical views about man's relationship to the universe', and 'it was immediately recognised as the greatest imaginative treatment by an English author of the Napoleonic Wars'. When on his birthday in 1921 Hardy received a Keats first edition and an address signed by 106 younger writers, it concluded, 'We thank you, Sir, for all you have written . . . but most of all, perhaps, for *The Dynasts*.' Sadly, it is little-read today, possibly because modern 'culture' is made up of so-called 'sound-bites', and a work on the scale of *The Dynasts* demands too much concentration and commitment. Perhaps the availability now of two finely edited editions – those of Harold Orel (Macmillan) and Samuel Hynes (Oxford University Press) – will help to remind the serious reader that it remains a majestic work of the creative imagination, notable, to quote Orel again, for its 'anger at the futility of war' and 'compassion for the defenceless and defeated'. Commenting on different interpretations, Hynes makes the valuable point that 'a great work shapes itself to history's occasions', and he concludes, 'Critics have found things to criticise in all of its parts – its verse, its language, its length, its spirit world – but they have also acknowledged its huge impressiveness, comparing it to a snow-covered mountain peak, and to Stonehenge. And it is something like that – irregular, imperfect perhaps, but massive, mysterious, brooding, an English epic, perhaps the last one.' It ends with just a note of hope that Consciousness will inform the Will, 'till it fashion all things fair'. Hardy at this time was still thinking of himself as an evolutionary meliorist.

Hardy was now in his sixties, and more and more of his friends and relations were 'going down into silence'. Emma's sister, Helen, whom Hardy had met in 1870 at the St Juliot Rectory, died in 1900, and two of her brothers in 1904. In April 1904 Hardy's mother died at the age of 91. It was a grievous loss for Hardy who had always been so close to her. 'She had been', said Hardy in *The Life*, 'a woman with an extraordinary store of local memories reaching back to the days when the ancient ballads were everywhere heard at country feasts, in weaving shops, and at spinning-wheels; and her good taste in literature was expressed by the books she selected for her children in circumstances in which opportunities for selection were not numerous' (p. 345). Emma did not attend her funeral. Another death in 1904 was that of Leslie Stephen who had been a friend of Hardy's since the 1870s, and in 1909 Swinburne and Meredith died within a month of each other. Hardy had never forgotten the excitement he had experienced when he first read Swinburne's *Poems and Ballads* in 1866, or Swinburne's comment to him on the amusement he had felt when he had seen a paragraph in a newspaper: 'Swinburne planteth, Hardy watereth, and Satan giveth the increase.' In March 1910 he visited Swinburne's grave on the Isle of Wight and 'gathered a spray of ivy and laid it on the grave of that brother-poet of whom he never spoke save in words of admiration and affection' (*Life*, p. 349). Hardy had known Meredith for forty years and paid

him a handsome tribute in his poem 'George Meredith' which he
wrote in time for it to appear in *The Times* on the day of the funeral.
A similar tribute was paid to Swinburne in 'A Singer Asleep'. Hardy
was an exceptionally competent, often very good, occasional poet.
That he was passed over for the appointment of Poet Laureate in
1913 is a measure of how much of a threat to moral standards he
was thought to be by the Establishment, which preferred the now
almost forgotten Robert Bridges.

But honours were now being conferred on Hardy. In 1905 he
received the first of several honorary degrees when he was given
an LL.D. at Aberdeen University. In London for the Season he was
still as active as ever, reading at the British Museum Library for
days at a time, going to concerts at the Queen's Hall and afternoon
services at St Paul's, visiting the Gosses and meeting Max Beerbohm,
W. B. Yeats and Henry James, and having tea at the House of Lords
as a guest of Gosse, who was now its Librarian, with Lord Salisbury
and other nobles and politicians. Very much of the same programme
of concerts, dinners, plays and social calls interspersed with work
at the British Museum was followed in 1906 when they were again
in London for about three months. Soon after his return to Max
Gate he was off on a tour with Henry, his brother, of Lincoln, Ely
and Canterbury, and then, on his return there were cycle-tours in
Dorset and Somerset. It was a full life, and there is every reason
to believe that Hardy was enjoying it. Nothing pleased him more
than writing poetry which he seemed to be able to do at any time
and anywhere. Those exhausting days of novel-writing were past,
he was a wealthy man, and his literary success was now beyond
question. Men and women of distinction sought his company, and
one woman of very little distinction had begun to make a considerable impression on him. It goes without saying that she was an
aspiring writer.

There is no certainty as to exactly how Florence Emily Dugdale
first met Hardy. Michael Millgate points out that she 'seems to have
given different accounts to different people', one being that she was
introduced by Florence Henniker in 1905. However, there is no
other evidence that the two Florences had met by then. What we do
know is that Hardy had received a letter from her in August 1905
asking for an interview with him. A letter from him to her dated 2
January 1906 makes it clear that the visit had taken place shortly
before. He thanks her for some flowers she has sent and concludes
'I do not think you stayed at all too long, and hope you will come

again some other time' (*C.L.*, 3, p. 193). The first mention of her in *The Life* is not until 1910 when we are told that among the visitors to Max Gate in the autumn of 1910 was 'Miss Dugdale, a literary friend of Mrs Hardy at the Lyceum Club, whose paternal ancestors were Dorset people dwelling near the Hardys, and had intermarried with them some 130 years earlier' (p. 378). This is deliberately obfuscating as she was a friend of Hardy's long before she became 'a literary friend' of Emma's, and the family relationship was tenuous in the extreme.

The Dugdales were a middle-class family living in Enfield, and the father, a headmaster, had five daughters of whom Florence, born in 1879, was the second. She was shy, quiet and so melancholy and sad about life that she could be moody and depressive. At one time she had intended to become a teacher but her poor health and inability to get on with the working-class children made her unsuitable for such a career and she tried without much success to earn her living as a writer. Her first and only real love was for a writer called Alfred Hyatt who worked hard to overcome a physical handicap and illness by journalistic work and compiling anthologies. One of these was *The Pocket Thomas Hardy*, published in 1906, and it may well have figured in the first contacts between Hardy and Florence. When Hyatt died in 1911 Florence described him as 'more to me than anything else in the world'. She would, she wrote to a friend in December 1914, 'gladly have given the rest of her life for one brief half-hour' with him. She had then been married to Hardy for nearly a year.

Florence was not a particularly good-looking woman but she had charm and Hardy's attraction to her had grown steadily after that first meeting in 1905. The annual visits to London provided them with opportunities for meeting and there was something about her that appealed to his paternal instinct. It was now more than ten years since his passions had been aroused by Florence Henniker and the hey-day in the blood was subsiding. Florence Dugdale was nearly forty years his junior but she admired his work and no doubt he was flattered by the interest in him of this young lady in her mid-twenties. He sent her two photographs of himself in September 1906 and shortly afterwards she was helping him with his work on Part III of *The Dynasts* by doing 'research' for him in the British Museum. By the spring of 1907 he is showing concern for her health. She mustn't go to the reading room on his behalf as it 'is just the place for you to catch a new influenza . . . and I should never forgive myself if you were to get it on my account' (*C.L.*, 3, p. 249). In April he suggests a meeting at the South Kensington Museum and in July he attempted unsuccessfully to get work for her with Macmillan and *The Daily Mail*. In September he used his influence with the *Cornhill* Editor to get her short story, 'The Apotheosis of the Minx' published and Hardy's part in writing the story is inescapable. In 1908 he was in London for the Season by himself, as Emma had not been well, but his attempts to get her to stay in Dorset even when she had recovered may result from his desire to be unhampered in his meetings with Florence rather than from a genuine concern for Emma. By 1909 the desire to spend time with Florence had become such that, somewhat indiscreetly, he asked his friend, Edward Clodd, to invite her to one of his Aldeburgh weekends and they were both there together in August and on several later occasions.

Of Hardy's affection for Florence there can be no doubt. He needed her companionship and with no reason to believe that Emma would die he had moments of depression and frustration which led to subterfuge and deception which must have worried him. It is unlikely that anything sexual occurred between them because, as Robert Gittings says in *The Second Mrs Hardy*, 'Florence . . . remained a true Victorian where sex was concerned.' Acknowledging a book sent by Marie Stopes, 'she was embarrassed and apologetic, "pray forgive me, I don't much appreciate the love-making, a lack of real feeling on my part, I suppose." ' There seems just a possibility that some closer association was contemplated in 1909 when a novelist called Netta Syrett met Florence at the Lyceum Club. Florence, described in Netta Syrret's book as Hardy's secretary, told her that she was looking for a *pied-à-terre* in London for Hardy and asked whether he could rent her rooms while Netta was in Italy. She was subsequently introduced to Hardy at the Club and described him as 'very much taken in hand and "run", I thought, by the efficient, business-like young woman, the hostess of the occasion, and the future Mrs Thomas Hardy. His first wife was still living at the time.' Hardy and Florence visited the rooms at Buckingham Palace Road. 'Hardy seemed pleased with the place and said it would suit him admirably if he should find it possible to live in London for a few months. But of that he was by no means sure' (*The Sheltering Tree*, pp. 194–5). Netta Syrett heard no more and one can only conjecture why. Hardy's love for Florence finds expression, as one might expect, in two poems, 'On the Departure Platform' (*C.P.*, 170) and

'After the Visit' (*C.P.*, 250). The first of these was probably written in 1907 and published in 1909 with no indication of the person depicted:

> We kissed at the barrier; and passing through
> She left me, and moment by moment got
> Smaller and smaller, until to my view
>   She was but a spot;
>
> A wee white spot of muslin fluff
> That down the diminishing platform bore
> Through hustling crowds of gentle and rough
>   To the carriage door.
>
> Under the lamplight's fitful glowers
> Behind dark groups from far and near,
> Whose interests were apart from ours,
>   She would disappear,
>
> Then show again, till I ceased to see
> That flexible form, that nebulous white;
> And she who was more than my life to me
>   Had vanished quite.

'After the Visit' refers to a visit by Florence to Max Gate in the summer of 1910 and it was first published in *The Spectator* in August 1910 and again there was no reference to Florence. Did Emma, one wonders, if she saw it, recognise the reference to the woman with 'large luminous living eyes' who was weighing up the question of

> what life was,
> And why we were there, and by whose strange laws
>   That which mattered most could not be.

By the time of its next printing in *Satires of Circumstance* Emma was dead and Hardy added under the title '(To F.E.D.)'.

It was desirable whether by design or accident that Emma should meet Florence, and the opportunity arose when in June 1910 Emma gave a talk at the Lyceum Club in London, Florence was introduced to her, praised the talk, and offered to type it out for her. Invited by Emma to their rented flat in Maida Vale, Florence immediately showed her usefulness by pouring out the tea and offering help and flattery. Emma loved it and invited Florence to spend a week at Max Gate where Florence soon became aware of the hostility and tension that existed. Writing to Clodd in November she was able to say, 'I am intensely sorry for her, sorry indeed for both.' Much has been made of the fact that Emma asked Florence whether she had noticed the resemblance of Hardy to the wife-murderer, Dr Crippen, but Emma might have been having her little joke. Emma, so anxious that the world should realise that she, too, was a writer, produced her manuscripts for Florence to read, and Florence in her helpful but possibly ingratiating way offered not just to type them but even to try to find a publisher for them. Of course, she never did, and this was not surprising as so much of Emma's writing was unpublishable. She did, in fact, publish some of her poetry privately and here is a typical piece:

There's a song of a bird in a tree, –
    A song that is fresh, gay, and free,
The voice of a last summer's thrush,
    Shaking out his trills – hush! hush!
'Tis sunshine and rain both together,
    And wind of March weather.

Before the end of the year Hardy had introduced Florence to Florence Henniker as a possible secretary-help and the two women became friends. One wonders if they ever discussed Hardy together and just what thoughts went through Florence Henniker's mind as she became aware, as she must have done, of Hardy's obsessive interest in his young 'assistant'.

While the Florence Dugdale relationship was developing, the Emma relationship was steadily deteriorating, as was her health. In a letter to Clodd in May 1909 Hardy apologised for not being able to 'return hospitalities received' because of 'my domestic circumstances' (*C.L.*, 4, p. 21). Christine Wood Homer describes Emma as becoming 'steadily worse with advancing age'. She 'became very queer and talked curiously' (Toucan Press Monograph). She had always feared and disliked Roman Catholicism and she now began to hand out extreme Protestant booklets to people in Dorchester. In April 1912 she completed a small prose work called 'Spaces' about the 'High Delights of Heaven', a work which Millgate very rightly calls 'the product of a mind at once obsessed, muddled, and naive' (p. 479).

The Florence 'affair' was taking place in the years 1906–12 at a time when Hardy, now in his sixties, was still living a full and active life. During the thirty years of concentration on poetry he seems to have written on average about one poem a fortnight. With the success of *The Dynasts*, more and more journal editors wanted to publish his poems, and some 200 of the 947 poems which now appear in Hardy's *Complete Poems* were first published as contributions to journals and newspapers. Most of those published in *The Times* were occasional poems such as that written on the outbreak of the 1914–18 war, 'Song of the Soldiers'. For several of them, including 'The Oxen', Hardy very generously added the words 'No Copyright reserved' and thus saved anthologists and others considerable sums of money. The fact that *The Times* printed so many of his occasional poems makes it all the sadder that he was never made Poet Laureate. His new publishers Macmillan found the demand for his books such that in 1906 they began the publication of the Pocket Edition which sold in tens of thousands for many years. Simon Gatrell, in his *Hardy the Creator*, gives the sales of Hardy's fiction in the Pocket Edition between 1906 and 1939 as 1 096 150. This was a profitable venture for both Hardy and Macmillan who were able to cut costs by using the plates of the Uniform Edition with a smaller page. On the Continent, too, his works were becoming ever better known with Tauchnitz publishing nearly all his novels in English and writers like Madeleine Rolland, who visited Max Gate in 1907, translating some of the major novels.

In December 1909 *Time's Laughingstocks*, his third book of verse, was published. Seven years had passed since *Poems of the Past and the Present*, and it contains 94 poems of an astonishing variety of subject matter and dating. Eighteen were written before 1900 and of these ten dated back to the 1860s. In his Preface Hardy said that some lines in the early-dated poems had been rewritten, though they had been left substantially unchanged. The print-run for the first edition was 2000, not large but a considerable increase on the two previous volumes. Several narrative poems of considerable power and interest include 'A Trampwoman's Tragedy' which had been refused by the Editor of the *Cornhill* because of its 'not being a poem he could possibly print in a family periodical', and 'A Sunday Morning Tragedy', about an abortion which goes wrong, which was rejected by *The Fortnightly* for the same reason. Ford Madox Ford claimed to have founded *The English Review* so that the latter could be published and it appeared there in December 1908. There are poems about his grandmothers, his mother and father, his wife, his childhood, about Florence Dugdale, and Florence Henniker. With a few exceptions, the standard is good to very good, but few of this collection are among his greatest. 'Panthera', about a second-century legend that Christ was the illegitimate son of a Roman soldier, and 'One Ralph Blossom Soliloquises' about a man who has love-affairs with seven different women, show Hardy still at work 'fluttering the dovecotes'. With *The Dynasts* still fresh in their minds the reviewers were respectful even if they commented on his 'unvarying sadness' and described the poems as 'full of misunderstandings, forebodings, memories, endings, questionings'. For Edward Thomas, 'Mr Hardy looks at things as they are, and what is still more notable he does not adopt the genial consolation that they might be worse, that in spite of them many are happy, and that the unhappy live on and will not die. . . . The moan of his verse rouses an echo that is as brave as a trumpet.' It took a year for the book to reprint.

His selection of the poetry of William Barnes was published in 1908 and enabled him to pay a tribute to a man he had always greatly respected. His Preface reveals him as a singularly perceptive critic, one who saw Barnes not as 'a naif and rude bard who sings only because he must' but as one 'warbling his native wood-notes with a watchful eye on the predetermined score. . . . Primarily spontaneous he was academic closely after.' The Preface also contains that memorable sentence, 'But criticism is so easy, and art so hard.'

Other events of 1908 and 1909 included attending the Milton celebrations at Cambridge in July 1908 and, to his considerable disappointment, just failing to meet Rupert Brooke. However, Rupert Brooke does record meeting him 'at *Comus* time', and remembered him talking all the time about the best manure for turnips. In November there was the first performance by what was to become 'The Hardy Players' of a dramatised version of one of his novels, *The Trumpet-Major*. Keith Wilson, in his useful *Thomas Hardy on the Stage*, describes Hardy's 'unacknowledged fascination' with the theatre. The Hardy Players, who were amateur actors mostly based in Dorchester, continued to produce adaptations of his stories for some twenty years and obtained nation-wide publicity because of the Hardy connection. Hardy himself seemed to enjoy his association with the players, and they gave him an important local source of interest during his closing years. Distinguished guests were invited from London to witness the performances and he helped the Players with advice and even did some re-writing for them. However, when there was adverse criticism of the amateurism of the production and the acting, his attitude towards them became cautiously non-committal.

In 1910 he and Emma went to London for the Season for what was to be the very last time. Age was beginning to tell. While in London he and Emma watched the funeral procession of Edward VII and, shortly after, Hardy received what was to be for him the supreme honour, the award of the Order of Merit. This came after he had turned down the offer of a knighthood in 1908 because he thought 'that any writer who had expressed unpalatable or possibly subversive views on society, religious dogma, currrent morals . . . must feel hampered by accepting honours from any government' (*Life*, p. 352). Emma, who would have loved to be Lady Hardy, regarded him as selfish for turning down the offer. The O.M. is awarded for eminence in any field and is strictly limited to a small number of members. It was conferred on Hardy by George V on 19 July. Emma was suffering from a cold and arranged for Florence to look after him on the important day, and no doubt Miss Dugdale was happy to do so. A further honour followed in November when he received the Freedom of the Borough of Dorchester, something which, he said in his speech on that occasion, he had taken in his writing for a long time.

The very pronounced satirical note which had been obvious in *Time's Laughingstocks* is even more obvious in the eleven 'Satires of Circumstance' which were published in *The Fortnightly Review* in April 1911. Each of these is a short story-poem of between twelve and twenty-two lines describing some such incident as a husband, mortally sick, observing by chance his widow-to-be getting a great deal of pleasure choosing some fashionable mourning clothes. The view of humanity presented here is so jaundiced as to be more like Swift than Hardy. Later in the year he began work on an important new edition of his works, the Wessex Edition. It was a massive undertaking for a man now in his seventies. It required the complete re-reading of all his fiction and involved him in first revising the Uniform Edition which was used as the copy text and then checking all the proofs. His revisions, which were considerable, but not as substantial as those made for the 1895–6 Osgood, McIlvaine Edition, included alterations to the Dorset dialect, a greater explicitness of sexual allusion, and improvements to style and clarity. Once again we see what his second wife called his 'artistic inability to rest content with anything that he wrote until he brought the expression as near to his thought as language would allow' (*Life*, p. 489). In the Wessex Novels Edition of 1895–6 he had added prefaces to the novels as if he couldn't resist commenting on his own novels. For the Wessex Edition, in addition to providing a new map of 'Wessex' for topographical reasons, he revised these prefaces and added to them. Thus, in 1912, he adds to the 1896 Preface to *Under the Greenwood Tree*, which was mainly about the west-gallery musicians and their efforts which 'were really a labour of love', the comment that had it been written later it might have been written in 'a deeper, more essential, more transcendent' way. The Preface to *Tess* adds the information that the 1912 edition contains a few pages about the goings-on at Chaseborough which had not been printed in the novel before, while the Preface to *Jude* has an important addition of several pages headed 'Postscript'. Hardy describes the 'unhappy beginning of *Jude*'s career as a book', his determination as a result to give up novel-writing, the charges against him of his being responsible for the ' "shop-soiled" condition of the marriage theme', the disappointment of one reader who didn't find the book as lubricious as he had hoped, and the belief of another reader that Sue Bridehead 'was the first delineation in fiction of the woman who was coming into notice in her thousands every year – the woman of the feminist movement – the slight, pale "bachelor" girl – the intellectualised, emancipated bundle of nerves that modern conditions were producing ...'. Hardy also felt it necessary to provide a 'General Preface to the Novels and Poems' that is usually printed at the beginning of *Tess*. It begins with the important statement that this is, as far as he is concerned, 'the definitive edition of these productions'. Sadly, in most later editions the word 'definitive' has been misprinted as 'definite' which is a meaningless word in this context. He then spends some time discussing his concept of Wessex and his intention to 'preserve for my own satisfaction a fairly true record of a vanishing life'. There is an explanation – not an entirely convincing one – of his categorising of the novels under the headings, 'Novels of Character and Environment', 'Romances and Fantasies' and 'Novels of Ingenuity', and it is significant that the six great novels are all in the first category. The Preface ends:

It was my hope to add to these volumes of verse as many more as would make a fairly comprehensive cycle of the whole. I had wished that those in dramatic, ballad and narrative form should include most of the cardinal situations which occur in social and public life, and those in lyric form a round of emotional experiences of some completeness. But

The little done, the undone vast!

The more written the more seems to remain to be written; and the night cometh. I realise that these hopes and plans, except possibly to the extent of a volume or two, must remain unfulfilled.

It was to be sixteen years before the night did come, and he was to publish another five books of verse and much of his greatest poetry. Even so he did not quite complete his hope of making his verse into a great epic of human life and relationships; but he only just missed it. What he was to leave us is vast in its range of human feelings and activities. The first two volumes of the new edition were published at 7s. 6d. (about £7 a volume in today's money) in April 1912, and a further two volumes were published each month until there were twenty in all. A further four volumes were added later. On a 25 per cent royalty, Hardy would have been very well rewarded for his painstaking work.

In June, W. B. Yeats and Henry Newbold travelled to Max Gate to present him with the gold Medal of the Royal Society of Literature. At one of Ford Madox Hueffer's parties in London that year he was described as sitting quietly, listening to the pretentious literary talk when an inexplicable hush occurred. Turning to a lady near him he 'remarked with shattering effect, "And how is Johnny's whooping cough?"' (Douglas Goldring, *South Lodge*, p. 33). Hardy was a master of the art of undercutting and the enigmatic joke. Leonard Woolf describes how Hardy told him of an air-raid during the 1914–18 war where there had been gathered together in Barrie's flat in London a group of writers, including, he thought, Barrie, Shaw, Wells and himself:

'A bomb might have fallen on that room', he said. 'Just think! Well, all the chief English writers were there – there wouldn't have been much left of English literature.' It was said with extraordinary simplicity, without the slightest implication that he was himself to be included among the chief English writers in that room, indeed somehow with the implication that he was not to be included. And yet, unless I was entirely mistaken, there was at the same time a tiny, charming twinkle in his eye. (*The Nation*, 21 January 1928)

That charming twinkle in the eye was often missed by those who did not know him well, and what was said humorously or ironically was misunderstood. There was much in Hardy of the dry humour of the Dorset countryman.

Emma died on 27 November 1912. She had aged quickly and had frequently suffered from illnesses which were aggravated by her fear of doctors and refusal to secure professional advice. Her heart had begun to worry her for some months before her death and there were indications of gallstone trouble. As late as mid-November she was able to visit friends near Puddletown, and on 25 November she had tea at Max Gate with some visitors although obviously very unwell. When on the 26th a doctor was called, Emma seems to have been unwilling to let him examine her. On the morning of the 27th a maid went into the bedroom in the attic where Emma had slept by herself for some time and realised that she was seriously ill. Hardy was called but she died very quickly, the cause of death being given as impacted gallstones and heart failure.

Robert Gittings, once again anxious to see the worst in Hardy, made much of the maid's comment that Hardy criticised her for having a crooked collar before he went upstairs to see his dying wife, but maids are notoriously prejudiced witnesses and Hardy had no reason to believe that Emma was dying. If one lives with someone who has been in bad health for a long time the final moment when it comes is never expected and there is no doubt that it came as a shock to him. He could never have expected, either, that he would feel the intense grief which swept over him as he looked back on thirty-eight years of married life which had begun so happily and ended so sadly. That there had been difficulties he could not deny, yet how much of life they had shared together, and even at the end there was some kind of friendship between them. When Emma was buried in Stinsford churchyard a few days later, Hardy's wreath bore the message, 'From her Lonely Husband, with the Old Affection'. He was overcome with the grief that death brings, but for him grief was especially associated with remorse for the wasted years, for the differences which had arisen between them, and for the poignancy that it was once again a case of 'Too Late Beloved'. Among her papers he found diaries written in her latter years which were highly critical of him, and he found what is undoubtedly her best piece of written work, *Some Recollections*. In addition to the description of her first meeting with Hardy which has already been mentioned it contains a moving account of her years in Plymouth, her move to join her sister in St Juliot, and her life in Cornwall before Hardy arrived on the scene. It is a poignant document which in its conclusion must have brought Hardy to tears:

> The day we were married was a perfect September day – 17th, 1874 – not a brilliant sunshine, but wearing a soft, sunny luminousness; just as it should be.
> I have had various experiences, interesting some, sad others, since that lovely day, but all showing that an Unseen Power of great benevolence directs my ways; I have some philosophy and mysticism, and an ardent belief in Christianity and the life beyond this present one, all which makes any existence curiously interesting. As one watches *happenings* (and even if should occur *unhappy happenings*) outward circumstances are of less importance if Christ is our highest ideal. A strange unearthly brilliance shines around our path, penetrating and dispersing difficulties with its warmth and glow. (p. 37)

It is clear that Hardy took upon himself far more of the blame for their troubles than he need have done. Writing to Mrs Henniker on 17 December, Hardy said,

> In spite of the differences between us, which it would be affectation to deny, and certain painful delusions she suffered from at times, my life is intensely sad to me now without her. The saddest moments of all are when I go into the garden and to that long straight walk at the top that you know, where she used to walk every evening just before dusk, the cat trotting faithfully behind her . . . (*C.L.*, 4, p. 243)

It was entirely natural that Hardy should make poetry out of his emotions; pain and suffering were a substantial part of his creative impulse, and in that letter can be seen an incident in one of the earliest poems he was to write about Emma's death, 'The Going'.

> Why do you make me leave the house
> And think for a breath it is you I see

At the end of the alley of bending boughs
Where so often at dusk you used to be;
(*C.P.*, 277)

His poem 'During Wind and Rain' (*C.P.*, 441) is built around
Emma's Plymouth memories and echoes her remark, 'all has been
changed with the oncoming years'. Never having revisited St Juliot
with Emma in all the years of their married life, he now felt im-
pelled to make the journey and 'On March 6 – almost to a day
forty-three years after his first journey to Cornwall – he started for
St Juliot' (*Life*, p. 389). He visited Boscastle, and Pentargon Bay and
Beeny Cliff and once again that astonishingly retentive memory
brought back vivid recollections of the past, of Emma riding her
horse along the cliff, of a drinking-glass lost on a picnic in the
Valency river, of Emma waiting for him in her air-blue gown, and
many more. In the few months after her death he wrote more poems
than he had ever written before in the same space of time. 'Hardy',
he tells us, 'was "in flower" in these days' (*Life*, p. 389), and it is
ironic that it required Emma's death to bring this about. Believing
as he claims to have done that the only form of immortality was that
of being remembered by those still alive, he immortalised Emma in
these poems, maybe as some form of atonement, and he consoled
himself in his grief. As William Cowper so nicely put it, 'He who
cannot look forward in comfort must find what comfort he can in
looking backward.'

Meanwhile, Florence, another form of consolation, was waiting in the wings. For a great deal of the interim between Emma's
death and her marriage to Hardy in February 1914 she was living
at Max Gate, but almost always with a chaperone there in the form
of Kate Hardy or Lilian Gifford, Emma's niece, who with her brother,
Gordon, had spent long periods living at Max Gate since the 1890s.
With the prospect of marriage to this great man now almost a certainty, it is strange that she found it necessary to write a stream of
letters to Clodd complaining about Hardy for being so wrapped up
in memories of Emma. She was, of course, intensely jealous of the
dead woman and showed her own limitations in being so. In
marrying him when he was nearly 74 and she was almost forty
years his junior she had expectations that could not possibly have
been realised. He was astonishingly lively for a man of his age, but
he had no desire to travel the world and even the London Season
was no longer an attraction. He wrote to Gosse on 5 October 1913,

'My excursions this summer have been only into adjoining counties: I get more and more stationary, always asking myself what's
the use of going far, when there is more within a mile of me than
I shall ever comprehend' (*C.L.*, 4, p. 306). Instead of accepting this
and being grateful for her translation from an unknown journalist to the wife of one of the most distinguished men in England,
from a woman of humble means to the mistress of a large house with
a very wealthy husband, she spent far too much time grumbling
moodily about her married life which she had freely chosen. In
fairness to her it must be said that she made Hardy a good house-
keeper and secretary and that she did a great deal to protect him
from the importunities of the public. As if to justify the marriage,
Hardy wrote to Sydney Cockerell, 'We thought it the wisest thing
to do, seeing what a right hand Florence has become to me, and
there is a sort of continuity in it, and not a break, she having known
my first wife so very well' (*C.L.*, 5, p. 9). And of his fondness for
Florence there can be no doubt. In a letter to her of 29 January 1913
we find him saying 'If I once get you here again won't I clutch you
tight', a message which she immediately conveyed to Clodd. It was
as if she had to have some correspondent on whom to pour out her
feelings and for the moment it was Clodd.

1913 saw further honours conferred on him when he was
awarded an honorary degree by Cambridge University and subsequently made an Honorary Fellow of Magdalene College. In October he attended a première of a film of *Tess* and at the end of the
month Macmillan published his final book of fiction, *A Changed Man*.
Hardy was by nature a well-organised and self-disciplined man
who kept a very careful check on his writings and his royalties. After
his unfortunate experience over the contract for *Under the Greewood
Tree* he made himself a shrewd negotiator with the publishing
houses. He had been in at the beginning of the Society of Authors
and was a loyal supporter of it in its efforts to protect the rights of
authors. His poems of the 1860s had been kept carefully for thirty
years or more before they were published, and his short stories written for journal publication were also filed away ready for possible
book publication at some later date. His first two books of short
stories had been so successful that in 1894 he had collected another
nine stories which had been published previously in journals between 1882 and 1893 and published them with the title *Life's Little
Ironies*. It was so successful that it had four reprints in three months.
But it still left Hardy with a further twelve stories which he thought

were hardly worthy of collection. However, he found it difficult to leave anything he had written not earning its full keep and he approached Macmillan in 1913 with the suggestion that they should be published in a book to be called *A Changed Man and Other Tales*. Publication took place on 24 October in an edition of 10 000 copies with simultaneous publication in America where there had always been a demand for Hardy's books. Hardy's modesty once again led to his decrying his writings and he told Florence Henniker that she must not expect much from the stories as most of them had been written long before as mere stop-gaps. His pretext for publishing them was that people were asking for them and pirated editions were appearing in the States, but no doubt tidying-up had something to do with it.

Hardy does not even mention *A Changed Man* in *The Life* but the extracts from letters and notes in this period show him as interested as ever in the 'science of writing'. In June 1912 he observes, 'What should certainly be protested against, in cases where there is no authorisation, is the mixing of fact and fiction in unknown proportions. Infinite mischief would lie in that. . . . The power of getting lies believed about people through that channel after they are dead, by stirring in a few truths, is a horror to contemplate' (*Life*, p. 386). We in the 1990s can bear witness to the truth of that. In September 1913 he writes, 'Thoughts on the recent school of novel-writers. They forget in their insistence on life, and nothing but life, in a plain slice, that a story *must be worth the telling*' (*Life*, p. 391).

Of the two Max Gate maids who were many years later to draw attention to themselves by publicising their not altogether reliable recollections of service there, the more reliable is Nellie Titterington. Quite unreliable is Dolly Gale who was at Max Gate for less than a year in 1914 when she was a mere 15, and sixty years later claimed to remember events which included seeing T. E. Lawrence on his motorcycle seven years before his first visit to Dorset. Ellen (Nellie) Titterington was the Max Gate maid from 1921 until shortly after Hardy's death when she was in her twenties. Talking about her memories some fifty years later she said how delighted she was to be able to avenge old wrongs by criticising her two employers. Such an attitude is not conducive to accuracy and her evidence must be treated with caution. She is far more critical of Florence than of Hardy and describes him as speaking softly, as a man of very great compassion, never angry, looking like a little sparrow hopping about and with his pleasures all in the mind. Florence was difficult to work for, suspicious, and spent large sums of money on clothes and shoes. She also reports Florence as saying to her that when she had married Hardy she had not expected him to live as long as he did.

The months following the marriage were overshadowed by the threat of war. In his study at Max Gate in April Hardy could hear the fleet at gunnery practice in the Channel and he wrote the poem 'Channel Firing' with its final stanza,

> Again the guns disturbed the hour,
> Roaring their readiness to avenge,
> As far inland as Stourton Tower,
> And Camelot, and starlit Stonehenge.
> (*C.P.*, 247)

On 4 August war was declared on Germany. 'It was seldom he had felt so heavy at heart as in seeing his old view of the gradual bettering of human nature . . . completely shattered by the events of 1914 and onwards' (*Life*, p. 395). Most people thought that the war would be over by Christmas, but not Hardy. Horrified at the German invasion of Belgium, he wrote an almost jingoistic poem called 'Men Who March Away' (*C.P.*, 493) in September. Writing to Lady Hoare at Stourhead about this poem, Florence said, 'He asks me to tell you that he scribbled it hastily upon his return from church on Sunday last (where we had an awful sermon from a drivelling curate). Indeed he wrote the main part of the poem while we were at dinner. Bad for his digestion doubtless!' It seems that Hardy not only thought that poetry could be written about anything, and, as 'An August Midnight' shows, written at any time, but that it could be written anywhere!

Lady Hoare had known Hardy since 1910 and described her friendship with him as being 'of the greatest and most valued interest and happiness'. Emma had written some very unpleasant comments about Hardy to her which Lady Hoare dealt with tactfully and courteously and now she began to receive complaints about Hardy from wife No. 2. Florence's correspondence with her is saddening in its sycophancy and gush, and once again there are indiscretions about her husband which on one occasion led to her writing a letter to Lady Hoare and then, the following day, begging her to destroy the previous day's letter. Indiscretions also occurred in her letters to an American friend, Rebekah Owen, and again there was the same emotional and imprudent outpouring followed by guilty retraction of what had been written. Impulsiveness and a lack of self-confidence did not help.

Florence was quite unable to separate Hardy the poet from Hardy the husband, and when *Satires of Circumstance, Lyrics and Reveries*, his fourth book of verse, was published in November 1914, two years after Emma's death, Florence was so distressed by all the poems about Emma that further cries of despair went out to Lady Hoare. 'It seems to me that I am an utter failure if my husband can publish such a *sad sad* book. . . . If I had been a different sort of woman, and better fitted to be his wife – would he, I wonder, have published that volume?' The question reveals Florence's ignorance of Hardy's creative imperatives and shows a grievous lack of sensitivity. Meanwhile Lady Hoare must have been hoping that there would not be a third Mrs Hardy. *Satires of Circumstance* is a collection of 107 poems, mostly written between 1910 and 1914, and for many it is the greatest of all. Here is Hardy at his mature best. It consists of an opening group of twenty-five miscellaneous poems, with the title 'Lyrics and Reveries', of which we know that at least six are about women in his life. 'After the Visit' and 'To Meet, or Otherwise' about Florence come first, then there are three poems about Emma, and then one about Florence Henniker, 'A Thunderstorm in Town'. The order is interesting. Did he think that being placed first would please Florence and quash any resentment at the Emma poems, one of which was 'When I Set Out for Lyonnesse'? Did Florence Henniker recognise herself in 'A Thunderstorm in Town' or as the 'one rare fair woman' in 'Wessex Heights' about whom Hardy wrote 'Well, time cures hearts of tenderness, and now I can let her go' (*C.P.*, 261). This opening section also contains some of his finest occasional poems, 'The Convergence of the Twain', 'The Schreckhorn' and 'A Singer Asleep' together with several that could be called either occasional poems or moments of vision or both – 'Channel Firing', 'Beyond the Last Lamp' and 'Wessex Heights', for example. Among a wide variety of other works are a poem called 'God's Funeral', which Hardy told Gosse would have damned him for the laureateship, and 'Ah, Are You Digging on My Grave' which shows us that much as Hardy loved animals he refused to be sentimental about them.

The second section is called 'The Poems of 1912–13' and it has as an epigraph '*Veteris vestigia flammae*', a quotation from Virgil's *Aeneid* which can be translated as 'Memories of an old flame'. This group of eighteen poems (later increased to twenty-one) were all about the dead Emma and were all written in the two years since her death. It is a superb achievement, a remarkable example of a brilliantly creative catharsis, and poems like 'The Going', 'The Voice', 'After a Journey', 'Beeny Cliff' and 'At Castle Boterel' are universally acknowledged today as among the greatest and tenderest songs of lamentation in the English language. In the words of Irving Howe, writing about 'After a Journey',

> The struggle to remember and to salvage the debris of life – achieved in these lines through a rhythm of turn and return, offer and withdrawal, till it reaches the triumphant simplicity of the penultimate line, set off in its brevity and finality – this struggle to remember leads Hardy beyond the merely contingent and toward those elements of his experience that are not his alone and finally not even his at all. What begins as an obscure private hurt ends with the common wound of experience. (*Thomas Hardy*, p. 182)

The third section of some thirty-nine poems is correctly entitled 'Miscellaneous Pieces' and it ranges over a wide variety of material, most of it journeyman work with Hardy reaching a steady level of competence ranging from realistic retelling of the Biblical story of St Peter's denial of Christ, 'In the Servants' Quarters', to a cynical tale about a Vicar's young wife who is deceiving him, 'In the Days of Crinoline'. There are a few poems in this section which don't deserve their place and one wonders why Hardy published them. The fourth section is the group of poems already mentioned, 'Satires of Circumstance', which Hardy called 'caustically humorous productions'. The bitterness and cynicism which marks them is so different from the tone of the 1912–13 Poems that it can only be that once again Hardy was determined to collect everything, regardless of quality and appropriateness, although he did make the unconvincing excuse for doing so that although 'he would readily have suppressed them', they had 'already gained such currency from magazine publication that he could not do it' (*Life*, p. 396). In the first edition of the 1914 volume these 'Satires' were placed awkwardly in a group in the middle of 'Lyrics and Reveries' but in later editions they were sensibly moved to the end of the book where they make up the fourth section. Hardy still didn't explain why it was necessary to use the title of this offending group of poems as the title of the book.

November 1914 saw a distinguished company headed by Granville-Barker put on in London an abridged and adapted version of *The Dynasts*. Hardy was unwell and could not attend the first night but Florence went and met John Masefield and H. G. Wells. She was moving up in the world. Hardy was much depressed by the horrors that were becoming part of the story of the war, and describes the end of 1914 thus, 'A sad vigil during which no bells were heard at Max Gate brought in the first New Year of this unprecedented "breaking of nations".' It may be added here that so mad and brutal a war destroyed all Hardy's belief in 'the gradual ennoblement of man' (*Life*, p. 397). Yet some time in 1915 he was able to write his poem 'In Time of "The Breaking of Nations"' with its confident assertion that in spite of the militaristic machinations of the dynastic families of Europe,

> Yonder a maid and her wight
>   Come whispering by:
> War's annals will cloud into night
>   Ere their story die.
> (C.P., 500)

This is one of Hardy's 'little gems', a poem which says a great deal and expresses deep feelings with the utmost economy of statement and a technical proficiency which results from many years of studying and writing verse. 'I Look into My Glass', 'Drummer Hodge', 'The Self-Unseeing' and 'The Oxen' are in the same class.

In May Hardy was in London where Hamo Thornycroft was making a model of Hardy's head and shortly afterwards Florence was there having a minor operation. In June Hermann Lea took them in his car to Bridport, Lyme Regis, Torquay, and Exeter where they stayed overnight. On this visit they called on Eden Phillpotts. Occasionally Hardy would hire a car and his usual driver, Harold Voss, described him as a real gentleman, always calm, an enthusiastic cyclist, and a lover of ginger-beer shandy! Car-rides were soon to come to an end because of the rationing of petrol; and the death in action of his second cousin, Frank George during the Gallipoli campaign, a young man of whom he was very fond and had considered a possible heir, brought the war closely home to him. Several war poems were written during this period, including 'On the Belgian Expatriation', 'An Appeal to America on Behalf of the Belgian Destitute', 'The Pity of It' and 'Cry of the Homeless'. The death of Frank

George resulted in 'Before Marching and After', and 'A Jingle on the Times', written in December 1914, was possibly regarded as too bitter at that time, and did not receive full publication until *Complete Poems* was published in 1976. It ends,

'How shall we ply, then,
   Our old mysteries?'
'– Silly ones! Must we
   Show to you
What is the only
   Good, artistic
Cultured, Christian
   Thing to do?

'To manners, amenities,
   Bid we adieu, –
To the old lumber
   Of Right and True!
Fighting, smiting,
   Running through;
That's now the civilised
   Thing to do.'

Such sentiments would not have been acceptable in 1915.

In November Hardy's sister Mary died. She and sister Kate and brother Henry had moved into a house called Talbothays in 1913. It was about two miles from Max Gate, had been designed by Hardy and built in the early 1890s for Henry who had let it during the intervening years. Mary had been ill for some time and her death was a grievous blow to Kate who had lived with her for a good part of her life. They were both teachers, both unmarried, and both had been close to their mother who had bound the family together with such a strong sense of loyalty. Mary was born only a year after Hardy and they had grown up together and always enjoyed a very special relationship. So moved was he that he had to find relief in writing about her, and within a few weeks he had written three poems about his 'late-lamented' sister – 'Logs on the Hearth', 'Looking Across' and 'The Sun's Last Look on the Country Girl'. In *The Life* Hardy pays tribute to her, mentioning that her aptitude as a portrait-painter was such that she might have gone far in that career if she had not been 'doomed to school-teaching, and organ-playing in this or that village church' (*Life*, p. 402). She was 'buried under the yew-tree where the rest of us lie', and Hardy designed the stone for her grave in Stinsford churchyard just as he had designed the monumental stone for his 'late-lamented' Emma in St Juliot church.

The passing away of so many friends and relations made Hardy aware that he must prepare for his own end, and he not only wrote to the Society of Authors about the copyright of deceased authors but in February 1916 appointed Florence and Sydney Cockerell to be his literary executors, an arrangement which was to lead to considerable trouble after Hardy's death. Cockerell is described by Robert Gittings as 'tireless' and 'shameless' and 'powerful and insinuating'. (*The Older Hardy*, p. 143) and there seems to be a good deal of truth in this. To Cockerell Florence was 'dull beyond description – an inferior woman'. In 1911 he had urged Hardy to present his manuscripts to libraries and universities and Hardy, who was too modest to do so himself, entrusted this operation to Cockerell, described by Siegfried Sassoon as 'a first-class factotum', who had no hesitation as Director of the Fitzwilliam Museum, Cambridge, in acquiring two of the best – *Jude* and *Time's Laughingstocks* for his own Museum, together with several minor manuscripts which he begged for himself. It is a sign of Hardy's generosity that he asked not a penny for manuscripts now worth millions of pounds.

1916 also saw the publication of his *Selected Poems*, a collection of 120 poems selected by him from the first four books of verse and *The Dynasts*, together with nine poems from the as-yet unpublished *Moments of Vision*. This book, which was included in Macmillan's Golden Treasury series, sold well and is still of special interest as it was designed by Hardy for the 'General Reader' and is a guide to his own preference among the nearly 400 poems which were available for selection. In 1927, very near the end of his life, Hardy worked on a new edition of this book which he called *Chosen Poems*. He increased the number of poems to 161 by discarding a few of those previously selected and adding more than forty from the books of verse published since 1916. *Chosen Poems* was an important book to Hardy and it represents what was his final choice of his own poetry, and it must, therefore, be a matter of regret that Macmillan in 1940 replaced Hardy's selection with one depressingly inferior, chosen by G. M. Young.

During the war Hardy did what he could for the war effort. In 1916 he gave various manuscripts and autograph letters to the Red

Cross sale, and this was followed in 1918 by the gift of the manuscript of *Far from the Madding Crowd* which, as a result of the Red
Cross auction, went into private hands until, in the 1980s, it was
bequeathed to Yale University. After visiting the German prisoners
of war stationed near Dorchester he felt considerable pity for them.
While visiting the prison hospital, 'One Prussian, in much pain, died
while I was with him. . . . Men lie helpless here from wounds: in
the hospital a hundred yards off other men, English, lie helpless
from wounds – each scene of suffering caused by the other!' (*Life*,
p. 404) He sent the prisoners copies of his books, and employed
some of them in his gardens. Writing to Florence Henniker he described them as 'amiable young fellows', and he went on, 'it does
fill one with indignation that thousands of such are led to the
slaughter by the ambitions of Courts and Dynasties' (*C.L.*, 5, p. 204).
When the Government in 1917 tried to turn him into a recruiting
agent he wrote 'A Call to National Service', a poem weak because
of his lack of commitment to it. Writing to Siegfried Sassoon on
18 May 1917 he exclaimed, 'I don't know how I should stand the
suspense of this evil time if it were not for the sustaining power of
poetry' (*C.L.*, 5, p. 213). Hardy had become a county magistrate
in 1894 and although not often called on to serve on the bench he
did do so on a number of occasions towards the end of the war
when cases of food-profiteering were being heard. His kindness
also showed itself in the warm welcome that was always given to
any soldier who called at Max Gate. Private R. L. Ball of the RAMC
was invited to tea after he had written to Hardy about the pleasure
his books had given him and he was given an inscribed copy of
The Trumpet-Major when he left (Toucan Monograph No. 41), and
a young officer called Elliott Felkin paid several visits in 1918 and
1919 during which he and Hardy talked about Swinburne ('a
gentle, naive and charming creature'), Flaubert, Shelley ('a delightful person'), Lytton Strachey, George Eliot, and Browning. Hardy
told him of his dislike of critics and reviewers, his liking for owls,
and his belief that going to church was good for people because
it meant they made themselves clean and came together once a
week. He took Felkin to Stinsford churchyard and with tears in
his eyes discussed the engravings on the tombstones. 'One of the
extraordinary things about him', said Felkin, 'is the rapidity of his
change of moods. He seemed quite broken up round the graves,
then on the way home physically tired but mentally alert, then at
the garden gate he hopped on to the bank like a young man, to

put his hand over the wall and find the key' (*Encounter*, April 1962, pp. 27–33).

Another visitor to Max Gate, Stewart Ellis, wrote of him, 'The fact is, his was an extremely shy and sensitive nature, and the mask he wore to the outer world was an artificial protection of his inner self. To bores and intrusive journalists seeking "copy" he presented the "pessimism" they inspired and desired to find' and 'those people . . . little knew that the same eyes could twinkle with fun as he told or heard some amusing story' (*Fortnightly Review*, March 1928, p. 404). A note he made in March 1917 again stated what he had so often said in the past, 'Like so many critics Mr Courtney treats my works of art as if they were a scientific system of philosophy, although I have repeatedly stated in prefaces and elsewhere that the views in them are *seemings*, provisional impressions only . . .'. And he continues, 'although invidious critics had cast slurs upon him as Nonconformist, Agnostic, Atheist, Infidel, Immoralist, Heretic, Pessimist or something else equally opprobious in their eyes, they had never thought of calling him what they might have called him much more plausibly – churchy; not in an intellectual sense, but in so far as instincts and emotions ruled' (*Life*, pp. 406–7).

The renewed call of Cornwall took him again to Boscastle and St Juliot in September 1916, and this time he brought a somewhat jaundiced Florence with him. They had tea at the rectory where it had all begun forty-six years before and Hardy was now even more ready to admit that Elfride in *A Pair of Blue Eyes* was based to some extent on Emma. During this visit they went to Tintagel. It may have been on this occasion that the idea came to him for what was later to become *The Famous Tragedy of the Queen of Cornwall*. By now Hardy was becoming increasingly unwilling to travel and nights away from Max Gate were very few indeed. They were in London staying with Barrie for two nights in July 1917, the occasion of the Zeppelin raid, and were in Plymouth and Torquay in October for a short stay, mainly so that Hardy could visit places associated with Emma's childhood. Florence was having to resign herself to the fact that her hopes of exciting travel were not to be.

Although it was only three years since the publication of *Satires of Circumstance*, yet another book of verse, Hardy's largest, appeared in November 1917. *Moments of Vision* is a collection of 159 poems, almost all written in the three years since *Satires of Circumstance* and just five dating back to the nineteenth century. It is an astonishing piece of creative work for a person of any age, let alone one in his mid-seventies. The title *Moments of Vision*, with its implication of moments of heightened physical awareness caused by some transcendent experience, was exactly right for a book of poems at least thirty of which relate to the life and death of Emma. The title is used to cover all the poems in the book except for a group of seventeen poems with the title 'Poems of War and Patriotism' and a 'Finale' of two poems including the justly well-known 'Afterwards' which looks forward to Hardy's own death. Did he, one wonders, think that this might be his last book? It would have been an impressive finale as it contains a large number of his finest poems – 'Afternoon Service at Mellstock', 'The Blinded Bird', 'The Oxen', 'Great Things', 'The Five Students', 'During Wind and Rain', 'In Time of "The Breaking of Nations" ' and 'Afterwards', to mention just a few. The variety of subject, mood, tone and structure is greater than ever and yet there is an impressive unity about the book. In the words of Middleton Murry, 'Each work of his is a fragment of a whole.' This same variety within unity is experienced in the war poems which include both the patriotic 'Men Who March Away' and 'I Looked Up from My Writing' in which Hardy expresses his repugnance at man's inhumanity to man by picturing the moon looking in at him writing, and saying,

> 'And now I am curious to look
>   Into the blinkered mind
> Of one who wants to write a book
>   In a world of such a kind.'
>   (*C.P.*, 509)

War is now part of the dark madness of mankind rather than some punishment inflicted on mankind by an immanent will or a President of the Immortals. In the month of publication he made a note that 'I do not expect much notice will be taken of these poems: they mortify the human sense of self-importance by showing, or suggesting, that human beings are of no matter or appreciable value in this nonchalant universe' (*Life*, p. 408). In fact, as with *Satires of Circumstance*, there were many reviews and they were nearly all favourable and very deferential to this Grand Old Man of English Literature even if there was a good deal of muttering about 'macabre and cadaverous imaginings', and his 'morbid vision', and his 'halting and clumsy' technique. Hardy's irritation is revealed in his letter of 7 February 1918 to Florence Henniker, 'The publishers have sent me some fifty reviews – all of them, save 5 or 6, deplorably inept, purblind . . . though they were friendly enough, I must say' (*C.L.*, 5, p. 250). Why, he keeps on saying, cannot they recognise that his is an art that conceals art? The last entry in *The Life* for 1918 is 'My opinion is that a poet should express the emotion of all the ages and the thought of his own' (p. 417).

Another important literary activity was begun about the time of the publication of *Moments of Vision*, the writing of *The Life of Thomas Hardy* by Florence Emily Hardy. This was, of course, largely the work of Hardy himself, anxious to pre-empt the work of other biographers but among the probable reasons for allowing Florence to claim it as her own work were his worry about whether it might be regarded as immodest to write about himself, and his desire to please Florence who had so desperately wished to be a 'proper' author. Michael Millgate points out very well that 'The confessional and revelatory impulses were entirely foreign to him, and he had in any case woven his richest autobiographical experiences into the very texture of his novels and poems' (Millgate, p. 519). Although great care seems to have been taken to keep the secret, there is evidence that Hardy told at least one person that he was writing his autobiography, so was he disingenuous or was it yet another piece of double bluff, Hardy knowing very well that there was no possibility of keeping such a secret indefinitely? Robert Gittings begins his biography of Hardy by describing him as being both deceitful and stupid about the writing of *The Life*, a criticism which may be partly the result of his disappointment that it is so reticent about Hardy's private (and sexual) life, matters so important to the modern biographer. Hardy's failure in this respect has blinded many critics to the tremendous richness of *The Life*, its comments on life, current affairs and literary matters, its memories of the past and wealth of anecdote and reminiscence. For this biographer it is one of Hardy's greatest works.

The Life was published in two volumes after Hardy's death, the first with the title *The Early Life of Thomas Hardy* in November 1928, and the second, *The Later Years of Thomas Hardy* in April 1930. Hardy would have written the description of his own death if it had been possible but the closing chapters of *The Later Years* had to be left to Florence. At various stages she consulted James Barrie, E. M. Forster and Siegfried Sassoon – all of whom she appears, rather short-sightedly, to have regarded as possible second husbands – about the editing of the book, and it is probable that she had considerable help with the closing pages, which are very well written. However, she thought it necessary to delete Hardy's frequent vicious attacks on the reviewers who had been vicious in their attacks on him, and she also cut out some of the descriptions of the Society people Hardy had mentioned as having met during the London Season. This was an understandable editorial decision but it is difficult to excuse her use of the red pencil on some references to Emma, the result of her inordinate jealousy of the first wife. Fortunately, we now have *The Life and Work of Thomas Hardy* by Thomas Hardy, edited by Michael Millgate which not only makes a convincing attempt to restore Hardy's original text but also provides a list of 'Post Hardyan' revisions.

In November 1918 he met for the first time one of the many young writers who made the journey to Max Gate in the 1920s – Siegfried Sassoon. Writing later about his meeting with Hardy, Sassoon described the 'homeliness' he was offered at Max Gate, Hardy's 'octogenarian agility and quickness which matched his alertness of mind', and his 'sense of humour'. Hardy, he said, 'became more lovable all the time'; he was a 'great and simple man'. Sassoon was intrigued by the Hardys' unawareness of the significance of A. C. Benson's fondness for young men, and in his diary he recalls how this unawareness startled him: 'I realised once again how remote my secret affairs are from even the Hardys who are so fond of me' (28 June 1922). Never such innocence! On Hardy's seventy-ninth birthday he was presented with a book containing more than forty manuscript poems by contemporary poets, each written out by the individual contributor. Sassoon presented the volume to Hardy and commented on his modesty and his unawareness of the admiration which his verse had evoked in other writers. 'It was', Hardy wrote, 'almost his first awakening to the consciousness than an opinion had silently grown up, as it were in the night, that he was no mean power in the contemporary world of poetry' (*Life*, p. 422). He had by now, of course, been publishing verse for twenty years, and, just as with the novel, recognition of him as poet had been slow but was rapidly gathering momentum.

November, too, brought the end of the war but once again Hardy, prophetically, saw that this was not really the end of it. Talking to Eden Phillpotts a year or two later he felt 'that only a phantom peace rose from the accumulated bitterness of Versailles and that men were sowing another crop of dragons' teeth rather than the fruit of the olive' (*The Angle of 88*, p. 69). He showed more wisdom than the politicians. Just two years after Hardy's death Hitler's Nazi party secured six-and-a-half million votes in that year's election. 1918 in *The Life* ends with a typical note, 'It bridges over the years to think that Gray might have seen Wordsworth in his cradle, and Wordsworth might have seen me in mine' (p. 417).

The principal literary event of 1919 was the publication of his *Collected Poems* in two volumes, the first containing the poems, the second *The Dynasts*. The first five books of his poetry were collected together for Volume 1 and the three further books published in the 1920s were added to successive editions of *Collected Poems*, until, finally, in 1930, it contained all eight books of his poems. It remained in print continuously until in the 1970s the printing plates began to wear out from the frequent reprints required, and *Complete Poems* took its place. It is a tribute to him as poet that since 1919 his poetical works have never been out of print. A variorum edition was published by Macmillan in 1978, and the ending of the copyright on Hardy's published poetry in 1979 led to the appearance of a considerable number of selections of his verse and Samuel Hynes's fine complete edition published by the Oxford University Press between 1982 and 1985. Hardy, who said towards the end of his life that 'His only ambition, as far as he could remember, was to have some poem or poems in a good anthology like *The Golden Treasury*' (*Life*, p. 478) – was he joking? – would have been delighted to see the high regard in which his poetry is now held. Would Palgrave, who wanted poetry to be 'a fountain of innocent and exalted pleasure . . . leading us in higher and healthier ways than those of the world' have found anything to admire in Hardy's direct, earthy, outspoken, establishment-questioning verse? Hardy's was a verse which took the whole of life as its subject and was accessible to all: Palgrave's *Golden Treasury* was verse mostly written by middle-class poets for a middle-class audience. There was no room in his anthology for ruined maids or philosophical questionings.

In 1920 Hardy reached his eighties. In spite of Florence's letter to Cockerell reporting that 'He seems to have grown so much older though during the last few months. . . . He forgets things that have happened only a day or two before, and people he has seen or heard from' (*Friends of a Lifetime*, p. 302), he was still able to impress visitors with his alertness, serenity, briskness and joviality. To Marie Stopes he was like an 'eager, happy boy, the amused and sympathetic observer . . . a stimulating, bright, swift eager person. He reminded me of a red-breasted robin' (*John o'London's Weekly*,

27 December 1940). Was Florence guilty of wishful thinking, one wonders? There is certainly no sign of a mental deterioration in the letters of this period, nor at any time in the remaining years of his life. By 1919 he had completed *The Life* up to 1918 and he was then involved with Macmillan in the publication of the prestigious Mellstock Edition of his work in a limited edition of 500 copies. The thirty-seven volumes were published in 1919–20 and Hardy's work on this was much reduced by using the Wessex Edition as the copy-text. Hardy contributed five pages of corrections and additions and corrected the proofs of just *A Pair of Blue Eyes* and the volumes of verse. '. . . no human printer, or even one sent from Heaven direct, can be trusted with verse', said Hardy (*C.L.*, 6, p. 6). He had long wanted to see a *de luxe* edition of his work and the completion of this very successful publishing venture delighted him. And at last Oxford University (his Christminster) honoured him. In March 1920 he received an Honorary D. Litt. and then attended a perform-ance of *The Dynasts* put on by the University Dramatic Society, where he found many of the undergraduates handsome and possessed of great 'freshness and vivacity'. Some volumes of the Wessex Edition were now due for reprinting and Hardy, meticulous as ever, had his 'little list' of corrections ready for Macmillan. Just before his eightieth birthday he sent Macmillan a five-page list of questions about his sales in America and the copyright position there, and then, on his birthday he had messages of congratulations from the King, the Prime Minister, the Vice-Chancellor of Cambridge Univer-sity and countless more. He had also to receive a deputation from the Society of Authors and there were so many 'strangers unexpectedly entering' that he felt rather tired.

On 21 April he had made his last visit to London to be present at the marriage of Harold Macmillan, and now it was for the world to come to him, which they did. H. G. Wells and Rebecca West visited in February 1919 and Charlotte Mew, whom he regarded as 'far and away the best living woman poet' and whom he helped to get a Civil List Pension in 1924, had stayed with them for a couple of nights shortly before. Among other 1920 visitors were Robert Graves, who was delighted with Hardy's remark that his old mother had always said of baptism that at any rate there was no harm in it, and that she would not like her children to blame her in after-life for leaving any duty to them undone. He also commented on Hardy's loyalty to his friends and on his 'natural simplicity and goodness'. Vere H. Collins, friend of Edward Thomas, made five

visits between 1920 and 1922 and shortly after Hardy's death published his *Talks with Thomas Hardy*. He remarked on his 'vigour and
intellect . . . the quickness of his thought; the versatility of his interests; the alertness in his voice, his gestures; his keenness of sight;
the extraordinary clearness and steadiness of his handwriting'. Some
of the lyrics in *The Dynasts* were as good as anything in the *Collected
Poems* but would people think that they had been taken in if they
had to pay a second time for what they had already had? he asked
Collins. On Sunday afternoons soldiers from camps near Dorchester
would call and be entertained to tea. Occasionally Hardy would
talk about literature as he did in September 1920 when he told
W. M. Parker that he found so many 'goody' books dull and that
he had never heard farm folk talk in the way they did in Richard
Jefferies' books. The critic, Saintsbury, he maintained, had read too
much and did not possess sufficient insight. And so the life at Max
Gate went on and as if all these calls on this eighty-year old man
were not enough they had staying with them for several weeks
Florence's sister and her little boy who later remembered Hardy
winding the clocks every Monday morning after breakfast and said
he would never forget Hardy's kindly welcome.

As already mentioned, on his eighty-first birthday an event took
place which gave him great pleasure. He was presented with a first
edition of a volume of Keats's poetry with an address by one
hundred and six younger writers which paid him this tribute:

> We, who are your younger comrades in the craft of letters, wish
> on this your eighty-first birthday to do honour to ourselves by
> praising your work, and to thank you for the example of high
> endeavour and achievement which you have set before us. In
> your novels and poems you have given us a tragic vision of life
> which is informed by your knowledge of character and relieved
> by the charity of your humour, and sweetened by your sympathy
> with human suffering and endurance. . . . In all that you have
> written you have shown the spirit of man, nourished by tradition
> and sustained by pride, persisting through defeat.

Florence continued her writing of discreet and indiscreet letters
to her friends and in one, dated 26 December 1920, to Cockerell
she told him that Hardy 'is now – this afternoon – writing a poem
with great spirit: always a sign of well-being with him. Needless to
say it is an intensely dismal poem' (*Friends of a Lifetime*, p. 307). In

August of the following year she wrote to Barrie, declining an invitation to visit him because at 81 Hardy 'cannot go visiting any more'.
Among the visitors that year were Galsworthy, Sassoon, Cockerell,
E. M. Forster, Middleton Murry, Barrie, Walter de la Mare, and
Masefield who delighted Hardy with the gift of a full-rigged ship
which he had made himself and which bore the subtle dedication,
'To Thomas Hardy Poet from John Masefield poet'. Most of these
visitors stayed for a day or two and on one of Sassoon's many visits
his talk with Hardy lasted from 4.30 to 11 p.m. Middleton Murry
describes him drinking whisky at supper, Florence attributed his
recovery from an attack of 'flu to his drinking champagne, he himself
talked of his love of cider, and Ellen Titterington described bur-
gundy as one of his favourite drinks. And yet on another occasion
he claimed to drink very little of anything! Of his love of cats there
could be no doubt. E. M. Forster who described Florence as more
of a pessimist than her husband and 'very gloomy', wrote a hilari-
ous account of a visit with Hardy in 1922 to the Pets' Cemetery at
Max Gate:

> 'This is Snowbell – she was run over by a train . . . this is Pella,
> the same thing happened to her . . . this is Kitkin, she was cut
> clean in two, clean in two . . .'. How is it that so many of your cats
> have been run over, Mr Hardy? Is the railway near? – 'Not at all
> near . . . I don't know how it is. But of course we have only bur-
> ied here those pets whose bodies were recovered. Many were
> never seen again.' (Letter of 19 July 1922)

In May 1922 his sixth book of verse was published in an edition
of 3250 copies and it proved so popular that it was twice reprinted
before the end of the year. It had another catch-all title, *Late Lyrics
and Earlier*, and consisted of no fewer than 151 poems dating from
1861 to 1921 and with, once again, poems from almost every one of
the intervening decades. Twenty-two had been published previously
in newspapers, journals and books, and the volume is distinguished
from his other volumes of verse by the fact that it has a seven-page
'Apology' in place of the customary Preface. He had been ill in
January – cancer was wrongly suspected by his doctors – and the
idea of the 'Apology' had come to him then. It begins with what he
calls a few words of 'excuse or explanation'. The new book is submitted 'with great hesitation' and only because some 'illustrious men
of letters' requested it and because the poems were there waiting to

be published. After this weak and evasive start he once again brings all the weight of his attack on to those critics who have dared to call what are only 'questionings' in the exploration of reality 'pessimism'. He is one of those who believe that pain to all upon the globe whether 'tongued or dumb, shall be kept down to a minimum by loving-kindness, operating through scientific knowledge'. To regard poetry as the application of ideas to life is to lay oneself open to attack but if this is so he apologises but cannot help it. After the expression of regret that the Established Church has not replaced the supernatural with the rational, he attacks those who because of the juxtaposition of 'unrelated, even discordant effusions' in his books of verse have failed to realise that the grave and the satirical and humorous are often mixed together. The attack on 'mischievous' criticism leads on to the important statement that 'In any event, pure literature in general, religion – I include religion, in its essential and dogmatic sense, because poetry and religion touch each other, or rather modulate into each other; are, indeed, often but different names for the same thing – these, I say, the visible signs of mental and emotional life, must like all other things keep moving, becoming . . .'. It is a remarkable piece of writing from a dedicated writer and at one point it becomes prophetic:

> Whether owing to the barbarising of taste in the younger minds by the dark madness of the late war, the unabashed cultivation of selfishness in all classes, the plethoric growth of knowledge simultaneously with the stunting of wisdom, 'a degrading thirst after outrageous stimulation' (to quote Wordsworth . . .), or from any other cause, we seem threatened with a new Dark Age.

Florence was against publishing it and Gosse read it 'with surprise and some pain' but we must not forget that Hardy had been suffering from the stupidity and venom of Establishment critics for more than fifty years when he wrote this. As he said in *The Life*, 'Some of his friends regretted this preface, thinking that it betrayed an oversensitiveness to criticism which it were better the world should not know. But sensitiveness was one of Hardy's chief characteristics, and without it his poems would never have been written, nor indeed, the greatest of his novels' (p. 448).

What is particularly impressive about Hardy in these final years is his continuing professionalism as a writer. In the collecting together of his poems for the three final books of verse there is a meticulous attention to detail, and his mind, active as ever, continues to experiment with new verse forms and to draw on a diversity of subject matter. Could any two poems be more different than the engaging, lyrical and descriptive 'Weathers' which opens the book and the soul-searching 'Surview' with which it ends? Surprisingly, Hardy wrote very few simple, descriptive, rural poems and most of these are to be found in *Late Lyrics* and *Human Shows*. There are several poems about Emma, one called 'I Sometimes Think' which recognises his debt to Florence, and a few about other women. Among the very best are 'Going and Staying' with its memorable line, 'The silent bleed of a world decaying'; 'A Night in November'; 'The Fallow Deer at the Lonely House' with its distinct memory of his first home; 'At Lulworth Cove a Century Back' which remembers Keats in 1820 on his way to death in Rome; 'Last Words to a Dumb Friend', surely one of the finest elegies ever written about a dead pet; the poem about his father's death, 'On One Who Lived and Died Where He Was Born'; and 'An Ancient to Ancient', a poem of evocative retrospection and dignified farewell. But it is perhaps invidious to choose just a few from so much that is good. *Late Lyrics and Earlier* was followed later in the year by the publication of Hardy's poetic drama *The Famous Targedy of the Queen of Cornwall*. The inspiration for this was clearly his meeting in the 1870s with Emma and their visits to Tintagel. Hardy said of it that it was '53 years in contemplation, 800 lines in result, alas!' Its uniqueness, as Hardy saw it, was that it observes the three classical unities and requires no theatre or scenery, being in the nature of a mummers' play. So little impact has it made that it has been possible for biographers to write their books without a mention of it and, sadly, it has to be regarded as a work of little distinction, dull and – in the words of Ivor Brown – weak because of its 'combination of rare and strained words with a prosaic diction that approaches bathos' (*Saturday Review*, 8 December 1923).

No matter what Florence may have said, Hardy had not yet quite finished his visiting and in June 1923, shortly after the death of Mrs Henniker, he travelled to Oxford and stayed at the Queen's College for two nights, which was, in fact, the last occasion on which he slept away from Max Gate. The College had just elected him to an Honorary Fellowship and he was royally entertained and taken on tours of the College and the town. Hardy's interest in everything was intense and Godfrey (later Lord) Elton who acted as his host described him as 'an elderly country gentleman with a bird-like alertness and a rare and charming youthfulness . . . interested in everything he saw'. Hardy thought of this occasion as an outstanding one in the last years of his life, memorable no doubt because 'Jude' had finally triumphed.

1923 saw the departure of an old friend and the arrival of a new one. Sir Frederick Treves, who died on 7 December, had, like Hardy, grown up in Dorchester. He became an eminent surgeon, wrote a valuable guide to Dorset, and is now chiefly remembered by having operated on Edward VII just before his coronation and saved his life, and for the kindness he showed to the 'Elephant Man'. Hardy and Treves had known each other for many years and Treves's father had owned a shop from which Hardy had bought his first writing-desk. In *The Life* Hardy writes, 'The care which he took of all his possessions during his whole life is shown by the fact that this desk was in his study without a mark or scratch upon it at the time of his death' (p. 457). It was that same care which meant that he was still able to make use of poems written in the 1860s sixty years later. The new friend was T. E. Lawrence who was serving in the army at Bovington Camp, about ten miles from Dorchester, and had been given an introduction to Hardy by Robert Graves. Hardy and Lawrence took an immediate liking to each other and for the next two to three years until his departure for India at the end of 1926 Lawrence was a frequent visitor on his motorcycle. He told a friend that he generally saw Hardy 'every other Sunday'. Lawrence admired Hardy the writer: Hardy admired Lawrence the soldier. Both immensely valued their friendship and in a letter to Graves written in September 1923 Lawrence described Hardy as 'so pale, so quiet, so refined into an essence. . . . There is an unbelievable dignity and ripeness about Hardy: he is waiting so tranquilly for death, without a desire or ambition left in his spirit, as far as I can feel it: and yet he entertains so many illusions, and hopes for the world . . . and the standards of the man! He feels interest in everyone, and veneration for no-one.'

Another event of 1923 which deserves mention was the visit to Max Gate on 20 July for lunch of the Prince of Wales, who is reported to have said to Hardy, 'My mother tells me you have written a book called *Tess of the d'Urbervilles*. I must try to read it some time.' Having recently turned down an invitation to lecture at Yale University (*Life*, p. 471), it can only have been his dry sense of humour and boredom which prompted Hardy to ask a particularly pedantic American professor, who insisted on visiting him in 1923, whether

Harvard was a girls' school. The professor was astonished at his ignorance.

Someone who knew Hardy better than most during these last years of his life was May O'Rourke who was his secretary from 1923 onwards. A typewriter was obtained for the first time when Florence entered into residence and Max Gate had a telephone in 1919. Florence was both wife and secretary but with the growth in correspondence – the Max Gate correspondence stored in the Dorset County Museum and catalogued by Carl and Clara Weber in *Thomas Hardy's Correspondence at Max Gate* records some 2500 letters received in the last eight years of Hardy's life and this is by no means a complete record – Florence obviously decided that there must be a further 'secretary'. May O'Rourke was 25 and had written some poetry which Hardy had seen and then invited her (in 1918) to tea. As she was his secretary for so long and was obviously a very fair and sensible observer of the Max Gate life during those years some of her Monograph is worth quoting. She found Hardy charming, friendly and with a sense of fun. To her suggestion when she first met him that Stinsford was 'a Gray's Elegy sort of place', he replied 'It *is* Stoke Poges.' She described Max Gate as a 'household in which life and literature are one'. Hardy had constant problems with the tourists who waited outside the house in order to get his autograph or the visitors who wouldn't go. 'Have they gone yet?' he would ask her after creeping out of his study. Every morning at ten o'clock he went to his study and worked there for a fixed time. To Newman Flower he said, 'I may not write a word for a fortnight, but it is discipline – on one of those mornings of discipline the mood comes – and I write.' After lunch he rested, then went for a walk to Stinsford church or Came or some other loved place, after which there was tea – often with visitors present – and then in the evening Florence would read to him. In 1920 she read all of Jane Austen's novels. May O'Rourke mentions his remarkable memory, his sadness that he had had no children, and his constant concern for her welfare.

Siegfried Sassoon in a letter to Sydney Cockerell of 14 October 1940, three years after Florence's death, gave this impression of Florence: 'One sees her difficulties – and her limitations. Like many women, she had very little judgment about people, was easily prejudiced, and couldn't resist the lure of the second-rate (when it flattered her!). On the whole, I think she did her job very well. But she was a person who enjoyed being gloomy.' She certainly looked gloomy in the photograph of her taken with the Prince of Wales, but so do the Prince and Hardy and it should be remembered that in those days people always looked serious in photographs whereas today the command is 'Smile!' But that she was moody and melancholy there can be little doubt. E. M. Forster in 1924 described her as a 'pessimist – more so than her husband who grows gayer as the years increase'. Her low state of health did not help and a crisis developed in 1924 when it was thought that a lump in her throat might be cancerous. She went to London on 29 September and had what appeared to be a successful operation, but May O'Rourke thought that 'a grim bogey was then and henceforth never far away from her' and that this led on occasions to depression and a discolouring and distortion of life. It was partly this which led her to make so many complaints about her life at Max Gate. When the 'famous dog' Wessex died at the end of 1926 and she wrote to Cockerell, 'He was only a dog and not a good dog always but *thousands* (actually thousands) of afternoons and evenings I would have been alone but for him', she is talking nonsense. Thousands of afternoons would amount to several years and there is plenty of evidence that throughout the 1920s the visitors to Max Gate were unceasing. The wonder of it all is that Hardy, now a very old man, continued to write his poetry, attend to his correspondence, and lead such a busy life without any complaint. That was left to his wife. However, like May O'Rourke when she talks about Florence's 'strong sense of duty, her swift impulses to give pleasure or to serve a need', we must not forget that this moody woman had qualities which obviously endeared her to her husband. While she was in London having her operation he was distraught with worry, and the poem 'Nobody Comes' (*C.P.*, 715) reveals by its date '9 October 1924' that it was written probably as he was waiting anxiously for Florence's return from London after the operation and walked on to the road outside Max Gate in the hope of seeing the car bringing her home:

> Tree-leaves labour up and down,
>   And through them the fainting light
>   Succumbs to the crawl of night.
> Outside in the road the telegraph wire
>   To the town from the darkening land
> Intones to travellers like a spectral lyre
>   Swept by a spectral hand.

A car comes up, with lamps full-glare,
That flash upon a tree:
It has nothing to do with me,
And whangs along in a world of its own,
Leaving a blacker air;
And mute by the gate I stand again alone,
And nobody pulls up there.

What poems he might have written if Florence, who eventually died in 1937 of cancer, had predeceased him!

Another side of Florence's character, her quite unnecessary jealousy, manifested itself at the end of 1924 when the Hardy Players, the local amateur dramatic society which had received nationwide publicity because of its association with Hardy, produced his own adaptation of *Tess*. The actress playing the name-part was a local woman of considerable beauty and charm called Gertrude Bugler and Hardy had been so impressed by her acting in earlier productions of the Players that he took a special interest in her. He was overwhelmed by her performance as Tess because, as Norman Atkins, who had played Alec, wrote in his Monograph, 'she was the very incarnation of Tess Durbeyfield', and there was talk of Gertrude going to London to play the part in a professional production. That Hardy was greatly fond of her there is no doubt but that the relationship went any farther than that is ridiculous. She was sixty years younger than he, happily married and the mother of a child. If Florence had been sensible and level-headed she would not have taken it seriously, but in her moody way she was wracked with jealousy, prevented Gertrude from going to London and behaved disgracefully. She told Cockerell that she thought that she would go mad and there is a hint of paranoia about her actions. Later, after Hardy's death, as some kind of atonement she encouraged Gertrude to act the part of Tess professionally in London and this she did in 1929. Gertrude lived on until 1992, loved by all and always ready to talk about the past. She was particularly proud of Hardy's words to her when he was bidding her goodnight one evening at Max Gate: 'If anyone asks you if you knew Thomas Hardy, say "Yes, he was my friend".' Hardy had imagined a sixty-year old man in love with a twenty-year old woman in *The Well-Beloved*. Only Florence could have imagined an eighty-year old man in love with a twenty-year old woman. 1924 ended with Hardy sitting up to hear 'Big Ben and the London church bells by wireless ring in the New Year'.

The Max Gate Visitors' Book records about one hundred visitors in 1925 and they included Cockerell, the Granville-Barkers, Lawrence, Arthur Bliss, H. M. Tomlinson, Gwen Frangcon-Davies, Eden Phillpotts, Lady Ottoline Morrell, J. C. Squire, Siegfried Sassoon, Marie Stopes, Newman Flower, Middleton Murry and the members of the cast which was performing *Tess* at the Garrick Theatre in London who came down to act some of the scenes from the play in front of Hardy. 'He talked of Tess as if she was someone real whom he had known and liked tremendously', said one member of the cast. In May there was a suggestion of a Thomas Hardy Chair of Literature at a Wessex University but nothing came of this or of a later proposal that there should be such a Chair at the University College of Southampton. However, the honorary degrees continued to arrive and St Andrews and Bristol Universities brought his total in 1925 to five.

And still the books of verse came. *Human Shows, Far Phantasies, Songs and Trifles* was published on 20 November in an edition of 5000 copies – ten times that of *Wessex Poems* in 1897 – and it was almost completely sold out before publication. Two further impressions followed before the end of the year. It contains an astonishing 152 poems, most of them composed in the three years since *Late Lyrics* but two are dated in the 1860s, and five in the 1890s. Twenty-five of them had been published previously in journals, etc., and Hardy was receiving constant requests from editors for poems, far more than even he could satisfy. He was now so much the Grand Old Man of English literature that the reviewers found much to admire and little to dislike. They agreed that there was no falling-off in his standard. 'Here', said *The Times Literary Supplement*, 'is another volume of brief summings-up of his sense of the meaning of life, little scenes, short stories, brief and pregnant utterances of the questions which life has continually forced him to ask, and of the only answers he has been able to give to them.' The poems have a 'grave beauty' and they all 'exhibit the Hardy touch, with its strength which is not always afraid of being confused with roughness, its austerity which is as tender as it is stern'. The opening poem, 'Waiting Both' (*C.P.*, 663), sounds a chord which can be heard throughout in poems of great diversity:

A star looks down at me,
And says: 'Here I and you
Stand, each in our degree:

What do you mean to do, –
    Mean to do?'

I say: 'For all I know,
Wait, and let Time go by,
Till my change come.' – 'Just so,'
The star says: 'So mean I: –
    So mean I.'

One of the poems, 'On the Esplanade', is an interesting mixture of the old and the new, the romantic and the realistic and shows Hardy's Janus-like ability to look both ways. The carefully-chosen titles – and Hardy took great trouble to get his titles right – indicate the range of subject matter – 'Life and Death at Sunrise', 'Night-Time in Mid-Fall', 'A Sheep Fair', 'Snow in the Suburbs', 'Winter Night in Woodland', 'Green Slates' and 'Coming up Oxford Street: Evening', are typical examples. Here is Hardy's plenty.

And he was certainly not writing now just for financial reasons. His annual royalty cheque from Macmillan came to £4400, say £150 000 in today's money, and there were several other sources of income. In the same month, for example, *John o' London's Weekly* asked for permission to publish *Tess* again as a serial and he received £1000 for this of which Macmillan had to be paid one-third. Money was being received from the very many translations of his novels, and his poems were increasingly being anthologised. The Nonesuch Press was being charged at this time two guineas a poem for the poems it wished to use in an anthology, and Hardy, shrewd as ever, commented on the way 'some people are induced to buy an author by reading snatches of him by chance' (*C.L.*, 6, p. 316). His wish to have his poetry as widely read as possible was not based just upon the desire to earn money; he had a fervent belief that poetry not only entertained but instructed. There was something apostolic about his urge to write verse and publish it, and just as Verdi and Turner had produced some of their best work in old age, so would he. It would have been easy at his age to fall back on stanzaic forms and rhyme schemes and rhythmic patterns he had used in the past but the technical experimentation continued just as it had in the past and the poems on the page reveal as many different structures as an architect's notebook.

T. E. Lawrence pointed out that Hardy seldom commented on

the work of living writers. To do so would have been regarded by him as bad-mannered, but there is considerable evidence that right up to his last days he was reading widely among his contemporaries, or having their books read to him by Florence. Among the seventy or so people who signed the Visitors' Book in 1926 were E. M. Forster, Middleton Murry, John Masefield, John Drinkwater, T. E. Lawrence and Virginia Woolf, and being the kind of person he was he would have been acquainted with the works of all of them. Yet we shall probably never know what he thought of Virginia Woolf's work or that of other literary figures active at that time, such as T. S. Eliot, D. H. Lawrence, James Joyce, G. B. Shaw, Somerset Maugham or even Edith Wharton who had met him many years before and found him 'remote and uncommunicative'. It comes as a surprise, then, to find that he had read Ezra Pound's poetry, the reason being that Pound had sent him copies of *Quia Pauper Amavi* and *Hugh Selwyn Mauberley* in 1920. In a letter dated 3 December 1920 Hardy thanked him for this gift with the meaningful sentence, 'I will not try to express my appreciation of their contents, as I am a very slow reader; and as, moreover, your muse asks for considerable deliberation in estimating her' (*C.L.*, 6, p. 49). In a letter of 18 March 1921 in response to a request from Pound that Hardy should criticise his work, Hardy wrote back, 'As I am old-fashioned, and think lucidity a virtue in poetry, as in prose, I am at a disadvantage in criticising recent poets who apparently aim at obscurity. I do not mean that *you* do, but I gather that at least you do not care whether the many understand you or not' (*C.L.*, 6, p. 77). Pound, for his part, thought that Hardy 'gets through despite his funny way of writing verse. Have just had a poem from him, full of every sort of inversion verbal, but so DAMN straight in thought' (Letter to Ford Madox Ford, 26 May 1921).

E. M. Forster, in an attempt to impress, had told Virginia Woolf in 1922 that he had been staying with Hardy who was 'a very vain, quiet, conventional, uninteresting old gentleman . . . whose great pride was that county families asked him to tea'. It prompted Virginia to comment that 'perhaps at 82 one rots a little'. She might have commented on Forster's lack of loyalty to someone whose hospitality he had been enjoying. However, in her account of her meeting with him four years later there is no sign of rot. Hardy is 'cheerful', 'vigorous', 'extremely affable and aware of his duties', 'shrewd', 'perfectly aware of everything', 'sensible and sincere' and 'What impressed me most was his freedom, ease and vitality' (*A*

Writer's Diary, pp. 89–94). Clearly, if there was any rot it was that spoken by Forster indulging in that kind of malicious unpleasantness which seemed to come so naturally to some of the Bloomsbury Group and their friends.

In 1926 Macmillan came up with a clever new idea to capitalise on their most valuable property. They produced a *de luxe* edition of *Tess* signed by Hardy and limited to 325 copies. Sir Frederick Macmillan was worried about whether Hardy would have the strength to sign the signature sheets which were to be bound in but he need not have worried. For a very 'liberal' payment of £300 Hardy was more than willing to do the signing. So successful was this venture that a year later a similar *de luxe* signed edition of *The Dynasts* in three volumes was offered for sale and once again the edition, increased now to 525 copies, was sold out almost as soon as it was published. Plans were being made to repeat this highly lucrative venture with *The Return of the Native* in 1928 when death brought all such plans to an end.

Hardy's realistic outspokenness was not diminished with age. Asked by Marie Stopes to give his opinion on the censor's refusal to grant her a performance licence for her play *Vectia*, he replied in a letter of 16 April 1926 that the play's situation and events were improbable: 'I cannot conceive a young woman not an imbecile who has been married three years being in such crass ignorance of physiology, especially with a young man just through the party-wall ready to teach her' (*C.L.*, 7, p. 16).

1927 was the last full year of Hardy's life, and although he now very seldom went very far away from Max Gate, he did visit the Granville-Barkers in Devon on his birthday and lay the foundation-stone of the new Dorchester Grammar School in July on a cold and windy day. In August he drove with Gustav Holst to 'Egdon Heath' but sadly did not live long enough to hear the piece of music which resulted from this visit. Later in the month he spent the day in Bath where 'He seemed like a ghost revisiting scenes of a long-dead past' (*Life*, p. 474). It was fifty-four years since he had been there with Emma. Other short outings were to Ilminster, Yeovil and Lulworth Cove. But in spite of his age there was no let-up in the visits to Max Gate. 'They want to see me', he said, 'in my eleventh hour and fifty-ninth minute.' 'They' included, among many others, John Buchan, Henry Newbolt, Edmund Gosse, Sydney Cockerell, Llewelyn Powys, Siegfried Sassoon, John Masefield, John Galsworthy and Henry Williamson. Williamson's visit was on 31

October, only three months before Hardy's death. He called without any appointment but was graciously received by Florence
and Hardy, who had been resting, came down to meet the author
of *Tarka* and talk about the cruelty of otter-hunting. It is difficult
to reconcile this Hardy with the mean and inhospitable recluse
described by Robert Gittings.

With an unbelievable energy in one so old, and a meticulous thoroughness which had been one of his characteristics right through his
long life, he spent much of 1927 (1) gathering his short stories together for a collected edition which was published in 1928 after
his death, almost immediately reprinted and then allowed by its publishers to go out of print for some sixty years until the Desmond
Hawkins edition, *The Collected Short Stories of Thomas Hardy*, was
published in 1988; (2) revising and enlarging his *Selected Poems* for the
new volume *Chosen Poems*; and (3) beginning to put together new and
old poems for his eighth book of verse, to be entitled *Winter Words*.
He wrote a Preface which began, 'So far as I am aware, I happen
to be the only English poet who has brought out a new volume of
verse on his . . . birthday . . .' It seems that at one stage he hoped it
might be 'ninetieth birthday', but more realistically it looked like
being 'eighty-eighth'. He even wrote what was to be the final poem
in the final book with its apt title of 'He Resolves to Say No More'.
Of course, he had no intention of saying no more. He just knew
that a book, like a building, ought to be properly planned.

And death did silence him on 11 January 1928. His final illness
had begun a month earlier with no sign that it was serious. On that
morning 'he sat at the writing-table in his study and felt totally
unable to work. This, he said, was the first time that such a thing
had happened to him' (*Life*, p. 479). He became steadily weaker and
worried his wife as to whether she had sent what was presumably
his last poem, 'Christmas in the Elgin Room', to *The Times*. It was
a bitterly cold winter with snowdrifts several feet deep and after
Christmas he was confined to bed but the weakness increased. Even
so he insisted upon writing a cheque for his subscription to the
Pension Fund of the Society of Authors. On 11 January he seemed
better but in the evening he had a heart-attack and shortly after
nine he died. It is a sign of a brave spirit that on his deathbed he
asked Florence to read to him the verse of *Omar Khayyám*

Oh, Thou, who Man of baser Earth didst make,
And ev'n with Paradise devise the Snake:

For all the Sin wherewith the Face of Man
Is blackened – Man's forgiveness give – and take!

For Hardy there was to be no death-bed recantation.

The news of his death was telephoned to London by the ubiquitous Cockerell, who had been summoned to Max Gate by Florence, and it was announced on the wireless that evening. Meanwhile, Cockerell and Barrie and other members of the Establishment had decided – against all the evidence that Hardy wanted to rest with his family in the 'most hallowed spot on earth', Stinsford churchyard – that Hardy must have a public burial in Westminster Abbey. The Dean was just a little worried that someone who had so often declared himself to be an agnostic should be buried in his Christian shrine and wrote to the Vicar of Fordington church to ask for 'evidence of Hardy's Faith and practice as proofs of Christianity and Churchmanship'. The Rev. Bartelot's reply skilfully evades answering the questions asked and refers to the facts that he was baptised, subscribed to the restoration of his church, contributed to church funds, was interested in church music, had in the past attended St Peter's church twice a year and had led a life of 'absolute moral rectitude'. The Dean accepted this piece of equivocation and condescended to receive Hardy's body into his Abbey.

Poor Florence had no idea what to do and eventually agreed to a barbaric compromise. Hardy's heart was cut out of his body as he lay in his Max Gate bedroom and was buried in Stinsford, the rest of him was cremated and buried in the Abbey. Hardy would have used the ironies of the situation to write one of his satires of circumstance. The two funerals took place on the afternoon of 16 January with Henry Hardy the chief mourner at Stinsford, and Florence, leaning heavily on Cockerell's arm and thickly veiled, the chief mourner at the Abbey. The pall-bearers chosen to carry the coffin containing an urn with Hardy's ashes were Barrie, Galsworthy, Gosse, Housman, Kipling and G. B. Shaw representing literature, and Stanley Baldwin, the Prime Minister, and Ramsay MacDonald, the Leader of the Opposition, representing Parliament. No member of the Royal Family attended. Obviously the Prince of Wales had still not got round to reading *Tess*. The funeral did not pass without other satires of circumstance. According to Blanche Patch, G. B. Shaw's secretary, in her *Thirty Years with G.B.S.*, Kipling did not want to meet Shaw and 'shook hands hurriedly and at once turned away as if from the Evil One'. Arnold Bennett complained bitterly to the press about the way tickets for the Abbey funeral had been distributed and the absence of any member of the Royal Family. This was the end of any hope he might have had of a knighthood. William Rothenstein, the artist, decided to paint a picture of the scene with the pall-bearers but as Barrie refused to sit for this he abandoned the idea. Finally, there was a row between Cockerell and Florence about Cockerell's magnificent idea for a monument to Hardy on Rainbarrow to match that to Admiral Hardy on Blagdon Hill, and Hardy's admirers had eventually to be satisfied with Eric Kennington's nice but rather insignificant statue which has him looking at one of the busiest roads in Dorchester where the sound of traffic never ceases.

Throughout 1928 the tributes to Hardy appeared in newspapers and journals not only in England, but throughout the world. For *The Times* he was 'the greatest living master of English prose and verse . . . the last survivor of the Eminent Victorians.' *The Sunday Times* described him as having 'the greatest staying power and most consistent artistry of all great figures in English literature'. *The Daily Telegraph* thought that he was 'a great novelist by virtue of his ability to tell a story' while 'his poetry showed an astounding fertility of invention'. For *The Morning Post* he 'was of that race of genius which is too big for society or class, fashion or time, and embraces humanity.' Virginia Woolf in *The Times Literary Supplement* wrote, 'When Hardy lived "there was a king among us, and now we are without."' Hardy was an 'unconscious writer' whose 'moments of vision' resulted in 'passages of astonishing beauty and force' in every book he wrote. The most oratorial and impressive in its Victorian utterance was that of Edmund Gosse – so soon to die himself. With Hardy's death, he wrote, 'the throne is vacant, and Literature is gravely bereaved. . . . His modesty, his serenity, his equipoise of taste, combined with the really extraordinary persistence of his sympathy and curiosity, made him an object of affectionate respect to old and young alike.' Gosse, Hardy's friend for fifty-three years, recorded this tribute and it was broadcast to the nation. Listened to today it sounds like a voice 'left behind of a band gone distant', a relic of a truly great period of English literature.

It remains to record that *Winter Words* was published on 2 October 1928 in an edition of 5000 copies and was reprinted the same month. Only eight days after her husband's death the bereaved widow wrote to Macmillan to say that Hardy had been working on a new collection of verse. There would have been a good deal of revision, she said, if he had lived and she thought that the first and last poems had been arranged but she wasn't sure about the ones in the middle. The 105 poems, with the customary diversity of subject matter, style and quality, had mainly been written during the last three years of his life but the book contained work from every decade since the 1860s except the 1870s. Many of the poems are as good as anything contained in the earlier books and the vision is essentially that of thirty years earlier. Memories of the past are revived in 'Childhood among the Ferns', 'To Louisa in the Lane' and 'Family Portraits'. The dead dog, Wessex, inspires a haunting lyric about his passing, and Hardy's sympathy with animals and trees is strongly felt in 'The Lady in the Furs', 'The Mongrel' and 'Throwing a Tree'. 'The Clasped Skeletons' works its way through the great lovers of history using inescapably erotic overtones, and 'A Practical Woman' tells the story of a woman whose husband (?partner) has produced nothing but sickly children so she goes off to find a better sire. On her return with 'a blooming boy' she says:

'I found a father at last who'd suit
    The purpose in my head,
And used him till he'd done his job,'
    Was all thereon she said.

Who but Hardy could have written a poem on such a subject, or one about the sadness in the eighteenth century of a young attractive woman losing a front tooth ('The Gap in the White'), or one about a woman talking to her second husband in bed about how her first husband used to come home drunk, and to prevent his molesting her she had sewn him up in the sheets one evening and unfortunately he had suffocated ('Her Second Husband Hears Her Story')? Hardy was determined to go out, as he had begun, still challenging complacency and expressing his own realistic, honest view of life.

Although the mansion where he died was only two miles from the cottage in which he was born, he had come a long way in the nearly ninety years which separated the unknown little boy and the world-famous man of literature. Through his genius, industry, and professional discipline he left behind him fourteen novels, more than fifty short stories, and nearly a thousand poems. Almost seventy years after his death his work is as alive as ever and he would have been particularly pleased that his poetry is still so widely read. Siegfried Sassoon described his poems as the 'spiritual auto-biography of his maturity'. There could be no better way to end than with a poem which ended one of his own books of verse – 'Afterwards'. It tells us a great deal about him.

When the Present has latched its postern behind my tremulous
                stay
  And the May month flaps its glad green leaves like wings,
Delicate-filmed as new-spun silk, will the neighbours say,
  'He was a man who used to notice such things'?

If it be in the dusk when, like an eyelid's soundless blink,
  The dewfall-hawk comes crossing the shades to alight
Upon the wind-warped upland thorn, a gazer may think,
  'To him this must have been a familiar sight.'

If I pass during some nocturnal blackness, mothy and warm,
  When the hedgehog travels furtively over the lawn,
One may say, 'He strove that such innocent creatures should
               come to no harm,
  But he could do little for them; and now he is gone.'

If, when hearing that I have been stilled at last, they stand at the
                door,
  Watching the full-starred heavens that winter sees,
Will this thought rise on those who will meet my face no more,
  'He was one who had an eye for such mysteries'?

And will any say when my bell of quittance is heard in the gloom,
  And a crossing breeze cuts a pause in its outrollings,
Till they rise again, as they were a new bell's boom,
  'He hears it not now, but used to notice such things'?

Bibliography

Thomas Hardy: *The Life and Work of Thomas Hardy*, edited by Michael Millgate (London, 1984).
Thomas Hardy: *The Collected Letters of Thomas Hardy*, edited by R. L. Purdy and M. Millgate (Oxford, 1978–88).
Thomas Hardy's Personal Writings, ed. Harold Orel (London, 1967).
Thomas Hardy: *The Literary Notebooks of Thomas Hardy*, edited by Lennart A. Björk (London, 1985).
Thomas Hardy: *The Personal Notebooks of Thomas Hardy*, edited by Richard Taylor (London, 1978).
Thomas Hardy: *The Architectural Notebook of Thomas Hardy*, edited by Claudius Beatty (Dorchester, 1966).
Emma Hardy: *Some Recollections*, edited by Evelyn Hardy and Robert Gittings (Oxford, 1979).
Kristin Brady: *The Short Stories of Thomas Hardy* (London, 1982).
Jean Brooks: *Thomas Hardy: The Poetic Structure* (London, 1971).
Simon Gatrell: *Hardy the Creator* (Oxford, 1988).
Ian Gregor: *The Great Web* (London, 1974).
Robert Gittings: *Young Thomas Hardy* (London, 1975).
Robert Gittings: *The Older Hardy* (London, 1978).
Robert Gittings and Jo Manton: *The Second Mrs Hardy* (London, 1979).
Timothy Hands: *Thomas Hardy: Distracted Preacher?* (London, 1989).
Timothy Hands: *A Hardy Chronology* (London, 1992).
Evelyn Hardy: *Thomas Hardy* (London, 1954).
Desmond Hawkins: *Hardy: Novelist and Poet* (New York, 1976).
Desmond Hawkins: *Concerning Agnes* (Gloucester, 1982).
Desmond Hawkins: *The 'Tess' Opera* (Hardy Society Monograph, 1984).
Irving Howe: *Thomas Hardy* (London, 1967).
Arlene Jackson: *Illustration and the Novels of Thomas Hardy* (London, 1982).
Denys Kay-Robinson: *The First Mrs Thomas Hardy* (London, 1979).
D. H. Lawrence: *Study of Thomas Hardy* (Cambridge, 1985).
Michael Millgate: *Thomas Hardy: His Career as a Novelist* (London, 1971).
Michael Millgate: *Thomas Hardy: A Biography* (Oxford, 1982).
Charles Morgan: *The House of Macmillan* (London, 1943).
Rosemarie Morgan: *Women and Sexuality in the Novels of Thomas Hardy* (London, 1988).
Harold Orel: *The Final Years of Thomas Hardy* (London, 1976).
Norman Page: *Thomas Hardy* (London, 1977).
F. B. Pinion: *A Hardy Companion* (London, 1968).
F. B. Pinion: *Thomas Hardy: His Life and Friends* (London, 1992).
R. L. Purdy: *Thomas Hardy: A Bibliographical Study* (Oxford, 1954).
M. Seymour-Smith: *Hardy* (London, 1994).
J. I. M. Stewart: *Thomas Hardy* (London, 1971).

Rosemary Sumner: *Thomas Hardy: Psychological Novelist* (London, 1981).
Dennis Taylor: *Hardy's Poetry 1860–1928* (London, 1981).
Dennis Taylor: *Hardy's Metres and Victorian Prosody* (Oxford, 1988).
Richard Taylor: *The Neglected Hardy* (London, 1982).
Keith Wilson: *Thomas Hardy on the Stage* (London, 1995).
Virginia Woolf: *The Second Common Reader* (London, 1932).
Monographs on the Life, Times and Works of Thomas Hardy, Nos 1, 2, 4, 8, 18, 20, 29 and 41 (Beaminster and St Peter Port, various dates).

Index